FINANCIAL INSTITUTIONS AND SERVICES

FOREIGN EXCHANGE MARKET INTERVENTION

MARKET MICROSTRUCTURE MODELS AND EMPIRICAL INVESTIGATIONS

FINANCIAL INSTITUTIONS AND SERVICES

Additional books and e-books in this series can be found on Nova's website under the Series tab.

FINANCIAL INSTITUTIONS AND SERVICES

FOREIGN EXCHANGE MARKET INTERVENTION

MARKET MICROSTRUCTURE MODELS AND EMPIRICAL INVESTIGATIONS

NEVI DANILA
AND
SARDAR M. N. ISLAM

nova
science publishers
New York

Additional color graphics may be available in the e-book version of this book.

Library of Congress Cataloging-in-Publication Data

ISBN: 978-1-53614-710-0

Published by Nova Science Publishers, Inc. † New York

CONTENTS

Preface		**vii**
Acknowledgments		**xi**
Chapter 1	Introduction	**1**
Chapter 2	Foreign Exchange Intervention	**9**
Chapter 3	The Impact of Intervention on the Inventory-Control Mechanism	**51**
Chapter 4	The Bid-Ask Spread: The Market Microstructure Perspective	**73**
Chapter 5	The Empirical Decomposition of the Bid-Ask Spread for Exchange Rates	**93**
Chapter 6	Government Intervention on the Spread	**117**
Chapter 7	Findings: Foreign Exchange Intervention Effectiveness	**133**
Appendices		**139**
References		**203**
About the Authors		**215**
Index		**217**

PREFACE

Conventional macroeconomic fundamental models of exchange rates, which incorporate the role of government intervention, have not generally been able to explain the movements of the exchange rate in the short and medium term horizon. These shortcomings have motivated researchers to apply market microstructure models in an attempt to explain the impact of government intervention on the movements of exchange rates over these time horizons. Market microstructure is a branch in economics and finance that deals with the issues and institutions of exchange and intermediation in the market. This perspective is based on a multi-agent system characterized by the issues of information asymmetry and conflicts and the possibility of designing games for resolving these issues.

This book investigates the effectiveness of government intervention from the market microstructure perspective, especially focusing on its impact on the setting of bid-ask exchange rates (from the Plaza Agreement to the Louvre Accord). We test the effect of an intervention on dealer's behaviour in controlling his inventory to set the quotation of exchange rates. We also examine the relative importance of the inventory cost in three components of the bid-ask spread. Finally, we look into the impact of the intervention on the spread.

In Chapter 3, we find that government intervention by sales of US dollar is insignificant. This means the dealers did not in the period believe the signal, which was given by the government through coordinated government intervention.

Intervention by the purchase of the US dollar is significant but with a positive sign. Theory tells us it should be negative. The positive sign means that the dealers shifted down the quote to discourage their customers from selling US dollars (buy DM and Yen) and encourage them to buy US dollars (sell DM and Yen) as they anticipated the US dollar would depreciate. A purchase of the US dollar signals to the market that the government has an intention to appreciate the dollars in the future. Thus, the dealers reacted in the opposite direction of the government's intention. This was probably due to the lack of credibility of the government intervention. We also note that the large scale of G-3 (Japan, Germany and USA) intervention to support the US dollar (purchasing dollars against DM) after the stock market crash of October 1987 was perceived by market participants as a commitment of US to prevent a post-crash liquidity crisis rather than a commitment to support the dollars.

In summary, government intervention in the foreign exchange market for the US dollars during the period of Plaza agreement to Louvre accord was not effective in influencing the dealers' behaviour in controlling inventory position by shifting the quote up or down. This may have been due to a lack of commitment of the G-5 to policy coordination, although different schools of thought will provide different theoretical explanations for this finding.

In Chapter 4 and 5 we turn to analyse how important is the inventory cost in the components of foreign exchange bid-ask spreads. Our research shows that the component of bid-ask spread in foreign exchange market can be ranked, in order from most to least importance, as inventory holding cost, adverse selection, and order processing cost. High inventory holding cost is related to the impact of opportunity costs and the risk of changes in inventory value. Moreover, we find that small banks (traders) have less ability to unload inventory imbalances since they do not operate continuously. The lower adverse selection cost is consistent with the fact that the government is believed to have intervened secretly for about 40 percent of all intervention operations in our sample period. Moreover, our finding of lower importance for the adverse selection cost in the foreign exchange market compared to the equity market conforms to evidence that the potential loss for an informed trader is less in the foreign exchange market. This is because the traders will have same information about the government policy and the behaviour of the macroeconomy of a country. Highly competitive trading (price competition) in the foreign exchange market leads to a very small order processing cost.

Finally, we find that during 1985 to 1987 intervention in the Japanese yen widened the spread and intervention in the Deutsche mark did not have any influence on the spread. This finding is supported by several authors: Federal Reserve intervention either increased the volatility of yen/US dollar or had no impact on the volatility of DM/US$ during the period 1985-1991.

ACKNOWLEDGMENTS

The completion of research for the book was possible only through the help of those listed below. To them we give our extreme gratitude and acknowledgements for personal and academic help and contributions:

- To Professor Christopher M. Adam, who guided, helped and encouraged the research process extensively and substantially. The book owes academically and intellectually a lot to him for his contributions to the materials of the book.
- To the first author's parents whose support and understanding was necessary for the completion of her research.
- To Fawzan Rizqy Ananda, the first author's son, who gave her high motivation and encouragement to the completion this research.
- To Dr. Jianxin Wang, who gave the data and gave his highly valued opinion about this research.
- To the Federal Reserve Bank of New York and Board of Governors of the Federal Reserve System, who gave the important data for this research.
- To Anwaruddin Ambary for giving the first author motivations to finish up this work.

- To G. Mujtaba Mian and Robert Parker Gray for helping this research from beginning to end of the research process for the materials of the book.

Some articles were published from the original materials of this book and these materials are now included back in the present book with the permission of the publisher of these articles.

Chapter 1

INTRODUCTION

1.1. MARKET MICROSTRUCTURE AND FOREIGN EXCHANGE INTERVENTION

Studies of the effectiveness of foreign exchange market intervention using fundamental models (such as the monetary, sticky prices, and overshooting models) of the exchange rate determination have performed well for some periods, but they have not been able to explain the behaviour of the major exchange rates during the latter part of the flexible exchange rate regime (Almekinders, 1995; Dominguez, at. al., 2013).

Now researchers are beginning to apply market microstructure models in an attempt to explain the effectiveness of the intervention on exchange rates. Market microstructure is a relatively new branch in economics and finance that deals with the issues of how does the market operate, exchange takes place, and how different agents and institutions interact and coordinate information and strategies in the marketplace when the market is potentially characterised by the existence of information asymmetry, conflicts of interests, moral hazard and adverse selection. It is potentially based on a multi-agent system perspective and can adopt game theory as a framework for analysis and modelling. See also Spulber (1999) and Rasmussen (2007) for more details. The market microstructure perspective can give an improved framework for analyzing the issues of market operation and co-ordination since the models in this perpective can provide results and implications which are based on the resolution of the information asymmetry, agency theory and other related game theoretic issues.

Some market microstructure models are the following:

DeGrauwe's (1985) near-rationality model, the chartist channel of intervention, and noise trading signalling channel of intervention (Hung, 1991) are examples of some microstructural approaches. In the words of Frankel (1994, p.32) "we are somewhat more optimistic about the course of future research in international finance, in part because of the prospect of new developments that analyse the market for foreign exchange primarily from a microeconomic perspective."

This book examines the effectiveness of government intervention from the market microstructure perspective, especially focusing on its impact on the bid-ask prices. First, we investigate the impact of an intervention on the dealers' behaviour in controlling their inventory by shifting the quotes. Second, we inspect the relative importance of the inventory cost in the components[1] of the bid-ask spread since the dealers consider their optimal inventory every day, especially when there are events[2] that might influence the value of their inventory. We adapt a model from the equity market because the microstructure studies are well established in equity markets. Finally, we examine whether the intervention widens or narrows the bid-ask spread.

In this book, we use G-3 currencies as these three countries played the major role in the foreign exchange market during our sample period. Black (1991) suggests that the Deutsche mark and the Japanese yen are the second and third currencies traded in the three largest markets (New York, London, and Tokyo). The period of 1985 to 1987 (from Plaza Agreements to Louvre Accord) was chosen because these events (the agreements) were very pronounced for coordinated government intervention. According to Frankel and Dominguez (1993, p.327), market participants, central bankers

[1] The components of spread are transaction cost, inventory cost, and adverse selection cost.
[2] Such as the government intervention.

and academic economists believed that the intervention was ineffective policy tool in the early 1980s. Therefore the US government abstained from buying and selling foreign exchange.

The attitude of the US government changed in 1985. The government began to coordinate its intervention with that of other countries' central banks. The Federal Reserve has regularly intervened in the markets since that time. Thus, 1985 is the year when the government seemed to consider that the intervention had an important effect on the markets. We wish to determine whether the "conventional wisdom" of the ineffectiveness of intervention was still held by the markets or if the markets had changed their belief towards the effectiveness of government intervention. As Funabashi (1988, p. 213) notes "economic policy coordination initiated at the Plaza meeting should be studied critically as a possible model of success or failure for future policy coordination strategies. After all, the Plaza strategy was the first major venture to reform international economic policymaking among the industrial countries since Bretton Woods fell apart."

From the above analysis, the research problem of this book is defined as below:

- To understand, through the use of microstructure analysis, how intervention by authorities in foreign exchange markets affected the quotation of foreign exchange rates, in particular, the setting of bid-ask prices from 1985 to 1987 (from the Plaza Agreement to the Louvre Accord).
- To measure the relative importance of the inventory cost in the components of the bid-ask spread.
- To comprehend whether the intervention not only affects the quotation of bid-ask prices but whether it also influences the spread exchange rate spread.

1.2. Contributions of the Book

The authors believe that this book makes important contributions to the literature because:

- Intervention is now a vital part of monetary policy and we need to understand its impact; but that impact is not well understood, especially the variability of the duration of the impact.
- Existing models of intervention give ambiguous results, but the model used here is not ambiguous in its findings.
- The use of microstructure analysis allows a separate identification of intervention impacts, which are inventory effects (changes to foreign exchange portfolio balances of market participants) and signalling effects (policy authorities seeking to the guide planned trading of participants). Current models of intervention combine or fail to recognise the effects.

1.3. Organization of the Book

The chapters of the book are organised as follows.

Chapter 2 describes foreign exchange intervention. We review the objectives of intervention, the types of intervention, and a theory of intervention. One objective of intervention relates to its length of time, whether it is short, medium or long term. The effectiveness of intervention is mostly based on the type of the intervention: sterilised or non-sterilised. The theory of foreign exchange intervention provides a framework to link the elements of the intervention process. The inventory model is also described in more detail here in order to understand the behaviour of dealers who are always trying to manage their inventory imbalances. Finally, we demonstrate the expectation channel approach in modeling the dealers' behaviour regarding inventory control. We build on a model developed by Bessembinder (1994) to derive the equation, which can be used to test the effect of intervention on dealers' behaviour in controlling their inventory by setting the quotes.

Chapter 3 investigates the empirical analysis of the intervention on the dealers' behaviour in controlling their inventory.

Chapter 4 explains the concept of the bid-ask spread: the components of the spread, and the factors that influence the spread and the volatility of exchange rate. The volatility of exchange rates is one of the reasons for the government to intervene in the foreign exchange market. Moreover, volatility influences the spread. The more volatile the market, the wider/higher, in general, is the spread. Volatility relates to the risk of changes in the value of the exchange rate, and this is one of the factors that affect the inventory holding cost. Government intervention may also cause the market to become more volatile. In particular "secret" government intervention is considered as adverse selection in the foreign exchange market, and tends to widen the spread.

The relative importance of the inventory cost compare with the remaining costs in determinants of bid-ask spread is discussed in Chapter 5. Chapter 6 is the empirical analysis of the intervention's effect on spread.

Chapter 7 reports the conclusion and the summary of findings.

1.4. Empirical Results, Implications and Findings

We find that government intervention by *sales* of the US dollar in the 1985-1987 period is insignificant. This means the dealers did not believe the signal, which was given by the government through coordinated government intervention.

Intervention by the *purchase* of the US dollar was significant with a positive but incorrect sign. The positive sign means that the dealers shifted down the quote to discourage their customers from selling US dollars (buy DM and Yen) and to encourage them to buy US dollars (sell DM and Yen) as they anticipated the US dollar would depreciate. The purchase of US dollars signal led to the market believing that the government had an intention to appreciate the dollars in the future. Thus, the dealers reacted in the opposite direction to the government's intention[3]. We believe this was supposedly due to the lack of credibility of the government intervention. We also note that the large scale of G-3 (Japan, Germany and USA) intervention to support the US dollar (purchasing dollars against DM) after the stock market crash of October 1987 was perceived by market participants as a commitment of US to prevent a post-crash liquidity crisis rather than a commitment to support the dollars (Dominguez, 1990, p. 139).

In summary, the intervention during this period (1985 to 1987) was not credible. Consequently, the intervention was not effective in influencing the foreign exchange market. The ineffectiveness of the intervention was due to the lack of commitment of the monetary authorities (DeGrauwe, 1996; Broto, 2013). The G-5 needed to hasten their efforts to build a more credible and effective international monetary regime or they should have committed themselves fully to policy coordination (Funabashi, 1988, p.246). Of course, different theoretical explantions for this are possible depending on the school of thought adopted in the analysis of this issue (see Kreps, 1990 for different schools of thought).

As we noted above dealers shifted quotes down as US dollars kept depreciating, even though the government signalled an appreciation of the dollar. This meant that the dealer was most concerned with the inventory cost since holding a currency inventory to provide immediacy imposes opportunity costs and the risk of changes in inventory value. We find that the inventory holding cost is the most important component of the three determinants of spread in the foreign exchange market. Our empirical results here show that the least important component is the transaction cost because the foreign exchange market is a highly competitive market and adverse selection is the second most significant cost.

---

[3] The dealers' behavior conformed to the fact that the dollars kept depreciating at that time, although the Fed bought US dollar in large amounts.

Finally, we determine that intervention in the Japanese yen widened the exchange rate spread, and the intervention in the Deutsche mark did not have any influence on spread, during 1985 to 1987. This finding is supported by Neal and Tanner (1996): Federal Reserve intervention either increased the volatility of yen/US dollar or had no impact on the volatility of DM/US dollar during the period 1985-1991[4].

---

[4] There is evidence of a relationship between the spread and price volatility (Boothe, 1988; Bessembinder, 1994; Glassman, 1987).

Chapter 2

FOREIGN EXCHANGE INTERVENTION

In this Chapter, we build the tools that we require to analyze our chosen research problem. We need to understand the structure of foreign exchange markets (section 2.1) and the concepts of intervention in foreign exchange markets (section 2.2). We then consider the central role of expectations formation (section 2.3) before outlining the essential insights of inventory models for microstructure trading in Section 2.4. We finally draw the elements together in section 2.5 to show how intervention can work through inventory adjustment models based on expectations in foreign exchange markets. This model then is the basis for our tests and results outlined in Chapter 3.

2.1. THE FOREIGN EXCHANGE MARKET

In an open economy, the residents of one country can trade internationally. It requires a foreign currency market if the countries have different currencies. A foreign exchange market permits buyers and sellers of currencies to exchange one currency for another (Rivera-Batiz, 1994). Collectively foreign exchange markets are the largest markets in the world.

London, New York, and Tokyo are the three financial centers that dominate the foreign exchange trade.

The market participants are customers, market makers, foreign exchange brokers and central banks. Customers are people who need market makers to complete their transactions in international trade. Market makers (mostly commercial banks) are institutions who create the market by setting bid and ask prices upon demand in one or more currencies. Brokers are those who arrange trades between market makers but do not engage in trading on their account. Central banks enter the market to move the price of exchange rate or to influence the volatility by buying foreign currency if there is an excess supply of foreign currency, and selling foreign currency if there is an excess demand of foreign currency or to accomplish their international transactions.

Customers go directly to market makers, as do brokers. Thus, customers and brokers do not interact with each other. Brokers earn money by charging a fee for matching market makers. Using recent data for one month (April 1989), trade was generated mostly by direct interbank trades (55%). Trading through brokers and non-bank customers was about 39.9% and 5.1% respectively in the US. Most transactions occur between banks either directly or through brokers.

An exchange rate is the price of one currency vis-à-vis another. There are two quoting conventions: direct and indirect quotes. A direct quote is for units of local currency per unit of foreign currency. An indirect quotation is for units of foreign currency per unit of local currency. Foreign exchange markets are categorized as spot markets and forward markets. In spot markets, currencies are bought and sold for immediate delivery and payment (one or two days). In the forward markets, currencies are bought and sold for future delivery and payment.

2.2. Foreign Exchange Intervention

Although many countries have moved to a flexible exchange rate regime, governments have not stayed away from intervening in these systems. Indeed, governments have intervened to move the price of exchange rates in such flexible regimes more heavily than they did with fixed exchange rates[5].

Intervention is the buying or selling by a government of its currency against foreign currency in foreign exchange markets. According to Balbach (1978, p.2-7) in the US, intervention in foreign exchange markets can be undertaken by three distinct institutions: foreign central banks, the Federal Reserve System, and the Exchange Stabilisation Fund (EFS). Intervention by foreign central banks to support the dollar can be only described as the creation of their currency denominated deposits and buying the dollars in the foreign exchange market. This increase in the demand for dollars in the foreign exchange market and, consequently the price of dollars in terms of this foreign currency will rise (appreciate).

The Federal Reserve System intervenes in the foreign exchange market by activating the swap network. Swap arrangements permit the US Treasury or the Federal Reserve to borrow foreign currencies while giving dollar-denominated deposits at the Federal Reserve Banks as collateral. The deposits are usually converted into Treasury Securities, primarily of the nonnegotiable type. The acquired foreign currencies are then used to buy dollars in the foreign exchange market. The result is the same as intervention by a foreign central bank.

The Federal Reserve can also coordinate the intervention with the foreign central bank. For example, when the Federal Reserve coordinates intervention with Bank of Japan to support the dollar, the Federal Reserve and Bank of Japan will buy the dollars and sell yen in the same period. This action increases the demand for dollars in the foreign exchange market, and the dollar will appreciate.

Intervention by the Exchange Stabilisation Fund can use three types of assets (deposits at Federal Reserve Banks, Treasury Securities, or Special Drawing Rights (SDR)[6]). The Gold Reserve Act of 1934 created this institution to intervene in exchange markets, mainly, to protect the

---

[5] See DeGrauwe (1996), p.208 table 10.1 and Figure 10.1.

[6] SDRs (Special Drawing Rights) are special international reserve asset created by the IMF. They are issued as a substitute for gold as it is considered an undesirable choice due to the costs of mining and storing the quantities needed to finance growing world trade.

exchange value of the dollar during the fixed exchange rate regime (Schwartz, 1996). While the US Treasury owns the fund, it is a separate entity with its financial resources and with its account at the Federal Reserve Bank.

Intervention using deposits at the Federal Reserve Bank (FRB) can be explained as follows: because of the minimal amount of deposits at the FRB, the Exchange Stabilisation Fund sells SDR certificates to receive the deposits in return. It uses the deposits to buy the foreign currency at the foreign central bank; then it buys the dollars using the foreign currency. The institution will deposit these proceeds at the Federal Reserve Bank. This will increase the demand for the dollars, and the result is an appreciation of the dollar.

The second type of asset is Treasury securities. The Fund sells its Treasury securities to a foreign central bank and receives the foreign currency deposits. The Fund uses these deposits to buy the dollars and places these dollars with the Federal Reserve Bank, which causes the demand of dollars to increase in the foreign exchange market. The Fund can also intervene in the market by using SDRs. The Fund sells SDRs to the foreign central bank and receives foreign currency deposits, then uses these deposits to buy the dollars. The Fund deposits the proceeds at the Federal Reserve Bank. The result will be the same as with intervention previously discussed.

The U.S. Treasury has responsibility for foreign exchange policy in the US, but it always talks with the Federal Reserve before deciding to intervene. The Federal Reserve Bank of New York operates the intervention on behalf of the U.S. monetary authorities. The Federal Reserve Bank of New York has also undertaken foreign exchange intervention for the Federal Reserve's account since 1962. The Federal Reserve is the junior agency, and the decision that it should intervene is at the Treasury's initiative (Schwartz, 1996). Also, traders at the New York Federal Reserve observe market trends and developments to provide information to policymakers. However, they focus the activity on the U.S. market (FRBNY Fedpoints 44, [on line], Nov 1996).

The Federal Reserve typically deals in the spot market as opposed to the derivative market. The foreign currencies that are used to intervene in the market come equally from Federal Reserve holdings and the Exchange Stabilization Fund of the Treasury. The Federal Reserve publishes a report of its foreign exchange activity a month after every 3-month reporting period (FRBNY Fedpoints 44, [online], Nov 1996). However, newspapers regularly report the activities of the Federal Reserve and other central banks. A question is how accurate are the reports of foreign exchange intervention. Klein (1993) compared the actual intervention data (released by the Federal Reserve in the summer of 1991) to daily press reports of intervention (from The New York Times and The Wall Street Journal) from January 1985 to December 1989. He found that the overall conditional probability that intervention was reported given that occurred is 72 percent. In addition, the conditional probability that intervention occurred given that it was reported is 88 percent. Thus, the newspaper reports are accurate representations of actual intervention.

2.2.1. Type of Government Intervention

There are two types of intervention: non-sterilized and sterilized. Non-sterilized intervention is when the monetary authorities intervene in the foreign exchange market by buying and selling the foreign currencies that will affect the domestic money stock. The domestic money stocks (supply) are connected to changes in the monetary base that are related in turn to changes in the international reserves of the central bank and/or changes in central bank credit, given the money supply multiplier. For example, assuming that Bank Indonesia (the Indonesian central bank) holds its credit constant, the Indonesian monetary authority buys dollars in the foreign exchange market to decrease the value of the local currency, the rupiah, against the US dollar. The authority pays by issuing checks on itself and raising the money supply. It leads to a decrease in the interest rate to keep the money market in equilibrium at any given level of income. Thus, holdings of Indonesian assets will be less attractive, and the demand for the rupiah will decrease. Consequently, the value of the rupiah decreases.

Sterilized intervention is when the monetary authorities intervene without affecting the domestic money stock. For example, the Indonesian authority buys dollars, but at the same time, the government sells government securities in exchange for cash.

In the US, the Federal Reserve routinely "sterilizes" intervention in the foreign exchange market, which prevents intervention from moving the level of bank reserves away from levels consistent with established monetary policy goals. If intervention is undertaken on behalf of a foreign central bank or the Treasury and therefore uses funds which have not been newly created by the Federal Reserve, sterilization is not necessary (FRBNY Fedpoints 44, [online], Nov 1996).

Osterberg (1992) shows that most analyses concentrate on sterilized intervention. There are three channels through which sterilized intervention can influence the exchange rate: the portfolio balance channel, the market efficiency channel and the signaling channel (Loopesko, 1994 p.257-277). The portfolio balance channel mechanism means sterilized intervention changes the relative supplies of domestic and foreign bonds. Because the investors are risk averse and the domestic and foreign bonds are not perfect substitutes, intervention implies a readjustment of the exchange rates (rates of return). For example, the United States intervenes in the foreign exchange market to support the dollar relative to Japanese yen. The Federal Reserve buys dollars in the market with Japanese yen and sterilizes the intervention by buying Treasury bonds at the open market-desk. Assume that the Japanese also sterilize the intervention by selling the yen-denominated bonds. The Fed's action initially creates the excess demand for Treasury securities and lowers the US interest rates. In contrast, the Japanese sale of yen-denominated bonds creates the excess supply for securities and raises the Japanese interest rates. Because there is imperfect substitution between US and Japan bonds, the US bondholders are not willing to hold the excess of Japanese bonds. Lower US interest rates tend to increase US money demand, while higher Japan interest rates tend to decrease Japan money demand. With the money supplies in both countries held constant, and the expected future spot rate remains constant, the dollar will appreciate against the yen.

The extent to which intervention changes to exchange rates depends on the degree of substitutability between dollar-denominated and yen-denominated securities (Humpage, 1986, p.9). Other things equal, if the two securities are close substitutes, the impact on the exchange rate will be small. On the other hand, if they are not perfect substitutes, a significant change in exchange rate will be needed to offset the risks. Dominguez and Frankel (1993a) claim that sterilized interventions are effective if they can change the risk premium (regarding the portfolio effect). However, Marston (1988, cited in Schwartz, 1996, p.389) suggests that the indecisive results of the portfolio balance model are due to the following three reasons:

- ex-post interest differentials may reflect the failure of traders to take advantage of profit opportunities in the foreign exchange market but not reflect the risk premium
- the interest differentials may explain the risk premium, but the exchange of two securities may have a small impact on the exchange rate
- economists may lack the technical data and tools to measure the effects of the sterilized intervention on portfolio decisions.

The market efficiency channel is when investors know about the intervention and interpret it as relevant information in forming their spot-rate forecasts. In other words, if exchange rates are forward-looking and expectedly efficient for public information, then any policy action that conveys additional relevant information to the market can influence exchange rates (Dominguez, 1990 p.123).

The portfolio balance channel and the market efficiency channel are considered to be independent policy instruments because their influence is independent of the other present and prospective domestic policies. Numerous studies are exploring these two channels by testing the uncovered interest rate parity (Humpage, 1986; Du, et. al., 2018). The results are consistent with the hypothesis that sterilized intervention affects the exchange rates through one of these channels or both, but it cannot differentiate between the two.

However, Humpage (1986) suggests that empirical investigations generally do not find strong support for the argument that intervention affects the exchange rate through a portfolio balance channel. The enormous growth in financial market turnover during last decades seems to have diminished the potential for central banks to cause a significant imbalance in investors' portfolios. For this reason, current research focuses more on the expectational/ signaling channel (Almekinders, 1995, p.79).

If the monetary authorities have inside information, intervention may signal future monetary policies. It is the signaling channel mechanism. Intervention is an effective signal if a consistent monetary policy follows it. Hence, the signaling channel cannot be regarded as an independent policy instrument. Dominguez (1990) concludes that the effectiveness of the intervention as a signal depends on the credibility of the implied monetary policy. Goodhart and Hesse (1993) note that central banks only need to make a credible threat of intervention to influence speculative agents' behavior in markets. Accordingly, central banks can maintain that threat by only intervening occasionally in circumstances when they might want to influence exchange rates.

Furthermore, Obstfeld (1988) argues that one reason sterilized intervention may send more informative and more credible signals than announcements or other public debt-management policies is the effect of unanticipated exchange-rate changes on the government's net worth. For example, when the government sterilizes the intervention of supporting the dollar, it will lose more money when its currency appreciates by a percentage amount greater than the nominal interest rate differential. Thus, public finance lends credibility to a government that uses sterilized sales of foreign currency to signal a future appreciation of its currency, and sterilized purchases of foreign currency to signal a future depreciation (Obstfeld, 1988, p.39).

Bhattacharya and Weller (1997) examine sterilized intervention with an alternative model that is introducing asymmetric information into a standard model of rational speculative trade in the forward market. They conclude that rational speculators have a benefit at the expense of the central bank since they will not trade unless they are assured of receiving a benefit, thus, the effectiveness of the sterilized intervention is not questioned. Besides, the perverse response, which arises if the domestic currency depreciates when the central bank purchases domestic currency, only occurs when the market has a relatively precise estimate target exchange rate, but it is uncertain about the fundamentals. Furthermore, the central bank will never find it advantageous to reveal the scale of its intervention activity. If the central bank reveals its private information about the fundamental, an intervention will prove completely ineffective (p.254).

In the U.S., government intervention employs both market makers, who generally are commercial and investment banks, and brokers. According to Osterberg (1992, p.3), secret intervention occurs via brokers, since the brokers do not reveal the parties (maintain anonymity) until the transactions occur, or via a commercial bank which does not traditionally conduct foreign exchange business (Frenkel and Dominguez, 1993). This view is also supported by Peiers (1997). He says that in performing an intervention, a central bank can deal either directly with commercial banks as counterparties or go through the brokers' market. If a central bank wants to make knowledge of the intervention information widespread, the central bank has to select a particular counterparty as a price leader who may be followed by other traders. The passage of price leadership during the period of central bank intervention is as follows: suppose a central bank chooses a bank trader, X, as an intermediary bank. Then, a central bank will deal with X when intervening in the market. Since X has private information regarding the future authority's policy, it will adjust order flows and prices first. Therefore the bank trader X is receiving positive economic advantage from its insider information. Uninformed competitor bank, Y, observe X's price adjustment as a signal that it is dealing with an informed trader. Thus, Y follows X's movement by revising its price and adjusting its position to minimize its losses. Trader X's leadership status remains until all central bank operations are revealed to follower banks.

Peiers (1997) examines price leadership patterns in foreign exchange markets with a focus on central bank intervention as an informal stimulation for leadership positioning. He tested the hypothesis of Deutsche Bank price leadership between October 1, 1992, and September 30, 1993. He suggests that central bank activity is revealed to the market well before a public announcement, with Deutsche Bank perceived to be the early information insider to Bundesbank intervention. Deutsche Bank price leadership occurred between 60 and 25 minutes before Bundesbank intervention reports. Once the information was more broadly dispersed to the market, less informed banks learned from the informed trader's order flows and revised their prices for profit-taking. The reason behind selecting Deutsche Bank as an intermediary bank of Bundesbank was that the Deutsche Bank had the largest European customer base in 1993. In the same year, it also ranked as the 13th largest bank in the world regarding shareholder equity and asset value. Thus, Deutsche Bank's customer depth strengthened the bank's ability to gain early access to new information as well as to disseminate such information quickly. Moreover, its size advantage allowed Deutsche Bank to provide more rapid liquidity and volume turnover than most competitors in the DM/US dollar market (p.1590, p.1595).

Regarding the impact of government intervention (reported or secret) on the volatility of exchange rates, Dominguez (1993) finds that secret intervention increases the volatility of exchange rates because it gives an ambiguous signal. The result is more likely to increase uncertainty in the market, and the volatility will widen the spreads. Osterberg (1992) supports this view: intervention via market makers will widen the spreads because market makers could view the intervening central bank as having inside information[7]. Secret interventions make up less than 20% of all intervention. However, Hung (1997) suggests that Federal Reserve secret intervention is approximately 40% of all intervention in the US market. In contrast, reported central bank intervention leads to a reduction in both daily and weekly exchange rate volatility because it provides clearer

[7] In contrast with Lyons (1995), who argues that the foreign exchange market not have inside information.

signals of intervention policy (Dominguez, 1993). The decrease of exchange rate volatility is expected to reduce the spread.

Neal and Tanner (1996) test the effects of central bank intervention on the ex-ante volatility of US dollar/DM and US dollar/yen exchange rates between 1985 and 1991. They use the implied volatility of currency option prices to estimate the ex-ante volatility. They also control for the effects of other macroeconomic announcements. They find no evidence that central bank intervention is associated with a decrease in ex-ante exchange rate volatility over the period 1985 to 1991. The Federal Reserve intervention increases the volatility of US dollar/DM and US dollar/yen but is insignificant for US dollar/DM and significant for US dollar/yen. On the other hand, the Bank of Japan intervention significantly increases the volatility of US dollar/DM and US dollar/yen. The intervention of the Bundesbank does not have any impact on the volatility of US dollar/DM and US dollar/yen. Overall, intervention by central banks during the period 1985 to 1991 is associated with favorable changes in ex-ante volatility, or with no change (p.865).

Hung (1997) has a different view of the positive correlation between secret intervention and exchange rate volatility. He explains the correlation between them from the perspective of the noise trading channel. A central bank can enter a relatively thin market to manipulate the exchange rate. It is common knowledge that the sterilized intervention is most likely having a short effect. If this transitory effect is captured by chartists (noise traders) and the prevailing trend broken and a trend reversal formed, they may adjust their positions based on the reversed trend. This action extends the effect of the intervention. Thus, to make the noise trading channel work successfully, "the central bank must have not only up-to-date market intelligence and familiarity with noise traders' reaction functions, but also be capable of conducting intervention secretly" (p.783). For example, suppose the Bundesbank considers the Deutsche mark is overvalued. Then, the intervention to lower the currency value is required. Bundesbank enters the thin market secretly, and noise traders will not be able to know the sources of dollar supply. At that point, they include the downward pressure in their trendline analysis. Since chartists weigh more heavily the most recent exchange rate movement in their forecast, they will sell the Deutsche mark to follow the change of the market direction.

Furthermore, Hung (1997) advises that authorities may use "volatility-enhancing" intervention to reverse the direction of the exchange rate movement with strong momentum to manage the exchange rate level. The procedure of a "volatility-enhancing" strategy is as follows: suppose DM rises and is about to reach the upper band, and the Bundesbank wants to bring the DM down. When the DM is still rising sharply, the Bundesbank is not likely to accomplish its goal by selling DM with its limited sources. However, the Bundesbank may sell DM secretly when the DM is showing short-run downward fluctuation in the prevailing upward trend and do nothing if the dollar is rising. This will encourage traders to have a second opinion of the market direction, and it will be useful in discouraging one-way speculation and breaking the undesirable upward trend (p.783).

Hung (1997) also implies that intervention during the 1985-1986 post-Plaza Accord period reduced both yen/dollar and DM/dollar exchange rate volatility. It can be explained by a volatility-reducing strategy: the policy objective was to bring down the dollar in an orderly fashion when the dollar was already on a downward trend. The intervention in 1987-1989 post-Louvre period increased the exchange rate volatility, which is evidence of a volatility-enhancing strategy because the dollar was approximately at the desired level and the policy objective shifted to maintaining an implicit target band (p.790).

Osterberg (1992) examines the relation between G-3 (Germany, Japan, and the United States) central bank intervention and the bid-ask spreads of the DM/dollar and Yen/dollar spot and forward foreign exchange rates. He compares the bid-ask spreads during intervention periods to nonintervention periods. Moreover, he examines the spreads over periods usually thought of as times of intervention as opposed to nonintervention periods. He reports no evidence to support the conclusion that anticipation of intervention widens spreads. In other words, spreads are lower when actual intervention is expected than when intervention is neither expected nor realized.

2.2.2. The Theory of Foreign Exchange Intervention

Almekinders (1995) allows the models of intervention (sterilized and non-sterilized) into two categories: flow models of the exchange rate and asset-market models of the exchange rate. The details of the categories are shown in the table below.

Table 2.1. Models of Intervention (Almekinders, 1995)

Flow models	Asset market models
Purchasing Power Parity	*The Flexible-Price monetary model*
The Mundell-Fleming model	*The Sticky-Price monetary model*
	The Portfolio Balance model
	Stock-Flow interaction in portfolio models of the exchange rate

2.2.2.1. Purchasing Power Parity

The purchasing power parity theory states that "the exchange rate between the home currency and any foreign currency will adjust to reflect changes in the price levels of the two countries" (Shapiro, 1992, p.153).

If the government intervenes in the market by increasing the domestic money supply (with the income velocity of money and the level of real income fixed), the domestic price will increase. Consequently, it will lead the exchange rate (S = domestic currency/foreign currency) to be higher, a depreciation of the domestic currency. The sterilized intervention is not effective since this intervention does not change the domestic money supply.

However, many empirical tests reject the validity of PPP in the short-run since the price levels are sticky and adjust slowly, whereas the currency prices vary minute by minute (Dornbusch, 1976; Frankel, 1979). Thus, in practice, the exchange rates are proximately determined in financial markets rather than in goods markets.

2.2.2.2. The Mundell-Fleming Model

Mundell (1963) and Fleming (1962) make the assumptions of the model as below:

- Demand determines the domestic output
- The price level and wages are constant
- Domestic and foreign bonds are perfect substitutes and have the same maturity
- Domestic and foreign currencies are non-substitutable; thus they are held in their own country.

When the government conducts unsterilized intervention by purchasing foreign bonds in the open market, the domestic money supply increases. It reduces the domestic interest rate (with the assumptions of static expectations and perfect international capital mobility). The lower interest rate induces a capital outflow, which leads to a depreciation of the domestic currency. The depreciation increases the competitiveness of the domestic industries, and this raises the domestic income. The domestic economy moves to a new equilibrium.

The sterilized government intervention changes the composition of domestic and foreign bonds held by the private sector, but not the volume. Because of the perfect substitution between domestic and foreign bonds, this intervention does not affect the exchange rate.

Black (1991) modified the model by assuming imperfect substitutability and rational expectations under imperfect information. The unsterilized intervention process is the same as discussed above. The sterilized intervention influences the exchange rate indirectly through decreased uncertainty among investors. The risk will be lower. Thus, it persuades the investors to hold a more substantial position in foreign currency, and speculative capital flows (assumed to be stabilizing) are increased.

However, Almekinders (1995) argues that this model seems to be unrealistic. He notes that in deriving the expression of the willingness of speculators to bear the risk, the model assumes a constant foreign interest rate. Further, the sterilized intervention leaves the domestic interest rate unaffected. Thus, the assumption of a constant domestic and foreign interest rate induces hesitancy about the realism of the effectiveness of the sterilized intervention.

2.2.2.3. The Flexible-Price Monetary Model

This model assumes flexible prices, and that PPP holds continuously. The model says that the bilateral nominal exchange rate depends on the current and expected future values of relative money supplies and relative outputs in both countries.

When the government intervenes in the market with an unsterilized purchase of foreign bonds through open market transactions, the money supply increases. The excess supply of money is followed by an increase in the domestic price level. Consequently, the domestic currency has to depreciate, due to the PPP effect.

Sterilized intervention affects the exchange rate through the signaling/expectation channel (Mussa, 1981; Humpage, 1986).

2.2.2.4. The Sticky-Price Monetary Model

Dornbusch (1976) assumes that the price level adjusts in proportion to excess demand, and exchange market participants form their expectations regressively. Moreover, this model also assumes that the capital mobility and substitutability of bonds denominated in different currencies are perfect.

In the short-run, unsterilized purchases of foreign currency increase the real money balances (the price is still unchanged). The domestic interest rate falls, and investors expect a long-run depreciation of the domestic currency. Both factors decrease the attractiveness of domestic bonds. This model forces the exchange rate to overshoot in the short-run to a value higher than its long-run value. The real depreciation and the lower domestic interest rate increase the demand for domestic goods. Eventually, domestic prices rise, so the economy gradually moves back to its long-run equilibrium.

Sterilized intervention leaves the exchange market unchanged since the intervention lacks a money-market effect. The effectiveness of foreign exchange intervention in both flexible and sticky-price model depends on the money-market effect.

2.2.2.5. The Portfolio Balance Model

Branson, Halttunen, and Masson (1977) present a basic portfolio model of the exchange rate. This model assumes static expectations and a small country. The demand functions for money, domestic bonds, and foreign bonds are assumed to depend on wealth. Unsterilised intervention by buying the foreign currency cannot be affected since the small country residents are assumed to hold their currency. Thus, the government intervenes by purchasing foreign bonds in exchange for domestic money. This action leads to an excess supply of money and an excess demand for foreign bonds. The excess supply of money causes a depreciation of the domestic currency, which means an increase in the value of foreign currency and lower interest rates. Thus, the proportion of wealth in the form of foreign bonds increases. It absorbs the excess demand for foreign bonds.

Sterilized intervention is already discussed in section 2.3.1 above. The only difference here is that we hold the assumption of small-country and static expectations. Thus, the government intervenes by purchasing foreign bonds instead of by buying foreign currency in exchange for domestic bonds.

2.2.2.6. Stock-Flow Interaction in Portfolio Models of the Exchange Rate

Branson (1983) extends the standard small-country portfolio model. He assumes slow adjustment of the price level to monetary shocks, and that the domestic country has acquired a net foreign asset position by running a current account surplus in previous periods.

Unsterilized intervention by purchasing foreign bonds leads to a depreciation of the domestic currency and the decrease of the domestic interest rate. With no initial change of the domestic price, the real exchange rate depreciates along with the nominal exchange rate. This leads to an improvement of the trade balance and a current account surplus. The domestic economy accumulates additional foreign assets, and eventually, the current account surplus leads to an appreciation of the domestic currency. Accompanying the increase in the domestic price level; the real exchange rate appreciates more sharply. This appreciation reduces the trade surplus, even though the higher interest earnings on foreign assets keep the trade flow in surplus. Therefore, the domestic economy continues accumulating foreign assets. There is more appreciation of the real exchange rate. The adjustment process is complete when the current account is in equilibrium.

Hallwood and MacDonald (1986) extend the standard small-country portfolio model to analyze sterilized intervention. They divide the goods sector into traded goods and non-traded goods sectors in the domestic economy. The sterilized intervention leads to a depreciation of the currency. The depreciation means a higher price for traded goods. The domestic producers will shift resources to traded goods, while domestic consumers will buy more non-traded goods. The excess supply of traded goods is exported which improves the trade balance. Moreover, the higher price of traded goods raises the overall domestic price level and drives real wealth below the desired level. The domestic residents reduce consumption to accumulate real wealth. The improved trade balance assists the deficit on the capital account, which encourages the purchase of foreign assets by domestic residents. The current account surplus, eventually, appreciates the domestic currency, and the rate of accumulation of net foreign assets gradually declines to zero.

All the theoretical studies above assume that the structural model contributes a valid framework for the analysis of the effectiveness of foreign exchange market intervention. However, MacDonald and Taylor (1992) confirm that "the asset approach models have performed well for some time periods, such as the interwar period, and, to some extent, for the first part of the recent floating experience (1973-1978); but they have provided largely inadequate explanations for the major exchange rates during the latter part of the float"(p.24).

For that reason, researchers have adopted a new strategy in exploring the government intervention, based on the microstructure or non-fundamentalist point of view as discussed in section 2.3.1. For example, Hung (1997) approaches government intervention through a chartist or noise trader channel intervention. Central banks can influence the course of exchange rates when the market is sufficiently thin, and the intervention is carried out through brokers. The upward or downward pressure on the currency, which is incorporated in the Chartists' trendline analysis, induces them to strengthen the movement of the exchange rate in the direction favored by the central bank. She also says that the highly visible interventions conducted via the interbank market will effectively give a signal to noise traders about the course of the exchange rate (Hung, 1991).

2.2.3. The Objective of Government Intervention

According to FRBNY Fedpoint 44 (online), the U.S. monetary authorities may sometimes intervene in the foreign exchange market to influence market conditions and/or the value of the dollar. Besides, Almekinders (1995) stated that in the short term all central banks have a common objective of "countering disorderly exchange market conditions." A disorderly market means that the daily movements of exchange market are above or below the mean (average) daily value. According to Schwartz (1996), exchange rates are less disorderly than the prices of other financial assets. He also suggests that the explanation of a high degree of exchange rate volatility is the fact that foreign exchange markets efficiently spread the effects of economic shocks. Moreover, the volatility is evidence of bandwagon effects, destabilizing speculation, or market inefficiency.

The medium-term objectives relate to resisting large short-term exchange rate movements or "erratic fluctuations" which exceed a certain size. Fluctuations in the level make changes in other economic variables (aggregate and sectoral output, price level, a volume of international trade, and foreign investment flows) (Schwartz, 1996). A strong (weak) dollar leads to trade deficits (surpluses), produces unemployment in export (import) industries, and encourages protectionist pressures. A weak dollar increases inflation, which is expected to pass through to non-tradable goods prices and wages. Thus, the fluctuations in the level of exchange rates impose adjustment and uncertainty costs on the economy. The long-term objectives attempt to give some space to monetary policy by lessening the impact of foreign shocks on domestic monetary conditions, to resist depreciation because of its inflationary effects, and resist appreciation to maintain competitiveness.

However, Schwartz (1996) doubts that the intervention can accomplish the goals that are sought, for the following reasons:

- Intervention may be able to reduce the massive and reversible transitory movements of exchange rates and to decrease the spread temporarily. But, there is no sign that any lasting change has been the result of the action of the US authorities. "Who has benefited from such intervention?" (p. 394).
- Intervention does not confront the fundamental economic conditions that underlie medium-term change in the exchange value of the dollar. The feared consequences of medium-term variations in the dollar's exchange value have not arisen. When the dollar is strong, shifts in employment from traded to non-traded goods industries result, but such shifts among industries are common whether or not the exchange value of the dollar is involved. Similarly, when the dollar is weak, it can induce inflation. It may be true for a small open economy, but not for a large, relatively closed economy like the United States. "If inflation has at times manifested itself, it has been home-grown by Federal Reserve monetary policy, not an import-driven rise in prices" (p.394).

German economists divide the intervention objectives into four categories (Almekinders, 1995). First is "Anpassungs"-interventions (smoothing-interventions) "grosso modo" which refer to interventions undertaken to give a "leaning against the wind" policy. The central bank tries to resist large short-term exchange rate movements without affecting the underlying trend. Second is "Erhaltungs"-interventions (trend-breaking-interventions), which alter the trend in the development of the exchange rate for economic or political reasons. The third objective is "Gestaltungs"-interventions (direction indicating-interventions) which are applied to the situation where the exchange rate is moving out of control.

Finally, other interventions involve sales and purchases of foreign currencies owing to the management of the volume and composition of the foreign exchange market reserves of the central bank.

Almekinders and Eijffinger (1996) investigated the objective of daily Bundesbank and Federal Reserve intervention in the DM/US dollar market and the Japanese yen/US dollar from the post-Louvre period February 23, 1987, to October 31, 1989. They concluded that German and US central bank leaned against the wind in the DM/US dollar and US dollar/DM markets and the Yen/US dollar market and they tried to counteract appreciation of their currency more strongly than depreciation. It was also found that an increase in the conditional variance led the central banks to increase the volume of intervention due to their leaning against the wind policy. Moreover, the Bundesbank and the Federal Reserve have taken action to lower exchange market uncertainty.

2.2.4. Unilateral and Coordinated Central Bank Intervention

Coordinated intervention is assumed to be simultaneous (same day) sterilized intervention operations by more than one central bank in support of (or against) the same currency (Dominguez, 1990).

Two assumptions make the intervention effective through the signaling channel. First, the central bank is believed to have inside information about the future monetary policy. Second, the central bank has the incentive to reveal that information is accurate. Motivations behind coordinated interventions are as follows (Dominguez, 1990):

- Multiple signals increase the total amount of inside information conveyed by intervention operations. Furthermore, the probability that the signals are correct will increase. The additional costs of lost reputation among the coordinating central banks will make central banks reluctant to give the wrong signals.
- Alternatively, central banks want to coordinate intervention because they want to free-ride on other central banks' reputations for providing informative signals. The market will have more

difficulty learning the wrong signal from a given central bank when intervention is coordinated.

- Furthermore, Schwartz (1996) also states that "those not participating in coordinated intervention might be regarded as displaying a lapse of good citizenship in the world community." If central banks do not participate in programs of coordinated intervention by an international group of countries, they will be assumed to be a neglectful country in the world community. However, it is clear that countries have their interests at times rather than devotion to the collectivity, for example, when they are more concerned about the appreciation of their currencies than the depreciation of the dollar. Thus, the success of a coordinated intervention depends more on whether the countries support the direction of the market movement than on whether the countries want to regard as members with good standing in this community.

The United States has conducted unilateral and coordinated interventions several times since the Bretton Woods era. An outline of the interventions from the Bretton Woods era to 1994 is as follows (Schwartz, 1996):

2.2.4.1. Bretton Woods Era

The Bretton Woods Agreement in 1945 anticipated that short-run payments imbalances would be met by drawings on official exchange reserves and IMF credits to ensure that the economy would be insulated from external shocks. It implies that sterilized intervention was utilized. Nevertheless, in operation, the Bretton Woods system had a different set of rules for the US and other countries outside the US. The US became the center country, which did not have a responsibility to intervene directly in foreign exchange markets as other industrialized countries did. The US gold stock was not threatened since the industrialized countries invested the official reserves in interest-earning US Treasury securities. However, the collapse of the dollar-based par value system was the result of the voluntary growth of dollar claims relative to the size of the gold stock. It induced the US to depart from the conservative monetary policy. In 1962, an intervention was designed to achieve (Schwartz, 1996):

- offset pressure on the US monetary gold stock when it was believed to be temporary (reversible)
- smooth disequilibrating movements in exchange rates
- supplement international arrangements through the IMF
- satisfy the world demand for liquidity.
- The intervention was not intended to affect the deficit in the US balance of payments; and that the US would continue to supply dollars in payment for the goods and services which the rest of the world provided.

In conclusion, protecting the value of dollars held by foreign central banks to prevent their exchange for US gold was the goal of the intervention during the Bretton Woods era.

2.2.4.2. September 1971 - 1974

In July 1973 the Federal Reserve intervened with its small holdings of foreign currency, and with a significant amount of foreign currencies resources available through swap agreements. Then, the dollar depreciation worried the US authorities because of a rise in inflation, the prospect of higher oil imports, and the political fallout from the Watergate incident. Moreover, the European currencies appreciated at the same time. It induced the US to intervene again with modest sales of Deutsche marks. From the start of floating exchange rates until September 1974, the authorities intervened sporadically to counter disorderly markets.

2.2.4.3. October 1974 - 1981

From October 1974 to March 1975, the Federal Reserve, the Bundesbank, and the Swiss National Bank coordinated intervention to offset volatility in the dollar-Deutsche Mark and dollar-Swiss franc rates and to slow depreciation of the dollar. They used swap lines to finance the intervention.

From September 1977 to December 1979, the Bank of Japan joined the team of coordinated intervention to stop the decline in the dollar. During November and December 1978, the amount of the US intervention in support of the dollar was S6.7 billion, and the three countries (Germany, Japan, and Switzerland) bought the dollars in insignificant amounts.

By the end of 1980, the Federal Reserve was intervening in the foreign exchange markets practically on a day-to-day basis. The trading desk positioned simultaneous bid and ask prices to neutralize disorderly markets. From September 1980 to February 1981, the goal of the intervention was to slow the rise in the dollar and to acquire hard currencies to pay off swap debts.

2.2.4.4. 1981 - 1987

On January 17, 1985, the Ministers of Finance and the Central Bank Governors of the G-5 countries (France, Germany, Japan, the United Kingdom, and the United States) met in Washington and agreed to undertake coordinated intervention in the markets. The Bundesbank sold a total of $3.5 billion from January to March 1985. The United States and Japan sold $600 million. The United States backed up the intervention by reducing its discount rate by half a percentage point to 7.5%. There was confusion in the market about the intervention: it seemed the market was misinformed about the level and the degree of intervention coordination over this period, and the market did not recognize that the Bundesbank was active in the market by selling dollars. Central banks were also confused with the achievement of the coordinated intervention during this first period (Dominguez, 1990).

On September 22, 1985, the Plaza Agreement was announced. The reason behind it was that the dollar was high, the growth abroad was slow, U.S. exports were shaky, and imports were soaring. This situation caused the U.S trade deficit to swell during summer 1985. Protectionism was called for by the U.S. Congress. It worried America's trading partners. The Plaza Agreement communiqué stated that "in view of the present and prospective changes in fundamentals, some orderly appreciation of the main non-dollar currencies against the dollar is desirable. They (the

Ministers and Governors) stand ready to cooperate more closely to encourage this when to do so would be helpful" (G-5 Announcement, September 22, 1985, cited in Dominguez 1990, p.133). The paper stated, "a 10-12 percent downward adjustment of the dollar from present levels would be manageable over the term." It was also agreed that "further downward movement should be avoided" (Funabashi, 1988, p.17). In conclusion, the G-5 agreed to lower the dollar in the short and long term without losing control of the market. The strategy was to maximize the intervention when the dollar was strong and to support the dollar when it declined excessively. The period of intervention was six weeks with the total amount $18 billion. The maximum daily intervention for each participant was in the range of $300-400 million. The currencies used for intervention were the dollar, yen and Deutsche mark, and the proportion of intervention was shared as follows: the United States 30%, Germany 25%, Japan 30%, United Kingdom 5%, and France 10% (Funabashi, 1988).

On May 5, 1986, the Tokyo Summit of the G-7 countries (Canada and Italy in addition to the G-5 countries) took place. From the Plaza agreement to the Tokyo summit, the yen appreciated from 240 to 170 yen to the dollar. This movement affected the small and medium-sized firms in Japan. Japanese exports were hurt. The policymakers worried that a further appreciation would slow the economy and perhaps cause a recession. Japan pleaded to stabilize the yen-dollar exchange rate, but the G-7 came up with two innovations in the new cooperation strategy of which currency stabilization was only one component. First, the G-7 intended to engage in more intervention policy coordination in the future, or they would frequently meet between summits, at least once a year. Second, the G-7 would assess the economic performance of the participants by using the G-7 economic indicators ("multilateral surveillance"). These are GNP growth rates, inflation rates, interest rates, unemployment, fiscal deficit ratios, current account and trade balances, monetary growth rates, reserves, and currency rates. If there was a substantial deviation in the indicators, a discussion of "appropriate remedial measures" was to be called. In mid-January 1987 the Bank of Japan bought a large number of dollars since the yen-dollar rate approached the 150 level. Then, the Bundesbank coordinated the intervention with the Bank of Japan to support the dollar and backed up the intervention with a reduction of the discount rate. The Federal Reserve also joined the Bank of Japan in supporting the dollar by purchasing $50 million against the sale of yen (Dominguez, 1990).

On February 22, 1987, the G-6 (excepting Italy) produced the Louvre Accord. The finance ministers and central bank governors declared that their currencies were "within ranges broadly consistent with underlying economic fundamentals." The policy makers indicated that they were ready to intervene to help stabilize exchange rates at "around current levels." Two specified midpoint rates were agreed: 1.8250 Deutsche marks to the dollar and 153.50 yen to the dollar; plus or minus 2.5 percent was determined as the first line of defense for mutual intervention on a voluntary basis, while at 5 percent consultation on policy adjustment was to be obligatory; between these limits of 2.5 percent to 5 percent, intervention efforts were expected to intensify (Funabashi, 1988, p.186). In early August 1987, the Federal Reserve and the Bundesbank intervened in the market to support the Deutschmark to maintain the Louvre Deutschemark-dollar target. In mid-August, the G-3 coordinated small-scale interventions to support the dollar. To back up the intervention, the Federal Reserve increased the discount rate from one-half percent to 6%.

From late October through December 1987 the G-3 central banks engaged in numerous large-scale coordinated dollar supporting intervention operations. The US purchased $3,876 million, and the Bundesbank purchased $2,704 million. Moreover, the Bundesbank cut the discount rate to 2.5 percent to back up its intervention operations (Dominguez, 1990).

2.2.4.5. 1988 - 1994

In 1988 US intervened moderately as the authorities both bought and sold foreign currencies. In October 1989, the Federal Reserve coordinated intervention to depreciate the dollar value as the dollar became stronger. The Federal Reserve purchased yen and mark in more significant amounts than the previous years, and the G-7 sold dollars twice in amounts higher than the amounts of US intervention.

In 1990 to 1992 the US authorities bought and sold yen and mark. In 1993, the intervention was limited to the yen, and in 1994 the Federal Reserve sold yen and mark. At the end of 1994 and during the first months of 1995 it intervened again to support the dollar since the value of the dollar fell against the yen and the mark (Schwartz, 1996).

Does coordinated central bank intervention have more power in market responses than unilateral central bank intervention? Dominguez (1990) investigated the impact of unilateral and coordinated central bank interventions on market responses in the period 1985-1987. She divided the samples into five subperiods. In the first subperiod, G-5 (January-March 1985 Dominguez found that unilateral Bundesbank intervention was more credible than coordinated intervention. The sale of one million-dollar amount by the Bundesbank increased the overnight dollar-mark (57 basis points), and dollar-yen (37 basis points) return differential. The coordinated intervention had a smaller impact, 19 basis points and nine basis points for dollar-mark and dollar-yen respectively. However, the magnitude of the impact of Bundesbank and coordinated intervention on market expectations decreased for the longer maturity of dollar-mark and dollar-yen return differential.

In the second subperiod, Plaza (September-December 1985), Dominguez showed that unilateral Fed intervention was significant and the impact of intervention did not decrease as the length of the investment maturity increased. Moreover, coordinated government intervention had a tremendous impact on the one, and three-month dollar returns differential. In the third subperiod, September 1986 - January 1987, Dominguez suggests “mixed signals” by G-3. Unilateral Bundesbank and coordinated intervention had little impact on the market. The fourth subperiod, Louvre (February-June 1987), showed a little evidence of unilateral and coordinated intervention. Unilateral Fed intervention was significant, and the size of the impact decreased as the investment maturity increased in the last subperiod sample, Crash (October-December 1987). The coordinated intervention had a smaller impact on returns than unilateral Fed intervention. Finally, the three years’ periods unilateral and coordinated government interventions showed that coordinated central bank intervention was significant for one month and three months dollar return differential. Unilateral Bundesbank intervention was insignificant, while unilateral Fed intervention was significant in two out of six excess dollar return regressions over the three-year period. Dominguez (1990) concludes that there are different effects on market expectations between unilateral and coordinated interventions. The unilateral intervention significantly influences market expectations in some periods, and the coordinated intervention consistently influences longer-term market expectations.

2.3. PRICE EXPECTATION

According to Flood (1991, p.60), models posit probability distributions that produce the prices of orders in the market. Modelers may generate order prices by objective distributions, that is, by stochastic processes exogenous to the market. Alternatively, they may use a participant's (market maker) subjective beliefs to generate the price. To derive the subjective beliefs, market makers may use Bayesian learning that is "a player holds prior beliefs concerning the types of the other players, and as he sees them take actions, he updates his beliefs under the assumption that they are following equilibrium behavior" (Rasmusen, 1994 p.52).

This subjectivization of the pricing process is significant because it allows for heterogeneous expectations. The microstructure of the foreign exchange market presumes heterogeneity of expectations among market makers since numerous market makers are unlikely to have identical views. This belief is confirmed by empirical evidence that claims that market participants appear to use shared information differently in making their forecast (MacDonald and Marsh, 1996, p.680). Frankel (1994, p.35) captures the heterogeneity of expectations in two ways: different patterns of expectations formation among different classes of actors and a relation between the dispersion of opinion and other microstructure variables of interest.

Regarding the heterogeneity of the actors, Ito (1990) finds that different institutions have different expectations. It is most apparent between export industries and import industries. Focusing on the yen, he suggests that in the short run (one month), both exporters and importers might expect an appreciation in the yen, but the exporters have a lower expectation in yen. In the long run (six months), exporters expect the yen to depreciate, while importers still expect the yen to appreciate, even though it is not as much as in the short run. The basis for the difference is simple: exporters want a depreciation in the yen to make their goods cheaper, while on the contrary, importers want to create gain as the yen appreciates.

Moreover, MacDonald and Marsh (1996) observe the heterogeneity of expectations for both three and twelve months forecast horizons among economists, foreign exchange dealers, and executives in over 150 companies and institutions in the G-7 nations. This observation strengthens Ito's finding: international foreign exchange market participants interpret the critical variables in different ways, and they uphold individual biases relative to their rivals. They also indicate that good forecasters of one currency are not necessary good forecasters of another currency. Nevertheless, good short horizon (three-months) forecasters appear more likely to be good long horizon forecasters (twelve-months).

In the formation of expectations, Beng and Siong (1993, p.369) define the expectation of market participants to be rational if the subjective expectation of the market participants is identical to the mathematical expectation of the particular variable. It makes the forecast (on average) an unbiased predictor of the actual change in the exchange rate. They argue that another property of rationality is that the market participants can use all the information that is relevant for predicting the spot rate. With respect to those properties, Beng and Siong (1993) find that there is empirical evidence of a violation of unbiasedness; market participants cannot predict changes in the exchange rate correctly, and there is evidence that the forecaster expectations are stabilising in the short term and long term (using the Singapore dollar against the US dollars).

De Grauwe supports this view: rational behavior forms the market's expectations, even though another theory assumes that rationality in the expectations formation is limited. The agents not only use available and relevant information, but they also use the history of the exchange rates in making reliable forecasts. Then, they will use a model which describes the relationship between the news and the exchange rate. In the words of De Grauwe, "the subjective distribution of the future expected exchange rate is equal to the objective distribution, i.e., the one produced by the model" (p.82).

Moreover, he says this expectations theory stresses the forward-looking nature of the exchange rate which implies that in the flexible exchange rate regime the future expected exchange rate is unlikely to be fixed for very long.

In contrast, Ito (1990) presents evidence that expectations are formed "irrationally": heterogeneity in expectations formation is due to a constant bias rather than a reaction to the recent changes in exchange rates. However, he suggests that there is an inconsistency between short-term and long-term expectations. The long-term expectation is more stabilizing than the short-term expectation (using yen against US dollar).

Given an analysis of price expectation, we might ask about the preferences of dealers in discovering price. Do they prefer slower price discovery or faster price discovery? Usually, dealers prefer more rapid price revelation because they can allocate resources efficiently. But not all dealers prefer this. They may prefer a slower price discovery if order flow is observable because it induces additional risk sharing and additional trading with customers before revelation. It reduces the variance of unavoidable position disturbances and possible trading losses (Lyons, 1993).

2.4. Inventory Models

Many studies address the behavior of market prices and spread based on the inventory model. The similarity of these studies is that the specialist deals with the problem of how to balance his inventory. In the long run, the imbalance of inventory is irrelevant because the models assume that the deviations of inflows and outflows are not related to the future value of stock since the specialist can adjust his position and prices. However, the imbalance of inventory determines the market behavior in the short run. Consequently, the price effect is temporary, and it will revert to "true" levels when the balance of order flows is achieved (O'Hara, 1997).

The first work was done by Garman (1976). He developed a model that described the "temporal microstructure" or moment to moment trading activities in asset markets. He focuses on the nature of order flow in determining security-trading prices (O'Hara, p.13). He suggests that "the specialist must pursue a policy of relating their prices to their inventories to avoid failure, it cannot be the case that they simply respond to temporary fluctuations in demand and supply" (p.267).

Amihud and Mendelson (1980) continued Garman's work incorporating inventory into the dealer's pricing problem. The crux of their analysis is that the quoted bid and ask prices depend on the market maker's stock. A market maker controls the parameters of the inventory development process. Thus, they obtain a semi-Markov decision process where inventory is the state variable. Then, the decision made for a given inventory level is bid and ask prices which determine the respective supply and demand rates. Moreover, the inventory is assumed to be bounded from above and below some constant level. This assumption eliminates the possibility that the dealer can run out of inventory or the possibility of failing. The model produces three main findings. First, the prices are monotone decreasing functions of inventory. It means a dealer increases his bid and ask prices as his inventory falls, and he decreases his prices as his inventory increases. Second, they deduce that the spread is always positive. Finally, they conclude that the optimal pricing policy implies the existence of a "preferred" inventory position (p.32). As the dealer realizes the inventory is deviating from the "preferred" level, he will adjust the prices to restore that position.

Focusing on the dealer "preferred" inventory level, Madhavan, and Smidt (1993) also examine the behavior of market making related to a target inventory level. Their model combines the effects of both asymmetric information and inventory control formally. They also provide a new insight into the specialist's role: acting both as a dealer who provides liquidity and as an active investor whose behavior reflects investment and speculative motives. As an active investor, the specialist seeks to maintain a long-term position and may periodically adjust the size of these positions in the stock consistent with his portfolio objectives, while he takes a profit in the short-term from information about the future order imbalances. As a dealer, the specialist quotes optimally to induce the inventory towards the long-term target inventory level. In other words, he adjusts quoted prices to control fluctuations in inventory. Madhavan and Smidt show theoretically that the target inventory may shift over time in response to changes in the risk profile of the stock.

Moreover, under the assumption of constant desired inventory, the authors find (p.1597) that the mean reversion is very slow. It takes 49 trading days, on average, for an inventory imbalance to be reduced by 50 percent. After developing an econometric model that corrects for periodic, unobserved shifts in the specialist's desired inventory holdings, they find that it takes 7.3 trading days for an inventory imbalance to be reduced by 50 percent. It means there is strong evidence of mean reversion in inventories to these time-varying targets.

Hasbrouck and Sofianos (1993) produce another study of inventory adjustment. They analyze inventory adjustment, price determination, and trading profits for one significant class of dealers, New York Stock Exchange specialists. They assume that the inventory level eventually reverts to its mean, and they examine the speed of adjustment with the autocorrelation. They conclude that frequently traded stocks have a faster speed adjustment of inventory. The median autocorrelation is above 0.1 at lag of 10 trading days. It means that if on day 0 the closing inventory exceeds the optimum by 1,000 shares, the expected excess inventory will be above 100 shares on day 10. For the least frequently traded stocks, the median autocorrelations are 0.1 at a lag of about 42 days. This slow adjustment is due to the shifts in the desired level of holdings, and this is the result of changes in long-term investment positions. The long persistence in inventory levels indicates that the specialists adjust inventory levels toward time-varying targets. However, when the estimation of mean inventory is taken daily, the adjustment is more rapid, primarily when the exogenous shocks occur. It suggests that short-term variation reflect classic dealer behavior, while the long-term variation stems from investment holdings. This finding confirms the Madhavan and Smidt (1993) finding.

Also, Hasbrouck (1988) and Hasbrouck and Sofianos (1993) provide evidence that shocks to inventories lead to at least transient effects on quotes, especially if the specialist is the counterparty to the trade. In other words, the trades in which the specialist participates have a more significant impact on the quotes than trades with no specialist participant.

In contrast to Garman, and Amihud and Mendelson work above, Stoll (1978) investigates the behavior of securities prices through the dealer's optimization problem. The dealer's decision problem, now, focuses on the appropriateness of the compensation to offset the costs in providing the services. Stoll (1978) analyses this notion explicitly. Moreover, he constrains the study on the supply side.

The cost of immediacy developed in Stoll's model (1978, p.1133) is the sum of:

- Holding costs, the price risk and the opportunity cost of holding securities
- Order costs, the costs of arranging trades, recording, and clearing a transaction
- Adverse information cost which arises from trading with individuals who possess superior information

His study mainly focuses on holding costs. Stoll sees a dealer as an investor who has the desired portfolio based on the opportunities and his preferences. Then, providing immediacy means that the dealer is willing to move away from his desired portfolio to supply the other investor's desires of buying or selling a stock. This condition places the dealer on to a level of risk and returns that may be not compatible with his preferences. In response, he must be compensated enough to offset the loss of utility due to deviating from his initial portfolio.

The holding cost of taking a position in stock i is as follows (Stoll, 1978):

$$\frac{C_i}{Q_i} = c_i = \frac{z}{W_0}\sigma_{ip}Q_p + \frac{1}{2}\frac{z}{W_0}\sigma_i^2 Q_i \tag{2.1}$$

Where:

Q_i = "true dollar value of the transaction in stock i, the stock in which immediacy is being provided. (-) Value indicates a sale, (+) value indicates a purchase.

C_i = present dollar cost to the dealer of trading the amount Q_i. The cost is positive or negative accordingly as the transaction in stock i raises or lowers the costs of holding the inventory Q_p..

The dealer's cost, C_i, is not paid at the time the dealer provides the immediacy. The cost is reflected in the bid and ask prices which are different from the "true" price of the stock. Thus, the dealer borrows Q_i - C_i to finance a purchase for which Q_i is the "true" value. On the other hand, the dealer earns Q_i + C_i for a short sale.

Thus, the holding cost of taking a position in stock i depends on several factors:

- Dealer characteristics — relative risk aversion *z*, and dealer equity W_0. The higher the risk aversion of the dealer the higher the cost; and the smaller the dealer's initial wealth, the dealer charges a higher fee for taking a position of given size; or, at the same fee, the dealer will take smaller positions.
- The size of the transaction in stock i, Q_i. Total cost rises as the square of Q_i, while the percentage cost rises linearly with Q_i.
- The characteristics of the stock, i.e., the variance of return and the variance between the return on stock i and the return on the initial trading account portfolio.
- The size of the initial position in the trading account, Q_p. If the dealer holds the initial position and the σ_{ip} is positive, the cost of

buying stock i is larger than if the dealer does not hold the inventory. On the other hand, the cost of selling stock i is smaller when the dealer holds the inventory compared to when the dealer has no inventory.

The bid and ask prices are set to encourage transactions which reduce the risk of holding the initial portfolio. If the dealer already has a long position, and the return is positively correlated with stock i's return, the bid and ask prices are set to encourage sales by the dealer of stock i and to discourage purchases by the dealer of stock i. Thus, the bid and ask prices will be lower than if there is no initial position. However, the bid and ask prices compensate the dealer's cost for accepting the trade, if the dealer has no initial position in the stock. The percentage-spread function is as follows:

$$s_i = \frac{P_i^a - P_i^b}{P_i^*} = c_i\left(Q_i^b\right) - c_i\left(Q_i^a\right) = \frac{z}{W_0}\sigma_i^2\left|Q_i\right|$$
$$for\left|Q_i^a\right| = \left|Q_i^b\right| = \left|Q_i\right| \tag{2.2}$$

It is shown that the spread is independent of the initial inventory of the dealer, and does not involve any covariance term. This means that if the dealer prices to cover the costs of each transaction, the spread is independent of the initial inventory. Moreover, the linearity of percentage costs in trade size means that the spread increases linearly with trade size. The dealer's inventory affects the placement of the bid and asks prices but not its size. Ho and Macris (1984) confirm this result. They conclude that the dealer's percentage spread is positively related to the asset risk and is larger than the percentage reservation; and that the dealer adjusts his quotes in response to his inventory position. He will lower both his buy and sell quotes when he has accumulated a positive inventory. Conversely, he will raise both his buy and sell quotes when his inventory levels are below his optimal target. Finally, since the dealer can induce trading, the timing of a transaction and the nature of the transaction may also depend on his inventory position. Ho and Stoll (1981) extend Stoll's (1978) model to the transactions uncertainty, multiperiod framework, and the introduction of the demand side. The paper is limited to the behavior of a single dealer making a market in a single stock. Its primary concern is the risk of the uncertainty about the return on his inventory and the uncertainty about the future transactions. Under these stochastic returns and stochastic transactions, the dealer maximizes expected utility of terminal wealth by adjusting bid and ask prices through time. The authors present a dynamic programming solution to this general problem.

The model is not concerned with bankruptcy. Ho and Stoll assume that the time horizon is sufficiently short and the collateral is large enough to avoid bankruptcy. The objective of the dealer is to maximize the expected utility of his total wealth at time T.

At time T, the dealer is assumed to liquidate his inventory and base wealth at their market values without transaction costs. To find the optimal strategy for choosing the values of *a* (dealer sale) and *b* (dealer purchase) that maximize the dealer's preference function, Ho and Stoll employ dynamic programming.

Rather than describe the detail of how they solve the optimal strategy using dynamic programming, it is more useful to consider the model's conclusions. There are several important properties of the dealer's optimal pricing behavior. The spread consists of a risk-neutral spread plus a risk premium. A risk neutral spread maximizes expected profits for the given stochastic demand function. The more inelastic the demand for the dealer services the larger the spread.

The risk premium depends on transaction size, the return variance of the stock and the dealer's attitude toward risk. Moreover, the spread depends on the time horizon of the dealer. When the time remaining is equal to zero, the dealer does not look beyond the current moment and is concerned only with the fee he can collect from a purchase or sale. Hence only the risk-neutral spread is relevant to this matter. However, when the horizon of the dealer is lengthened, the spread is higher since all the variables of the risk premium/adjustment are positive. In other words, as the time horizon lengthens, the spread increases to compensate the risk-averse dealer for bearing inventory and portfolio risks. Furthermore, the transaction uncertainty per se does not affect the spread because it increases the uncertainty of the return on the dealer's portfolio by making uncertain how large an unbalanced position must be held. Thus, the transaction uncertainty affects the result indirectly through the dealer's overall portfolio position.

The final property is that the spread is independent of the inventory level. It means that the spread is not affected by the dealer's inventory position since the transaction uncertainty also does not matter. This property is consistent with the one period model of Stoll (1978). However, dealer price adjustment depends on inventory. When inventory increases, both bid and ask prices decline. On the other hand, the prices will increase when the inventory decreases. Thus, the dealer affects the order arrival by moving the placement of the spread relative to the true price, not increasing or decreasing the size of the spread itself.

O'Hara and Oldfield (1986) confirm this finding. They conclude that the inventory effects are complex since inventory imposes two types of risk on the dealer: the variability in market orders and the variability of stock's price. O'Hara and Oldfield isolate these two effects by solving separately for the optimal spread. First, suppose the dealer only faces price variability with his supply and demand fixed, the dealer incorporates uncertainty about future inventory value by moving the bid and ask prices symmetrically. On the other hand, suppose the dealer faces market order variability at a constant price, the spread now contains a risk adjustment, and the level of inventory does not affect the spread. It means whether the dealer faces either order uncertainty or price uncertainty alone, he will move the prices symmetrically. Furthermore, the spread is independent of the level of inventory.

Each model of the dealer's optimization approach suggests that inventory introduces risks for the dealer, and the dealer maximizes his pricing strategy to minimize these risks. The spread is independent of the inventory; however, the inventory burdens some cost on the dealer, which is reflected in his bid and ask prices.

Finally, Ho and Stoll (1983) extend the model incorporating multiple dealers. They allow market makers to trade either directly with the public or between themselves in an interdealer market. Thus, dealers not only face the uncertainty of their returns on inventory and the uncertainty of the transaction arrival, but also they deal with the actions of other dealers. Further, each dealer sets bid and ask prices to maximize his own expected utility of terminal wealth. Ho and Stoll restrict the analysis to two dealers whom each makes a market in two stocks. The dealers are assumed to have homogenous opinions about the true value of each stock. Each dealer's wealth is composed of an inventory of each of the stocks, cash, and base wealth (similar to Ho and Stoll (1981)).

With independent transactions in M and N and with one period left to the horizon date, a dealer with inventories of M and N has reservation buying and selling fees for stock M[8]:

$$b_M = \frac{1}{2}\sigma_M^2 R(Q + 2I_M) \tag{2.3}$$

$$a_M = \frac{1}{2}\sigma_M^2 R(Q - 2I_M)$$

where:

$$I_M = M + \beta_{NM} N \tag{2.4}$$

$$\beta_{NM} = \sigma_{NM} / \sigma_M^2$$

$\sigma_M^2 =$ per period variance of return of stock M

$\sigma_{NM} =$ per period covariance of return between stock M and N

$R = \frac{-U''(W)}{(1+r)U'(W)}$, a discounted coefficient of absolute risk aversion

From the equation above, it is shown that the dealer's fee depends on the stock's risk, on the dealer's attitude toward risk, on the transaction size,

[8] The same result holds for stock N.

and on the current inventory of the dealer in his stocks (M and N). Given buying and selling fees, the dealer's spread for stock M is:

$$s_M = \sigma_M^2 RQ \qquad (2.5)$$

It is clear that the dealer's inventory affects a or b alone, but the reservation spread is independent of inventory. A negative inventory reduces the buying fee but increases the selling fee. Hence the dealer moves the placement of bid and ask prices relative to the true price without changing the distance between them in adjusting his inventory. The diversification of the dealer's inventory beyond one or two stocks does not affect his reservation spread. The reason is that bid and ask are adjusted to the dealer's inventory with the result that the spread reflects only the risk of the incremental transaction. The independence of transactions in stocks produces the independence between the spread and the number of stocks.

Furthermore, under homogeneous preferences and opinions, the equilibrium market bid-ask spread in stock depends on the number of dealers making a market in the stock:

- Two dealers, $s \geq R\sigma^2Q$
- Three dealers, $s = R\sigma^2Q$
- More than three dealers, $0 \leq s \leq R\sigma^2Q$

where $R\sigma^2Q$ is the reservation spread of any dealer.

Ho and Stoll[9] show that the equilibrium market spread must be non-negative. If the number of dealers is at least four, the equilibrium of the market spread may be zero. However, the zero spread is not stable over time because the flow of incoming orders will drive the spread to the reservation spread of an individual dealer. Besides, if the unwanted inventory difference between second dealers exceeds Q, the dealers will trade with each other. In equilibrium, pessimistic dealers have acquired a short position and inventory risk that is reflected in a high bid and ask price

[9] Ho and Stoll conclude that this result holds for the market under heterogeneous opinions.

relative to their opinion of the true price. In contrast, the optimistic dealers have acquired a long position and inventory risk, which is reflected in a low bid and ask price.

Moreover, Stoll (1989) observes that the inventory holding cost is the smallest components of spread. On the other hand, Wang (1998) finds that the inventory holding cost is the most significant component of the bid-ask spread in the Sydney Futures Exchange (SFE).

Consistent with a standard inventory-control mechanism above, Bessembinder (1994) and Lyons (1993) confirm that a dealer will reduce (shift down) the quotes to unload the undesired inventory and he will increase (shift up) the quotes when he is in short position. In other words, the dealer will adjust the inventory position by shifting the quotes but not modifying the spread. Moreover, they find strong evidence of inventory effects in the foreign exchange market.

Thus, we can conclude that, first, most of the models explained above suggest the spread is independent of the inventory level. Second, the inventory position influences the placement of the bid and ask prices but not the size of the spread.

In line with the inventory adjustment theory above, our model shows how inventory position, which is influenced by intervention, shifts the quotation of the bid and ask prices (not the size of spread). The explanation of our model will be discussed in the subsequent section.

2.5. The Impact of the Intervention on the Inventory-Control Mechanism

To investigate the impact of foreign exchange intervention on the portfolio inventory-control mechanism, we build the model through the expectations channel. As Almekinders (1995) notes research on the effectiveness of intervention through the portfolio balance channel has shifted to the expectation channel. The reason is that "the enormous growth in financial market turnovers during the last decades seems to have diminished the potential for the central bank to cause a significant imbalance in investors' portfolios" (p.79).

We apply regressive expectations as a basic model. Pilbeam (1992, p.240) lends theoretical support for use of the regressive expectations model when he notes that "the regressive expectations mechanism, rational expectations, and perfect foresight models are from a theoretical viewpoint much better suited to dealing with the exchange rates because they all allow for economic agents using a far wider set of information." Rudiger Dornbusch (1976) also made the regressive expectations model popular since "it is a more elegant specification, consistent with dynamic models in which variables such as goods prices converge toward their long-run equilibrium values over time" (Frankel, 1993, p.281).

In the equilibrium of the international asset market, the interest rate differential is equal to the expected change of the exchange rate. Empirically, there is abundant evidence that the interest rate differentials forecast subsequent exchange rate changes (Froot and Thaler, 1990). The equilibrium asset market is as follows.

$$X_t = E(s) - s_t \tag{2.6}$$

X_t is the differential between domestic and foreign interest rates

$E(s)$ is the expected future exchange rate

s_t is the spot exchange rate; that is the amount of local currency per unit foreign currency.

Let $E(s)$ be formed by the regressive expectations: $E(s) = (1 - \sigma) s_t + \sigma s^*$

s^* = the long-run equilibrium exchange rate.

$$[(1 - \sigma) s_t + \sigma s^*] - s_t = X_t \tag{2.7}$$

$$\Leftrightarrow s_t - \sigma s_t + \sigma s^* - s_t = X_t \tag{2.8}$$

$$\Leftrightarrow -\sigma s_t = X_t - \sigma s^* \tag{2.9}$$

Let α_t denote a time t location parameter, defined in relation to the ask quote (A_t), bid quote (B_t), and unobservable value (V_t) by Bessembinder (1994):

$$V_t = \alpha_t A_t + (1-\alpha_t)B_t \tag{2.10}$$

We make a further assumption V_t = the spot rate (s_t).

$$s_t = \alpha_t A_t + (1-\alpha_t)B_t \tag{2.11}$$

Then;

$$-\sigma[\alpha_t A_t + (1-\alpha_t)B_t] = X_t - \sigma s^* \tag{2.12}$$

Define $S_t \equiv A_t - B_t$; S_t = bid-ask spread

$$\text{Then, } -\sigma(\alpha_t S_t + B_t) = X_t - \sigma s^* \tag{2.13}$$

$$\Leftrightarrow -\sigma B_t = X_t - \sigma s^* + \sigma\alpha_t S_t \tag{2.14}$$

The equation (2.14) is divided by $-\sigma$:

$$\Leftrightarrow B_t = -(1/\sigma)X_t + s^* - \alpha_t S_t \tag{2.15}$$

Let α_t be a linear function of an observable variable: $\alpha_t = \alpha_o + \gamma_1 Z_t$, where Z_t is a variable that influences the placement of quotes in relation to the spot value (Bessembinder, 1994). In our case Z_t represents government intervention.

Then from (2.15):

$$B_t = -(1/\sigma)X_t + s^* - \alpha_o S_t - \gamma_1 Z_t S_t \tag{2.16}$$

Assume s* is constant; taking the difference of all variables in (2.16):

$$\Leftrightarrow B_t - B_{t-1} = -(1/\sigma)(X_t - X_{t-1}) - \alpha_0(S_t - S_{t-1}) - \gamma_1(Z_tS_t - Z_{t-1}S_{t-1}$$

$$\Leftrightarrow B_t - B_{t-1} = (1/\sigma)(X_{t-1} - X_t) + \alpha_0(S_{t-1} - S_t) + \gamma_1(Z_{t-1}S_{t-1} - Z_tS_t) \quad (2.17)$$

We restate the equation (2.17) in a multiple regression as follows[10].

$$B_t - B_{t-1} = \alpha_0(S_{t-1} - S_t) + \beta_1 (X_{t-1} - X_t) + \gamma_1(Z_{t-1}S_{t-1} - Z_tS_t) + \varepsilon_t \quad (2.18)$$

Where $\beta_1 \equiv 1/\sigma$.

We, then test the following hypotheses under the model above.

$H_0: \beta_1 = 0$: the change in the interest rate differential does not have an impact on the expected change in the quotation.

$H_1: \beta_1 \neq 0$: the change in the interest rate differential has an impact on the expected change in the quotation.

$H_0: \gamma_1 = 0$: government intervention does not influence the level of quotes through the size of spread.

$H_1: \gamma_1 \neq 0$: government intervention influences the level of quotes through the size of spread.

A positive estimate of β_1 means that when the change in the interest rate differential becomes smaller (narrows down), then the quotes are being reduced, i.e., the value of US dollars depreciates. A positive estimate of γ_1 implies that quotes are being reduced in relation to value when there is government intervention (Z_{t-1} rises) and vice versa. Moreover, we expect the value of σ be between 0 and 1, i.e., $0 < \sigma < 1$ so $1 < \beta_1 < \infty$. Next, we review the empirical results of our model.

---

[10] The regression is without a constant since the difference of s* is zero.

Chapter 3

THE IMPACT OF INTERVENTION ON THE INVENTORY-CONTROL MECHANISM

As we outlined in the previous Chapter, we built our model of the impacts of intervention on the shift of foreign exchange quotes (inventory-control mechanism) through the expectations channel. We now turn to analyze the model empirically in more detail. Before doing so, first, we discuss the sources of the data. The tests for stationarity and the appropriateness of Ordinary Least Squares are examined thoroughly in Appendix 8.

3.1. SOURCES OF DATA

The exchange rate data (DM/US dollar and Yen/US dollar) have been obtained from the Federal Reserve Bank of New York. The data are bid and ask prices at New York closing times (5 p.m.) excluding weekends and holidays from 1 January 1985 to 31 December 1987. The Board of Governors of the Federal Reserve System provided the daily government intervention data and the daily interest rate data. The intervention data are daily purchases or sales of the US dollar against DM and daily purchases or sales of the US dollar against Yen in millions from 1 January 1985 to 31 December 1987. The interest rate data consist of daily Euro-dollar rates (3-month), daily German domestic interbank rates (3-month domestic interbank loan rate), and daily Japanese domestic interbank rates (3-month domestic interbank CD rate) excluding weekends and holidays from 1 January 1985 to 31 December 1987. Daily Euro-mark and Euro-yen rates are appropriate rates to use, but they are not used here because of the difficulty of obtaining them. However, Marston (1995) noted: "Once the most onerous controls were lifted in February 1974; the differential fell to -0.30 percent during the rest of the decade and to -0.16 percent in the 1980s. The average differentials are statistically different from zero in all three periods. In two non-control periods, however, the differentials are small enough to be attributable to minor differences in risk and other characteristics of the two instruments. So by the early 1980s, at least, the mark-denominated markets in London and Frankfurt were effectively integrated" (p.58-59).

Moreover, he had the same opinion for the Japanese interest rates, "once the controls were removed following the December 1980 law, the differential dropped to 0.25 percent. This differential is statistically different from zero but small enough to be attributed to transactions costs" (p.64-65).

Thus, we used the daily German domestic interbank and Japanese domestic rates to represent the daily Euro-mark and Euro-yen rates respectively. Moreover, the interest-rate differentials are defined as 3-month Eurodollar rates minus 3-month German interbank loan rate and 3-month Eurodollar rates minus 3-month Japanese interbank CD rate.

3.2. THE EMPIRICAL ANALYSIS

We separate the intervention data into two types: intervention purchases of US dollar and intervention sales of US dollar. The reason is that we want to know whether the purchases and sales of intervention give different impacts on the dealers' behavior (relating to the quotes shifting) because the intervention by buying and selling the currency sends different signals to the market. Purchasing (selling) US dollar by the Fed signals to the market that the government wants to appreciate (depreciate) the dollar. Besides, we use two sets of data: dummy intervention (purchases and sales), and the size of intervention (purchases and sales).

Restating the multiple regressions in the equation (2.18):

$$B_t - B_{t-1} = \alpha_0(S_{t-1} - S_t) + \beta_1(X_{t-1} - X_t) + \gamma_1(Z_{t-1}S_{t-1} - Z_tS_t) + \varepsilon_t{}^{11} \quad (3.1)$$

X = the change in the interest-rates differential (the change in the differential of US interest rate and German interest rate; US interest rate and Japanese interest rate)

S = spread (ask-bid)

Z = government intervention

ε= error term.

First, we use two dummy variables: dummy for purchases of US dollar (1=purchases, 0=no intervention) and a dummy for sale of US dollar (1=sale, 0=no intervention). Then, we apply the size of intervention data: purchases and sales of US dollar.

Using the dummy variables, the regression may be restated as:

$$B_t - B_{t-1} = \alpha_0(S_{t-1} - S_t) + \beta_1(X_{t-1} - X_t) + \gamma_1(\text{dummypurchase}_{t-1} - \text{dummypurchase}_t) + \gamma_1(\text{dummysales}_{t-1} - \text{dummysales}_t) + \varepsilon_t \quad (3.2)$$

Using the size of intervention, the regression may be restated as:

$$B_t - B_{t-1} = \beta_0 + \alpha_C(S_{t-1} - S_t) + \beta_1(X_{t-1} - X_t) + \gamma_1(\text{Intvpurchase}_{t-1} - \text{Intvpurchase}_t) + \gamma_2(\text{Intvsales}_{t-1} - \text{Intvsales}_t) + \varepsilon_t \quad (3.3)$$

---

[11] t denotes time and the regression is without a constant.

3.2.1. Dummy Variable

As noted in Appendix 8, heteroscedasticity is the only linear regression assumption violated by both the Deutsche mark-dollar and Japanese yen exchanges rate data. After correcting the heteroscedasticity problem, the estimators become valid for the model used. Thus, appropriate statistical inferences can be made about the true parameter values. The Table 3.1 and 3.2 display the results of the regression.

We observe from the data that the size of spread does not fluctuate over time. Then, we make another assumption — the spread is constant — to check whether we obtain a different result. These results are given in Tables 3.3 and 3.4. Before we discuss the result in detail, we can explain the sign of the coefficient. It is essential since the sign describes the behavior of dealers. A positive sign means that if there is government intervention (sales or purchases) the quotes are being reduced (shifted down) in relation to value. Shifting down the quotes will encourage the customers to buy the US dollar and discourage them from selling the dollar. A negative sign means the opposite: if there is government intervention (sales or purchases), the quotes will shift up. Increasing the quotes motivates the customers to sell the dollar and discourage them from buying the dollar.

In the case of the interest rate differential (X); a positive sign means that the quotes are being reduced in relation to value if the change in the interest rate differential (the interest rate spread) becomes smaller. Then, the dealers shift up the quotation if the interest rate spread widens. On the other hand, a negative sign means that the quotes are being reduced (increased) when the interest rate spread becomes wider (smaller).

We can notice that only the coefficients of dummy sales and dummy purchases change significantly for both the Deutsche mark-dollar series (Table 3.1 and 3.3) and the Japanese yen-dollar (Table 3.2 and 3.4) series. Dummy purchases are significant at 5% level, and dummy sales are not significant for both cases: whether we allow the spread flexible or constant.

Table 3.1. Regression Result
(Deutsche mark-dollar/dummy variables)

Dependent Variable: BID				
Method: Least Squares				
White heteroscedasticity-Consistent Standard Errors & Covariance				
Variable	Coefficient	Std. Error	t-Statistic	Prob.
SPREAD	5.089317	1.008257	5.047638	0.0000
X	-0.018937	0.008843	-2.141360	0.0326
DUMMYPURCHASE	12.16657	2.953805	4.118949	0.0000
DUMMYSALES	1.265583	4.042597	0.313062	0.7543
R-squared	0.043773	Schwarz criterion		-4.816789
Adjusted R-squared	0.039799	Durbin-Watson stat		2.063731

Table 3.2. Regression Result
(Japanese yen-dollar/dummy variables)

Dependent Variable: BID				
Method: Least Squares				
White heteroscedasticity-Consistent Standard Errors & Covariance				
Variable	Coefficient	Std. Error	t-Statistic	Prob.
SPREAD	0.845814	1.459721	0.579436	0.5625
X	-0.849099	0.623336	-1.362187	0.1736
DUMMYPURCHASE	9.473061	1.929362	4.909946	0.0000
DUMMYSALES	4.227555	5.196441	0.813548	0.4162
R-squared	0.014246	Schwarz criterion		3.464636
Adjusted R-squared	0.010027	Durbin-Watson stat		2.062171

For the Deutsche mark-dollar (Table 3.1 and 3.3), the change of the interest rate spread (X) is significant at 5% level. Also, the sign is negative. The negative sign means that the value of the US dollar will be higher when the change of the interest rate spread narrows down. However, the implied value of σ is outside the interval $0 < \sigma < 1$, i.e., ≈ -52[12]. According to the regressive expectations hypothesis, the exchange rate is expected to converge towards its long-run equilibrium, i.e., $0 < \sigma < 1$. Obviously, this is

[12] From the model: $\beta_1 = (1/\sigma)$; $\beta_1 = -0.0189$ and -0.0195, then the value of σ are -52.91 and 51.12.

not the case in our sample ($\sigma \approx -52$). In other words, the exchange rate was further away from the equilibrium during this period.

Table 3.3. Regression result (Deutsche mark-dollar)

Dummy variables with a constant spread Dependent Variable: BID				
Method: Least Squares				
White Heteroskedasticity-Consistent Standard Errors & Covariance				
Variable	Coefficient	Std. Error	t-Statistic	Prob.
DUMMYPURCHASE	0.013431	0.002660	5.049279	0.0000
DUMMYSALES	0.002022	0.005866	0.344748	0.7304
X	-0.019564	0.009126	-2.143740	0.0324
R-squared	0.012733	Schwarz criterion		-4.793917
Adjusted R-squared	0.010002	Durbin-Watson stat		2.045883

Table 3.4. Regression result (Japanese yen-dollar/dummy variables with a constant spread)

Dependent Variable: BID				
Method: Least Squares				
White Heteroskedasticity-Consistent Standard Errors & Covariance				
Variable	Coefficient	Std. Error	t-Statistic	Prob.
X	-0.868075	0.632752	-1.371905	0.1705
DUMMYPURCHASE	0.781261	0.169550	4.607837	0.0000
DUMMYSALES	0.578509	0.950564	0.608595	0.5430
R-squared	0.010652	Schwarz criterion		3.458973
Adjusted R-squared	0.007833	Durbin-Watson stat		2.066212

Dummy purchases are significant at conventional values with a positive sign. A positive sign means that the dealers will shift down the quotes when the government intervenes in the market by purchasing the dollars. It is not what the theory tells us; it should be a negative sign because the purchase of the US dollar signals to the market that the government has an intention to appreciate the dollar in the future. Thus, the dealers should shift up the quotes instead of shifting down the quotes to discourage their customers from buying the dollars and encourage them to buy the dollars. Apparently, the dealers reacted in the opposite direction of the government's intention.

In the case of the Japanese yen-dollar exchange rate, the change of interest rate differential (X) and the sale of the US dollar are not significant. Only dummy purchases are significant at 1% critical value with a positive sign. It is similar to the Deutsche mark-dollar series: the dealers will shift down the quotes as they anticipate the US dollar will appreciate in the future. The dealers altered their inventory in the different direction from the government's intention.

To investigate the impact of an intervention on the shift of quotes, the size of intervention data in the regression (3.3) will be reviewed in the following section.

3.2.2. Size of Intervention Variable

After examining the assumptions of the underlying OLS (in Appendix 8), we can conclude that we have to correct the estimates of the coefficient covariances due to the presence of heteroscedasticity for both the Deutsche mark-dollar and the Japanese yen-dollar series. The results of the regressions after correcting the heteroscedasticity are presented in Table 3.5 and 3.6. The outcomes of using dummy variables and using the size of intervention are different in coefficient but not in the level of significance. The coefficients are different (but not variable X) because we use different scales: 0 and 1 for dummy variables and millions of dollars for the size of intervention variables. However, we are only concerned with the level of significant since this relates to the behavior of the dealers in controlling their inventory by shifting down or up the quotes.

Again, the results are similar to those for the dummy variables: only the coefficients of intervention purchases and sales change considerably but not the level of significance for both series.

As in previous section (dummy variable), we make a further assumption; i.e., the spread is constant. Table 3.7 and 3.8 below display the results.

Table 3.5. The Regression Result
(Deutsche mark-dollar/size of intervention)

Dependent Variable: BID				
Method: Least Squares				
White Heteroskedasticity-Consistent Standard Errors & Covariance				
Variable	Coefficient	Std. Error	t-Statistic	Prob.
SPREAD	5.267453	0.989955	5.320904	0.0000
X	-0.018406	0.008774	-2.097713	0.0363
INTVPURCHASE	0.077503	0.014936	5.189140	0.0000
INTVSALES	0.010886	0.014817	0.734717	0.4628
R-squared	0.045980	Schwarz criterion		-4.819100
Adjusted R-squared	0.042016	Durbin-Watson stat		2.052574

Table 3.6. The Regression Result
(Japanese yen-dollar/size of intervention)

Dependent Variable: BID				
Method: Least Squares				
White Heteroskedasticity-Consistent Standard Errors & Covariance				
Variable	Coefficient	Std. Error	t-Statistic	Prob.
SPREAD	1.778081	1.408770	1.262151	0.2073
X	-0.777805	0.614173	-1.266425	0.2058
INTVPURCHASE	0.049355	0.009822	5.024734	0.0000
INTVSALES	0.012714	0.040467	0.314190	0.7535
R-squared	0.006931	Schwarz criterion		3.472028
Adjusted R-squared	0.002681	Durbin-Watson stat		2.053611

Table 3.7. The Regression result
(Deutsche mark-dollar/size of intervention with a constant spread)

Dependent Variable: BID				
Method: Least Squares				
White Heteroskedasticity-Consistent Standard Errors & Covariance				
Variable	Coefficient	Std. Error	t-Statistic	Prob.
X	-0.019008	0.009027	-2.105651	0.0356
INTVPURCHASE	7.10E-05	1.35E-05	5.237151	0.0000
INTVSALES	1.27E-05	1.71E-05	0.739287	0.4600
R-squared	0.011728	Schwarz criterion		-4.792900
Adjusted R-squared	0.008995	Durbin-Watson stat		2.037568

Table 3.8. The Regression result
(Japanese yen-dollar/size of intervention with a constant spread)

Dependent Variable: BID				
Method: Least Squares				
White Heteroskedasticity-Consistent Standard Errors & Covariance				
Variable	Coefficient	Std. Error	t-Statistic	Prob.
X	-0.806291	0.625031	-1.290003	0.1975
INTVPURCHASE	0.002785	0.000739	3.770488	0.0002
INTVSALES	0.002065	0.004610	0.447981	0.6543
R-squared	0.001386	Schwarz criterion		3.468294
Adjusted R-squared	-0.001459	Durbin-Watson stat		2.055161

For the Deutsche mark-dollar (Table 3.5 and Table 3.7), we can observe that the change of the interest rate differential (X) is significant at 5% level with the negative sign. However, the value of σ is outside the interval $0 < \sigma < 1$, i.e., ≈ -53[13].

Moreover, the intervention by purchasing the US dollar is significant at a conventional value with the positive sign. It means that every 1 million purchase of the US dollar will shift down the quotation around 0.0771. It confirms the result of using the dummy variables.

In the case of the Japanese yen-dollar exchange rate, only intervention by purchasing the US dollar is significant at 1% critical value with a positive sign. It means the dealers will shift down the quotes around 0.0491 point every 1 million purchase of the US dollar. In both series, the dealers are supposed to shift up the quotes. The empirical result does not confirm this outcome in our sample.

We now discuss in detail the reasons behind the ineffectiveness[14] of the coordinated government intervention in the period 1985 – 1987 in the following section.

---

[13] $\beta = 1/\sigma$; $\sigma = 1/-0.0184$ and $1/-0.019$.

[14] Either the intervention did not have any influence on the dealer's behavior or the dealers reacted in the opposite direction of the government's intention.

3.3. The Events of Intervention from 1985 to 1987

Between August 1984 and August 1987, the United States had three approaches to exchange rate intervention. Prior to the Plaza meeting (September 1985), the approach was to continue the policy established in March 1981, i.e., to calm disorderly markets. The second approach was after the G-5 meeting, to encourage dollar depreciation through coordinated government intervention. The third approach followed the G-7 meeting in February 1987, i.e., to stabilize the dollar (Humpage, 1988). On this basis, we divided the data into three events: pre-Plaza Agreement, Plaza Agreement, and Louvre Accord[15].

3.3.1. Pre-Plaza Agreement

In this section, we investigate the behavior of dealers on intervention before the remarkable coordinated intervention by G-3. As in the previous section, we set the data (Deutsche mark-dollar and Japanese yen-dollar) into two: dummy (purchase and sales) and the size of intervention (purchase and sales). The results are presented in the following Tables[16].

First of all, we obtain the similar results for both dummy variable and the size of intervention equation. Second, both of the series also have the similar outputs. The only significant variable is the change of the interest rate differential, and the sign is negative. It means that the dealers shift up the quotes in the Deutsche mark-dollar and the Japanese yen-dollar when the interest rate differential becomes smaller. Thus, during this period the dealers reacted to the change of interest rate spread by shifting down the quotation of the Deutsche mark-dollar and the Japanese yen-dollar to

[15] We do not include Tokyo Summit (4th of May 1986) since there was no intervention at all by the Fed during 1986.

[16] We check all the violations of assumptions of underlying OLS. However, we do not include them in the discussion (Appendix 8), we directly remedy the violations if they present in the regression.

anticipate the depreciation of the US dollar when the interest rate spread widened. The dealers preferred to hold foreign currency to US dollar when the US interest rate rose, or Germany/Japan interest rate fell. It contradicts the evidence that the currency with the higher interest rate appreciates on average against the currency with the lower interest rate (Froot and Thaler, 1990). However, it is consistent with the International Fisher Effect. The value of σ is outside the interval between 0 and 1: $\sigma = 1/-0.0687 = -14.55$ and $\sigma = 1/-3.0836 = -0.3244$ for the Deutsche mark-dollar and the Japanese yen-dollar respectively. According to the regressive expectations model, the value of σ lies between 0 and 1, which means the exchange rate is expected to converge towards its long-run equilibrium value. In contrast, our empirical results ($\sigma = -14.55$ and $\sigma = -0.3244$) suggest that the exchange rate was further away from the long-run equilibrium during the pre-Plaza period.

Before the Plaza Agreement, there was no purchase intervention; all the government intervention was as sales of dollars. Table 3.9 – 3.12 show that the intervention by selling the US dollar did not have a significant impact on the dealers' behavior in controlling their inventory. In other words, the sale of government intervention is not significant. Humpage (1988) supports this view. He suggests that pre-G5 intervention period did not have a systematic impact on day to day exchange rate movements. The depreciation of the dollar in that period was due to foreign intervention and/or a statement of the Federal Reserve Chairman[17] rather than to US intervention. Furthermore, Humpage notes that the US intervention still had a previous intervention policy[18] also, the government did not give any signal to change the monetary or fiscal policies. Chairman Volker also restated that "intervention by itself was of limited usefulness in affecting exchange rates, and the US Treasury did not seem to favor increased intervention" (Humpage, 1988, p.8). 3.3.2 Plaza Agreement.

---

[17] "Intervention in January, and early February had not been sufficient to influence the exchange rate. He seemed to suggest that a larger volume of intervention was necessary on those occasions when central banks intervened" (Humpage, 1988, p.7).

[18] To calm disorderly markets or to prevent disruptive speculation.

Table 3.9. The Regression result[19]
(Deutsche mark-dollar/dummy variable pre-Plaza Agreement)

Dependent Variable: BID				
Method: Least Squares				
Variable	Coefficient	Std. Error	t-Statistic	Prob.
X	-0.068779	0.018285	-3.761485	0.0002
SPREAD	5.362693	1.670247	3.210719	0.0016
DUMMYSALES	3.631362	4.476230	0.811255	0.4183
R-squared	0.128344	Schwarz criterion		-4.107060
Adjusted R-squared	0.118325	Durbin-Watson stat		2.031834

Table 3.10. The Regression result
(Deutsche mark-dollar/size of intervention pre-Plaza Agreement)

Dependent Variable: BID				
Method: Least Squares				
Variable	Coefficient	Std. Error	t-Statistic	Prob.
X	-0.067488	0.018408	-3.666291	0.0003
SPREAD	5.554546	1.681811	3.302717	0.0012
INTVSALES	-0.008157	0.049252	-0.165615	0.8687
R-squared	0.125185	Schwarz criterion		-4.103442
Adjusted R-squared	0.115130	Durbin-Watson stat		2.021538

Table 3.11. The Regression result
(Japanese yen-dollar/dummy variable pre-Plaza Agreement)

Dependent Variable: BID				
Method: Least Squares				
Variable	Coefficient	Std. Error	t-Statistic	Prob.
X	-3.083611	0.997458	-3.091469	0.0024
SPREAD	1.294094	2.543761	0.508733	0.6117
DUMMYSALES	3.802808	6.539585	0.581506	0.5618
R-squared	0.060250	Schwarz criterion		3.509091
Adjusted R-squared	0.047884	Durbin-Watson stat		2.399406

[19] There is no the purchase intervention since the Fed only intervened by selling US dollars during that time. We also check the regression with a constant spread, but we do not include it in the discussion because the results are the same as the regression with a flexible spread.

Now we investigate how powerful the intervention when the G-5 countries had a meeting in the Plaza hotel on September 22, 1985, to coordinate the intervention. The Tables 3.13 – 3.16 below show the results of the intervention.

Table 3.12. The Regression result
(Japanese yen-dollar/size of intervention pre-Plaza Agreement)

Dependent Variable: BID				
Method: Least Squares				
Variable	Coefficient	Std. Error	t-Statistic	Prob.
X	-3.083611	0.997458	-3.091469	0.0024
SPREAD	1.294094	2.543761	0.508733	0.6117
INTVSALES	-0.077926	0.134008	-0.581506	0.5618
R-squared	0.060250	Schwarz criterion		3.509091
Adjusted R-squared	0.047884	Durbin-Watson stat		2.399406

Table 3.13. The Regression result[20]
(Deutsche mark-dollar/dummy variable Plaza Agreement)

Dependent Variable: BID				
Method: Least Squares				
Newey-West HAC Standard Errors & Covariance (lag truncation=3)				
Variable	Coefficient	Std. Error	t-Statistic	Prob.
X	-0.044112	0.052530	-0.839746	0.4034
SPREAD	2.199957	4.070258	0.540496	0.5903
DUMMYSALES	0.658737	6.093548	0.108104	0.9142
R-squared	-0.012389	Schwarz criterion		-4.438627
Adjusted R-squared	-0.036494	Durbin-Watson stat		2.102384

From the tables above, we can conclude that the intervention did not have any influence on dealers' behavior during the sample period. It is also shown that the change in the interest rate spread is not significant. Thus, during this period the dealers did not change the quotation to control their inventory when the interest rate spread widened or narrowed. Moreover,

[20] The explanation is the same as footnote 19.

the value of σ was outside the interval 0 and 1[21] that meant the exchange rate deviated away from the long-run equilibrium.

We obtain the same result for the sale intervention in Deutsche mark-dollar and Japanese yen-dollar equations, i.e., it is not significant at the conventional value with a positive sign. It suggests that the dealers did not shift down the quotes when the government signaled to the market that it

Table 3.14. The Regression result
(Deutsche mark-dollar/size of intervention Plaza Agreement)

Dependent Variable: BID				
Method: Least Squares				
Newey-West HAC Standard Errors & Covariance (lag truncation=3)				
Variable	Coefficient	Std. Error	t-Statistic	Prob.
X	-0.044925	0.061515	-0.730305	0.4672
SPREAD	2.215925	3.772315	0.587418	0.5585
INTVSALES	0.009557	0.013736	0.695762	0.4885
R-squared	-0.008585	Schwarz criterion		-4.442392
Adjusted R-squared	-0.032599	Durbin-Watson stat		2.106856

Table 3.15. The Regression result
(Japanese yen-dollar/dummy variable Plaza Agreement)

Dependent Variable: BID				
Method: Least Squares				
White Heteroskedasticity-Consistent Standard Errors & Covariance				
Variable	Coefficient	Std. Error	t-Statistic	Prob.
X	-2.253113	2.148694	-1.048597	0.2960
SPREAD	-1.612399	3.586749	-0.449543	0.6537
DUMMYSALES	5.553219	6.052345	0.917532	0.3603
R-squared	-0.019295	Schwarz criterion		4.087297
Adjusted R-squared	-0.032197	Durbin-Watson stat		1.892652

[21]-22.27 and –0.46 for Deutsche mark-dollar and Japanese yen-dollar series respectively.

Table 3.16. The Regression result
(Japanese yen-dollar/size of intervention Plaza Agreement)

Dependent Variable: BID				
Method: Least Squares				
White Heteroskedasticity-Consistent Standard Errors & Covariance				
Variable	Coefficient	Std. Error	t-Statistic	Prob.
X	-2.170190	2.245553	-0.966439	0.3353
SPREAD	1.286762	3.030772	0.424566	0.6717
INTVSALES	0.013308	0.041406	0.321405	0.7483
R-squared	-0.038362	Schwarz criterion		4.105831
Adjusted R-squared	-0.051506	Durbin-Watson stat		1.894020

wished to depreciate the dollar through intervention. Nonetheless, we recognize that the dollar depreciated during that time. As Humpage (1988) notes "intervention had a strong announcement effect on both the mark-dollar and yen-dollar exchange rates, which could have lasted through early October. Day to day movement in the dollar, however, was not correlated with day to day intervention. After October 4, the intervention did not seem to contribute to the dollar's depreciation" (p.10).

Furthermore, the intervention was "leaning with the wind"[22] Moreover, the market generally preferred the depreciation of the US dollar. The G-5 policymakers also did not encourage a belief in the expectation of additional intervention to bring the dollar lower. The United States and German policies did not support the intervention, and the central banks did not promote the policy (Humpage, 1988). Ito (1987) suggesting that the intervention not have a major role in the period immediately following the Plaza agreement. He finds that "five waves of yen appreciation were, respectively, caused by the U.S policy switch, the high-interest rate policy by the Bank of Japan, the decline in oil prices, and a mix of prospects of U.S. fiscal deficit reduction and a further decline in oil prices. In other words, the exchange rates respond to news on what we consider fundamentals and not to mere interventions by the monetary authorities" (p.297-298). According to Funabashi (1988, p.214), the G-5 strategy from

[22] The dollar already had been depreciating.

the Plaza meeting to the Louvre meeting was not meeting the expectations of the supporters of more powerful policy coordination. He states that there were many critics of the event. One commentator noted that "the Plaza meeting itself was a non-event. There was simply no need for it: the dollar had already started to depreciate, so there was no need to push it" (p. 214). Thus, the depreciation of dollar during that time was not due to the intervention itself, but because of other variables. It explains the insignificance of our coefficients here.

3.3.2. Louvre Accord

The last event of coordinated government intervention during 1985-1987 is Louvre Accord. During that period, the Fed intervened in the market by buying and selling the US dollar against Deutsche mark and by buying the US dollar against Japanese yen.

From the table below, we recognize that the change in the interest rate spread is significant and has a positive sign for both series. It implies that the dealers quoted down (up) the Deutsche mark and the Japanese yen relative to the value of a dollar when the interest rate spread became smaller (wider) as the dealers anticipated the value of the dollar would depreciate (appreciate). It is consistent with the fact that the currency of the country, which has a higher (lower) interest rate, will appreciate (depreciate) (Froot and Thaler, 1992). This finding is also consistent with the fact that the dollar kept depreciating at a more modest pace and the interest rate spread widened to attract private capital. In addition, the value of σ is in the interval 0 and 1, i.e., 0.65 (1/1.56 = 0.65) for the Japanese yen-dollar. This number means that the market weighed the long-run equilibrium exchange rate more than the spot exchange rate in forming the expectation of future exchange rate[23]. However, the value of σ is outside the interval 0 and 1 for the Deutsche mark-dollar, i.e., 96.15 (1/0.01 =96.15).

---

[23] Regressive expectations: $E(s) = (1 - \sigma)s_t + \sigma s^*$.

Table 3.17. The Regression result
(Deutsche mark-dollar/dummy variable Louvre Accord)

Dependent Variable: BID				
Method: Least Squares				
Variable	Coefficient	Std. Error	t-Statistic	Prob.
X	0.010403	0.005909	1.760526	0.0798
SPREAD	1.686147	2.643232	0.637911	0.5242
DUMMYPURCHASE	12.50840	2.394269	5.224310	0.0000
DUMMYSALES	-6.073788	4.882145	-1.244082	0.2149
R-squared	0.137311	Schwarz criterion		-6.056090
Adjusted R-squared	0.124686	Durbin-Watson stat		2.132180

Table 3.18. The Regression result
(Deutsche mark-dollar/size of intervention, Louvre Accord)

Dependent Variable: BID				
Method: Least Squares				
Variable	Coefficient	Std. Error	t-Statistic	Prob.
X	0.010340	0.005839	1.771077	0.0780
SPREAD	2.007663	2.573492	0.780132	0.4362
INTVPURCHASE	0.080256	0.013831	5.802785	0.0000
INTVSALES	0.017369	0.023060	0.753184	0.4522
R-squared	0.155547	Schwarz criterion		-6.077456
Adjusted R-squared	0.143189	Durbin-Watson stat		2.035993

Table 3.19. The Regression result
(Japanese yen-dollar/dummy variable, Louvre Accord)

Dependent Variable: BID				
Method: Least Squares				
White Heteroskedasticity-Consistent Standard Errors & Covariance				
Variable	Coefficient	Std. Error	t-Statistic	Prob.
X	1.525158	0.832492	1.832039	0.0684
SPREAD	2.316430	1.918816	1.207218	0.2288
DUMMYPURCHASE	9.190527	2.020315	4.549057	0.0000
R-squared	0.116625	Schwarz criterion		2.879465
Adjusted R-squared	0.107746	Durbin-Watson stat		2.067109

Table 3.20. The Regression result (Japanese yen-dollar/size of intervention, Louvre Accord)

Dependent Variable: BID				
Method: Least Squares				
White Heteroskedasticity-Consistent Standard Errors & Covariance				
Variable	Coefficient	Std. Error	t-Statistic	Prob.
X	1.567473	0.839112	1.868013	0.0632
SPREAD	2.553121	1.954850	1.306044	0.1930
INTVPURCHASE	0.046228	0.010161	4.549348	0.0000
R-squared	0.106500	Schwarz criterion		2.890861
Adjusted R-squared	0.097520	Durbin-Watson stat		2.059137

For the intervention variables, only the purchase intervention is significant at the conventional value with positive signs (wrong sign). The purchase intervention is supposed to signal to the market that the government intends to appreciate the dollar. Consequently, the dealers will shift up the quotes to discourage dollar selling and encourage dollar buying by customers. However, during this period, the dealers responded to the purchase intervention oppositely. Some events may explain the result.

The decline of dollars since early 1987 concerned the US Treasury due to its relation to the decline of foreign capital inflows into the United States. The Louvre Accord was intended to stabilize the dollar. During the first five weeks after the Louvre Accord, the dollar was stable against the Japanese yen and strengthened against the Deutsche mark. After mid-March, however, the dollar began to fall. It seemed to be due to a loss of confidence by investors in the dollar due to trade problems. Between March 23 and April 6, the New York Federal Reserve Bank bought dollars against yen daily. The interventions were coordinated with the Bank of Japan and several European central banks.

However, the trade issues (especially protectionism)[24] were coupled with the passage, in the US of House of Representatives, of the Gephardt

[24] This is the primary cause of the market's concern over the dollar.

amendment to the pending trade bill (29 April)[25]. It caused a huge sale of dollars in world currency markets. Furthermore, market participants turned to the April G-7 meeting in Washington for the signals of the commitment of the finance ministers to stabilize the exchange rate. However, "they indicated no changes in monetary or fiscal policies that might have altered the fundamentals in the exchange rate" (Humpage, 1988, p.12). The dollar fell after the meeting. The Federal Reserve conducted the intervention operations purchasing dollar in coordination with the Bank of Japan and European central banks. At the end of all, from February through the end of April, the dollar had declined 3 7/8% on a trade-weighted basis against all G-10 currencies (Funabashi, 1988, p.190), even though the Fed Reserve intervened in the market by purchasing the dollar to prop up its value.

"Unlike the G-5 episode, however, the central banks were leaning against the wind instead of with it" (Humpage, 1988, p.13). In addition, there was a contradictory statement between Treasury Secretary Baker and US Trade Representative Yeuter. Baker tried to convince the market that the United States did not want the dollar depreciates more, but Yeuter opposed Baker's statement. Therefore, the intervention did not have any impact on the exchange rate. The dollar continued to depreciate (Humpage, 1988).

Later in the year, the large scale of G-3 (Japan, Germany, and USA) intervention to support the dollar after the stock market crash of October 1987 was not credible. As Dominguez (1990) quoted that "newspaper accounts in this period suggest that while traders were well-informed of the timing and magnitude of central bank intervention operations, dollar supporting intervention by the Fed was not credible. Market participants perceived the U.S commitment to averting a post-crash liquidity crisis as stronger than its commitment to supporting the dollars" (Dominguez, 1990, p.139). That is why the dealers shifted the quotes down to unload the dollars since the value of the dollars kept going down, although the government was signaling to the market to bring up the value of the dollar.

---

[25] Which restricted imports from countries defined as having "excessive trade surpluses" with the United States.

In other words, the government action was not credible enough to make the markets believe its intention.

Conclusion

Now we turn to the conclusion of the empirical works above. Let us summarize all the empirical results in Table 3.21.

Table 3.21. Table estimates and (probability) (Deutsche mark-dollar and Japanese yen-dollar)

	Interest rate	Purchase of US dollar	Sale of US dollar
Pre-Plaza Agreement			
Dummy variables:			
Deutsche mark-dollar	-0.0687 (0.0002)	-	3.631 (0.4183)
Japanese yen-dollar	-3.083 (0.0024)	-	3.8028 (0.5618)
Size intervention:			
Deutsche mark-dollar	-0.0674 (0.0003)	-	-0.0082 (0.8687)
Japanese yen-dollar	-3.0836 (0.0024)	-	-0.0779 (0.5618)
Plaza Agreement			
Dummy variables:			
Deutsche mark-dollar	-0.0441 (0.1488)	-	0.6587 (0.8499)
Japanese yen-dollar	-2.2531 (0.2960)	-	5.553 (0.3603)
Size intervention:			
Deutsche mark-dollar	-0.0449 (0.1340)	-	0.0095 (0.5540)
Japanese yen-dollar	-2.1701 (0.3353)	-	0.0133 (0.7483)
Louvre Accord			
Dummy variables:			
Deutsche mark-dollar	0.0104 (0.0798)	12.508 (0.0000)	-6.0737 (0.2149)

	Interest rate	Purchase of US dollar	Sale of US dollar
Japanese yen-dollar	1.5251 (0.0684)	9.190 (0.0000)	-
Size intervention:			
Deutsche mark-dollar	0.0103 (0.0780)	0.0802 (0.0000)	0.0173 (0.4522)
Japanese yen-dollar	1.5674 (0.0163)	0.0462 (0.0000)	-
The whole sample: 1985-1987			
Dummy variables:			
Deutsche mark-dollar	-0.0192 (0.0295)	12.0727 (0.0000)	1.2673 (0.7531)
Japanese yen-dollar	-0.8912 (0.1538)	9.3500 (0.0000)	4.2475 (0.4063)
Size intervention:			
Deutsche mark-dollar	-0.0186 (0.0327)	0.0771 (0.0000)	0.0108 (0.4487)
Japanese yen-dollar	-0.8253 (0.1824)	0.04911 (0.0000)	0.0126 (0.7520)

First, we obtain similar quantitative results for dummy variables and the size of intervention, even though some of these have different signs. This is not of any particular concern since the variables which give different signs (between dummy and size intervention) are not significant.

Second, most of the signs of the interest rate spread variables are negative. In addition, they are significant at the conventional values for the Deutsche mark-dollar series, but only during the period of Louvre Accord the interest rate spread is significant for the Japanese yen-dollar series. The negative sign means that the dealers responded to the change of interest rate spread by shifting down the quotes to anticipate the depreciation of the US dollar when the interest rate spread widened. It is consistent with the International Fisher Effect. However, the implied value of σ is outside the interval 0 and 1, which means that the exchange rate moved away from the long-run equilibrium value during that period.

For the intervention variable, only purchase intervention is significant at the conventional level with a positive sign for both series. It means that the dealers behaved in the opposite direction in controlling their inventory when there was a signal that the government was willing to increase the value of US dollar.

In conclusion, the intervention during this period (from 1985 to 1987) appeared not to be credible. Consequently, the intervention was not effective. The ineffectiveness of the intervention was mainly due to the lack of commitment of the monetary authorities (DeGrauwe, 1996). Moreover, there was a view that the G-5 had to hasten their efforts to build a more credible and effective international monetary regime or commit themselves fully to policy coordination (Funabashi, 1988, p.246).

It was indicated above that the dealers controlled their inventory level by shifting the quotes (in the opposite direction), even though the government's commitment to policy coordination was not credible. It means the dealers pay more attention to the inventory cost since the inventory level relates to the opportunity costs and the risk of shifting the value of the currency. Now, we turn to the relative significance of inventory cost compared with the other two components of spread. The following two chapters investigate this subject thoroughly.

Chapter 4

The Bid-Ask Spread: The Market Microstructure Perspective

As we noted in Chapter 3, the dealers shifted the quotes down as the US dollar kept depreciating, even though the government gave a signal to appreciate the dollar in the period 1985 to 1987. It meant that the dealers were most concerned with the inventory cost since holding currency inventories to provide immediacy imposes opportunity costs and the risk of changes in inventory value. The next question is how important is the inventory cost as a component of the bid-ask spreads. The theoretical background will be developed in this chapter, followed by the discussion of the empirical analysis in Chapter 5.

4.1. Concepts

The "study of securities market microstructure deals with the behavior of market participants in securities markets and with the effects of information, and institutional rules on the economic performance of those markets" (Flood, 1991 p.52). Thus, this literature focuses on the behavior of market agents and market characteristics rather than on the influence of macro fundamentals.

Traders' behavior is the central issue in the market microstructure. The behavior of market participants has an impact on market inefficiency. Flood (1991) measures the inefficiency by arbitrage opportunities, price dispersion, adjustment interval (the amount of time for convergence of the disequilibrium price to consensus), suboptimal allocation (the difference between the desired inventory and the actual inventory), and serial correlation. He finds from empirical work that a) as market makers become more numerous, arbitrage opportunities will increase but price dispersion, serial correlation, adjustment interval, and suboptimal allocation decrease; b) as brokers become numerous, price dispersion and serial correlation will increase, but there is a decrease in arbitrage opportunities and suboptimal allocations emerge, and there is no impact on the adjustment interval; c) as customers become more numerous, arbitrage opportunities, adjustment interval, and suboptimal allocation will increase too, but dispersion and serial correlation will decrease. Thus, a market composition has an impact on inefficiency. Furthermore, centralization of price information will reduce inefficiency.

> The interaction of institutional and behavioral factors generates the bid-ask spread. A bid is the buying price (from a market maker's point of view), and ask is the selling price (from the same point of view). The spread is the difference between the ask price and bid price. In the data used in this study, the major currency quotation spreads have a tendency to cluster in the value of 10 points for 53% of the quotations and the values of 5, 15 and 20 for 23% of the quotations when stated in conventional terms. However, spreads in non-conventional terms are substantially less clustered (Bessembinder, 1994, p.322).
>
> Quoted prices are different from transaction prices. Quotes are only indicative, they do not represent the bid and ask prices at which a bank will enter into a transaction. The trade activity within the interbank market is different from the posting of indicative quotes. However, the trading and quote-making decisions are not made independently from one another (Evans, 1998).

Flood (1991, p.64) argues that the bid-ask spread violates the law of one price since it prices the same commodity differently. However, there are several reasons to explain this apparent inconsistency. We argue in the next section that the bid-ask spread covers three types of costs: order-processing costs, asymmetric-information costs, and inventory carrying costs (Bessembinder, 1994 p.322).

In the foreign exchange market, market makers do not act as brokers, and the brokers do not act as market makers *(Lehalle and Sophie, 2013)*. They have separate functions. Market makers determine the bid and ask spread, and brokers receive the bid price (limit orders) from market makers and the ask price (limit orders) from other market makers. The broker's spread is the combination of the best bid and best ask, received by a broker as separate limit orders. "One motive for trading through a foreign exchange broker is to maintain the anonymity-the name of the bank placing a limit order is not revealed unless a deal is consummated and then only to the counterparty" (Flood, 1991 p.67). However, the theoretical models of brokered spreads are few, and there is not a clear understanding of the differences in price information between a market maker's spread and a broker's spread.

Market microstructure classifies a market as an interbank direct market (decentralized, continuous, open bid, double-auction market), or a brokered market (quasi-centralized, continuous, limit book, single-auction market) (Flood, 1991; Chen, et. al., 2012). The concepts are defined as follows:

- A *decentralized* market is one in which market makers (banks) quote and transact privately. Thus, the price is quoted, and the transaction is done by a private meeting between two market makers (banks). A *quasi-centralized* market is one in which brokers accumulate a subset of market makers' limit orders. The market is not fully centralized, since there is a multiplicity of brokers in the foreign exchange market, and, each broker receives a subset of market maker's limit orders.
- *A continuous* market is when "trading occurs at its own pace, and transaction orders are processed as they arrive" (Flood, 1991 p.58).

With continuous trading, earlier transactions satisfy some consumers and producers, and this causes shifts in supply and demand that affect prices for later transactions.

- *"Open-bid"* and *"limit-book"* are the ways of communicating price information. "Open-bid" is when a buy or sell price is announced to all agents in the market. Any participant can contact a market maker at any time for a price quote. "Limit-book" refers to the book of market maker's limit orders that contains an order to buy or sell a specified quantity of foreign currency at a specified price. The brokers arrange trades by keeping this limit book from which they quote the best bid and ask orders upon request. They refer to the best bid and ask in this book as the inside spread. Thus, the market makers can contact brokers to obtain the inside spread.
- *"Double-auction"* and *"single-auction"* are the ways the prices are quoted. Double-auction occurs when prices of both bid and ask are provided by participants, while a single-auction is when prices are specified to buy or sell. Hence, market makers provide double-auction prices, and brokers collect single-auction quotes in both ways, bid and ask quotes.

We now consider the important aspect of spread that is the components of spread.

4.2. The Components of the Bid-Ask Spread

As mentioned above, the spread covers three costs: order-processing costs, asymmetric-information cost, and inventory carrying costs.

The order processing cost is compensation for the costs of the transactions (telephone and telex charges, salaries, etc.). Glassman (1987 p.487) predicts that transaction costs may decline monotonically over time as technology in communications improve, as the volume of transactions became larger, and with an increase in competition among market makers. Empirically, so far, there has been no tendency for transaction costs to decline: instead, they have varied from year to year. Glassman believes these changes can be explained by changes in government controls on the foreign exchange and capital markets.

The asymmetric-information cost (the cost of adverse selection) is explained as the compensation to market participants for losing to the "information-motivated traders." Bagehot (1971) suggests that market makers deal with liquidity-motivated transactors who pay the spread in exchange for the service of predictable immediacy and with traders who have inside information. Thus, the market makers must charge everyone a wider spread to compensate for their loss when trading with informed traders. Informed traders are potentially able to obtain short-term profit from their own customers' orders who are liquidity-based since the informed traders can identify their customers who trade due to financing international trade or corporate transactions from the customers who have superior information regarding the fundamental determinants of the spot exchange rate. Thus, the liquidity traders' strategies are designed to minimize losses when dealing with informed traders (Lyons, 1997).

Glosten and Milgrom (1985) develop a model to show how the spread arises from adverse selection. Their model uses a risk-neutral competitive specialist who faces no transaction costs, that is, a specialist who has unlimited inventories of cash and securities with which to transact and the holding cost of inventories is zero. The ask prices increase, and bid prices decrease if the insiders' information becomes better, or the insiders become more numerous relative to liquidity traders, or the elasticity of the expected supply and demand of a liquidity trader increases.

Chung and Charvenwong (1998, p.1) also suggest that the market makers protect themselves from the informed traders by maintaining larger spreads for stocks with a higher tendency of insider trading since they may not be able to detect the insider trading when it occurs. Furthermore, Glosten and Milgrom state that the spread from adverse selection and specialists' costs have a qualitatively different effect on the serial correlation of price changes. The spread from specialists' cost leads to negative serial correlation, while spreads due solely to adverse selection do not lead to serial correlation. Then, the correlation coefficient can be used to determine the relative magnitudes of the sources of the spread. In addition, over time, the value expectations of the specialist and the insiders tend to converge. It means the insider information tends to be fully disseminated into the market prices.

Glosten (1987) explores further the relation between bid-ask spreads and transaction price behavior by focusing on asymmetric information and gross profit components of the spread. He supports the Glosten and Milgrom (1985) results: the spread from the gross profit components source induces biases in the measurement of mean return and variances of the return, and that induces negative serial covariance in the measured returns. The gross profit component leads to a fluctuation in transaction prices about the true price, while the adverse selection component leads only to fluctuations in the true price.

To follow up Glosten's model (1985 and 1987), Glosten and Harris (1988) develop and implement a technique for estimating a model of the bid-ask spread. They decompose the spread into two components: due to asymmetry, and due to inventory costs, specialist monopoly power, and clearing costs. They use NYSE common stock transaction prices in the period 1981-1983. They call the inventory cost, clearing fees, and/or monopoly profits the transitory component since its effect on stock price time series is unrelated to the underlying value of the securities.

In contrast, they call the adverse selection component the permanent component, since it has a permanent effect on all future prices due to the revision of market maker expectations. They conclude that there is evidence of adverse selection in the components of spread. The adverse selection spread component should be positively related to the transitory spread component. The wider the transitory spread, the more likely liquidity motivates the trader's trade. When the transitory spread is small, the number of informed traders should increase, and the adverse selection should also increase.

In the foreign exchange market, Ito et al. (1998) define private information as information that satisfies two criteria: (1) it is not common knowledge, and (2) it is price relevant. They provide a taxonomy of private information by considering a two-period trading model in which trading occurs at prices P_0 and P_1, then a terminal payoff F is realized at t=2. They refer to information on the terminal payoff F as fundamental private information, e.g., a dealer who receives private signals of a country's trade balance long before published statistics are available and a dealer who receives a central bank's order has also received private information. The latter is part of "secret" government intervention: the Federal Reserve Bank intervenes secretly through the broker market, or through a commercial bank with which it does not usually do business. The broker or the bank has an incentive not to disclose this intervention if it wants to be privy to future intervention and business (Frenkel and Dominguez, 1993).

In contrast, the information unrelated to the payoff F but relevant to interim prices P_0 and P_1 is considered to be semi-fundamental private information. Ito et al. (1998) provide two examples to describe semi-fundamental private information. The first example is superior knowledge of the distribution of dealer inventories. Because the transparency of order flow in spot foreign exchange is low, a dealer often has superior knowledge of her own and others' inventories.

Moreover, Lyons (1993) confirms that the foreign exchange market is a phone and computer network over which dealers quote bid and ask prices, and then consummate transactions. These communications are purely bilateral so that the price and quantities traded are not as transparent as they are in other financial markets. He says that asymmetric information occurs if a market maker deals with a non-market maker customer and other market makers do not know about it. Thus, he concludes that order flow as the source of information asymmetry among dealers (Lyons, 1991).

A second example is when traders share common information on F, but they may still disagree on the meaning of this information, thereby affecting P_0 or P_1. Then, Ito et al. (1998) provide evidence of private information in the foreign exchange market. They introduce the trading in Tokyo over the lunch hour. "Lunch-return variance doubles with the introduction for trading, which cannot be due to public information since the flow of public information did not change with the trading rules" (p.1111).

Flood (1991 p.65) also says that the adverse selection applies in the foreign exchange market since the spread allows market makers some protection against arbitrage opportunities. Arbitrage opportunities are viewed as a form of inside information in a market where price information is not centralized. Besides, Bessembinder (1994) suggests that adverse selection (informed traders[26]) exists in the foreign exchange market even though the potential loss from informed traders is less than it is in the equity market.

Bossaerts and Hillion (1991) investigate the bid-ask spread in the spot and forward foreign exchange markets when some traders have superior information about government intervention using four continental European currencies with respect to the French franc. They observe that higher and asymmetric bid-ask spreads on Fridays reflect the market makers' reaction when they are confronted with the better-informed traders. The smaller and less asymmetric spreads on other days of the week than Fridays suggest that the superior information has value beyond one day, up to a whole week. They also find that there is a less volatile risk premium using currencies with respect to the French franc than currencies with respect to the U.S. dollar. It means that there is a different degree of uncertainty about government intervention. Higher uncertainty about the intervention will increase the asymmetry of the spreads. It makes the forward rate more biased as a predictor of the future spot rate (Bossaerts and Hilton, 1991, p.539).

The inventory carrying cost relates to an opportunity cost component and the risk of changes in inventory value (Bessembinder, 1994). The opportunity cost occurs because the interest rate that can be earned for holding currency inventory that is needed for the spot market is less than the interest rates that can be earned on less liquid deposits. This cost is also referred to as the risk component (Glassman, 1987, p.479). The inventory carrying cost (risk component) increases before weekends and holidays due to the increase of the opportunity cost and the risk of the probability of an exchange rate change that will affect the value of inventory. It will

[26] Uninformed traders (liquidity traders) are traders who trade but not because of the superior information they have.

widen the spreads; thus the currency bid-ask spreads widen with an increase in inventory carrying cost (Bessembinder, 1994 p.331; Glassman, 1987 p.486). Furthermore, the risk component of spreads appears to be influenced by the rate of transactions in the market that is measured by trading volume and the volatility of prices.

4.3. FACTORS THAT INFLUENCE THE BID-ASK SPREAD

Based on the previous writings, we argue that three factors influence the bid-ask spread: price volatility, the market's anticipation of price volatility, and trading volume. There is a positive relationship between the spread and price volatility. Many findings support this relationship. Boothe (1988, p.485) shows the evidence of a relation between exchange rate uncertainty (volatility) and the size of transaction costs (bid-ask spreads) for seven currencies. Bessembinder (1994) and Glassman (1987) also support this argument. Also, bid-ask spreads have been found to be wider under floating exchange rates than under fixed (Aliber, 1975; IMF Annual report, 1982).

The second factor is the market's anticipation of volatility. Wei (1994) uses a currency option to measure the market's ex-ante estimation of exchange rate volatility. "The implied standard deviation from options can be thought of as a market's anticipation of the average daily volatility over the lifetime of the contract" (Wei, 1994 p.9). He finds that a one percent increase in anticipated volatility will widen the bid-ask spreads as much as 0.015%.

The third factor is the trading volume. Glassman (1987 p.486) finds that there is a positive relation between trading volume and spreads. It can be explained by the amount of trader disagreement[27]. This finding is defended by Wei (1994, p.19). He argues that a one percent increase in

[27] There are three determinants of trading volume: (1) the rate of information flows, (2)the amount of trader disagreement, and (3)the number of active traders. Point (2) is relatively more important than (3) for the foreign exchange market, while the literature suggests that (3) is relatively more important for securities markets (Glassman, 1987, p.486).

trading volume leads to a widening of the spread by approximately 0.005% point. Furthermore, Glassman (1987) finds the same result as Wei, even though the estimate of the effect of the volume appears much less than the estimates obtained by Wei. Black (1991 p. 514), however, argues that spreads vary inversely with the expected volume of transactions in the market. Thus the spreads will widen as the volume decreases. Bessembinder (1994 p.329) decomposes volume as forecastable volume and unforecastable volume and finds that forecastable and unforecastable volumes have different effects on bid-ask spread. Bid-ask spreads decrease when forecastable volume increases and bid-ask spreads increase when unforecastable volume increases.

Research by Lyons (1993) finds trading volume also causes price movement through an inventory channel and an information channel. Information asymmetry induces a price increase of one pip[28] for every US$10 million purchase at quoted prices (against DM). Prices can move through the inventory channel by lowering (raising/appreciating) quoted DM price by 3/4 of one pip for every US$10 million of a long position in dollars to motivate dollar purchases (to unload undesired inventory).

Bollerslev and Domowitz (1993) find a strong relation between trading activity (quote arrivals) and bid-ask spreads but only for small banks. The authors conjecture this occurs because small banks have less information regarding retail order flow at the open hour. Thus the spreads might be higher at this time, and they will widen the quoted spreads as trading activity increases. Besides, small banks generate quoted arrivals only during business hours. Hence they are more concerned with their positions in the closing hour. In general, all banks seek to reduce foreign currency positions and increase dollar positions by reducing the quotes on Fridays (before weekends). Thus foreign currencies tend to depreciate against the dollar on weekends (Bessembinder, 1994 p.346).

---

[28] Foreign exchange dealer's term for 0.00001 of a unit, e.g., if the $/yen rate is quoted 220.20, then a rise of five pipe would yield 220.25.

4.4. The Volatility of Exchange Rates

After the Bretton Woods System collapsed in 1971-1973, many countries moved to flexible exchange rates and exchange rates became more volatile. Market participants compare the observed exchange rates with expected exchange rate changes. Interest parity theory implies that "the forward premium is the best available forecast of the future change in the exchange rates" (DeGrauwe, 1989 p.60). However, in the real world changes in the observed exchange rates are much larger than the expected changes measured by forward premia. Therefore DeGrauwe concludes that the forward premia or discounts do not forecast the size and the direction of a high degree of exchange rate movements.

Another benchmark to measure the nature of exchange rate volatility has been Purchasing Power Parity (PPP). This theory says the equilibrium exchange rate is determined by the ratio of the domestic and the foreign price level. However, again, observed exchange rates have moved much more than Purchasing Power Parity rates[29]. In other words, there is a strong correlation between the nominal and the real exchange rates as the nominal exchange rates fluctuate much more than national price levels (DeGrauwe, 1989).

Tae-Hwy Lee (1994) uses the spread between spot and forward exchange rates to predict the volatility of exchange rate changes. There is evidence that spot and forward exchange rates are strongly cointegrated, that is, there is a long-term equilibrium relationship between spot and forward exchange rates. Furthermore, it seems that the larger the spread between spot and forward rates, the more volatile and uncertain the exchange rates. The volatility can also be seen from the trading patterns in exchange rate markets. London and New York markets have U-shaped trading patterns, that is busy trade exists at the opening and closing of the market. It appears to be the same as in the Tokyo market, but it is much less busy. A systematic release of news might explain this U-shape trading pattern. Overall, the US market is the most volatile, followed by the

[29] See Pilbeam, Keith, *International Finance*, Macmillan, London, second edition, 1998.

European then the Asian markets (Baillie and Bollerslev, 1990; Bollerslev and Domowitz, 1993). Evans (1998) also examines the trading patterns of volatility in Deutsche mark market using quotes and transactions prices data. He comes to the same conclusion, i.e., some evidence of a U-shape trading pattern, even though the seasonal pattern of transaction prices is more pronounced than in the quote data.

Furthermore, Goodhart and Figliuoli (1991) suggest that foreign exchange spot rates (in ultra-high-frequency minute-by-minute data) show a unit root, significant first-order negative correlation, mild heteroscedasticity during quiet periods (more significant during disturbed market conditions), and a tendency towards inefficiency. Goodhart (1988) also says: “first, apart from ultra-high-frequency hourly data, where there are some signs of overshooting, it is hard to see any obvious signs of ‘overshooting,’ either in the time-series patterns or the reactions to major UK news events or (unanticipated) interest rate changes. Instead, the exchange rate in the short run appears, if anything, to be characterized by some slight persistence and inertia; second, it often remains misaligned for long periods, in the sense that the forces driving it back to a long-term equilibrium are notably weak; third, there is virtually no information contained in the pattern of forward rates” (p.446-447).

What are the sources of the volatility? According to De Grauwe, inflexible exchange rate systems, the volatility is determined by the expectations agents to hold about the future. Fundamental variables (such as price levels, interest rates, current account, or other economic variables) and irrelevant variables influence the agents’ expectations.

Different types of agents have different ways of forming expectations. Three types of agents influence the volatility (fluctuations) of the exchange rate: noise traders (chartists), fundamentalists, and rational speculators. They have different impacts on any volatility which is triggered by a random shock to the market. Noise traders are investors whose demand for currencies is influenced by beliefs or sentiments that are not fully consistent with economic fundamentals (Hung, 1997, p.781). Many noise traders are chartists. Chartists are market participants who have extrapolative expectations, i.e., they compare the current change in the exchange rate with the change in the previous period. "Some chartists use moving averages of exchange rates of different periods to generate buying or selling signals, while other use trendlines to clarify the direction of market movements" (p.781).

Fundamentalists are market participants who have regressive expectations. They assume that the exchange rate will finally move towards a perceived equilibrium value based on macroeconomics movements, which are congruent with exchange rate determination. Rational speculators are market participants who notice the changes of the exchange rate stimulated by the behavior of chartists and fundamentalists. Thus, the difference between the expected exchange rate next period and the current exchange rate determines their demand for foreign exchange (Frenkel, 1996).

How do the different groups affect the volatility of the exchange rate when there is a random shock to the market? Assume that the equilibrium of the exchange rate is initially at the level determined by fundamentals. When there is a random shock, chartists induce fluctuations around the initial equilibrium. The fluctuations depend on the values of the demand elasticity of the exchange rate. The fluctuations can be converging, constant, or diverging. The fluctuation will be converging if the demand elasticity is less than one. A constant fluctuation is the result of the demand elasticity being equal to one, while diverging volatility exists when the demand elasticity is more than one (Frenkel, 1997).

There is a different story when fundamentalists enter the market. They reduce the volatility of the exchange rate, with the assumption that they recognize the long-run exchange rate. The higher the ratio of fundamentalists to speculators, the lower is the volatility of exchange rate. On the other hand, if fundamentalists do not know the long-run exchange rate, the more often fundamentalists revise their beliefs about the future time path of fundamental, the more volatile is the exchange rate.

Finally, the presence of rational speculators further discourages fluctuations in the exchange rate as long as the speculators correctly anticipate the beliefs of fundamentalists, the actual development of fundamentals is not different from the expected value, and random shocks do not occur (Frenkel, 1997).

Another source of volatility is news. Melvin and Yin (1996) find the rate of information arrival at the market fluctuates positively with the volatility of the mark/dollar exchange rate, and public information plays an essential role in the evolution of the foreign exchange market. Furthermore, Baillie and Bollerslev (1990) detect autocorrelation in the news which is consistent with a "heat-wave" type, that is a high (low) volatility today at a certain hour is likely to increase (decrease) the volatility at the same time the following day. The heat-wave contrasts with a "meteor shower," that is a transmission of news through time and across different market locations. MacDonald and Marsh (1996) also suggest that "informational asymmetries between nations are small and that it is appropriate to think of a global foreign exchange market with a common information set" (p.669). The source of a meteor shower is the heterogeneous expectations of market participants. New information causes exchange rates to change but does not necessarily lead to an increase in exchange rate volatility around the world (Hogan and Melvin, 1994).

4.5. Price Changes Due to the Spread

The theories about spreads are theories of "quoted" spreads, that is the difference between the ask price quoted by the market maker and the bid price quoted by the market maker. "Realised" spreads are the difference between the ask price at which a market maker makes a transaction and the bid price at which a market maker makes a transaction (Stoll, 1989). The quoted spreads are not necessarily the same as realized spreads. In theory, the quoted spread covers the order-processing cost, adverse selection cost, and inventory holding cost.

According to Stoll (1989), there are three alternative views of the trading process with an assumption of no new information: the transaction itself reveals the only information and the spread is constant.

- If the spread reflects only order processing costs, the ask (A) and the bid price (B) always straddles the "true" price. The market maker covers costs by buying at B_0 and selling at A_1 (on average)[30]. Sequences of purchases at the bid price are ultimately offset by sequences of sales at the ask price. The realized spread, A_1 - B_0, is the same as the quoted spread, A_0 - B_0.
- If the spread reflects inventory holding costs, the market maker will change the position of the spread relative to the "true" price to induce the transactions that will unload undesired inventory. For example, after a market maker purchase, the market maker will lower the bid and the ask price. The purpose is to motivate market maker sales (the ask price is lower) and to inhibit additional market maker purchases (the bid price is lower). Bessembinder (1994, p.339) confirms this view: "one method of decreasing a currency position is to decrease quotes in relation to value to increase the likelihood of customer purchases and decrease the likelihood of customer sales. Altering positions by shading quotes allows the bank to continue earning a spread on transactions." Also, Wei (1994, p.5) says that a market maker can only change the quotes after some transactions. In this case, under a linear inventory cost assumption, the spread is twice the inventory cost of a transaction (buy and sell). If the market maker buys, the inventory will be larger by one transaction amount. The bid price will be lower by -0.5S (where S is spread), and the ask price will be lower by 0.5S. If the next transaction is the reversal transaction (sell), the market maker will get a lower price (0.5S). Thus, the realized spread, (A_1 - B_0), is smaller than the quoted spread.
- If the spread reflects the adverse information costs, the prices will move like the inventory holding cost, but under adverse selection, there is a different reason. After a market maker purchase, bid and ask prices are lowered because a transaction at B_0 conveys information that the expected equilibrium price of the exchange

[30] 0 means previous time, while 1 means the later time.

rate is lower. Such information is conveyed under the assumption that some traders have superior information. Thus, the realized spread, (A_1 - B_0), is smaller than the quoted spread.

Stoll (1989) summarises the three views by the values of two parameters, θ, and π. The size of a price reversal is given by $(1-\theta)S$, where S is the spread and $0 \leq \theta \leq 1$. The probability of a price reversal is π. The price continuation is θS, and the probability of a continuation is $(1-\pi)$. Price reversals are assumed to be symmetric in the sense that a price increase after a transaction at the ask has the same size as a price decrease after a transaction at the bid. Price continuations are assumed to be symmetric in the same way.

- Under pure order processing, the amount of price continuation (θ) is 0 because the price reversal $(1-\theta)$ is equal to the spread. The probability of price reversal (π) is 0.5 because prices move between the bid and the ask.
- Under pure inventory holding cost, the amount of price reversal $(1-\theta)$ is 0.5, and the probability of price reversal (π) exceeds 0.5 because the dealer wants to modify a transaction in one direction or the other.
- Under pure adverse selection, the amount of price reversal $(1-\theta)$ is 0.5 and is equal to the price continuation. The probability of price reversal (π) is 0.5 because of the equilibrium price change. Thus, the dealer is indifferent whether the next trade is the same as the last trade or the opposite.

Stoll (1989) develops his model under three assumptions:

- The market is informationally efficient in the sense that the expected price change in a security is independent of current and past information. In the foreign exchange market, the market appears to be efficient since only unexpected changes in money supply lead to changes in exchange rates, and the exchange rate responses are rapid, often completed within twenty minutes of the announcement (Hakkio and Pearce, 1985).

- The spread, S, is constant over the period for which empirical work is carried out. In the foreign exchange market, the spread is clustered at the value of 10 for 53% of the quotations (Bessembinder, 1994; Goodhart, 1991). Thus, this assumption can be applied to the foreign exchange market.
- All transactions are carried out at the highest bid or the lowest ask price available in the market.

The total price change in a security may then be decomposed into three components (Stoll, 1989)[31]:

$$\Delta V_t = a + \Delta P_t + e_t \tag{4.1}$$

ΔV_t = total price change in a security between time t - 1 and time t

a= expected price change in the security in the absence of the bid-ask spread

ΔP_t= price change due to the spread, and

e_t= price change due to new information; $E(e_t) = 0$

Then

$$\text{cov}(\Delta V_t, \Delta V_{t+1}) = \text{cov}(\Delta P_t, \Delta P_{t+1}) + \text{cov}(\Delta P_t, e_{t+1}) + \text{cov}(e_t, \Delta P_{t+1}) + \text{cov}(e_t, e_{t+1}) \tag{4.2}$$

In an efficient market, changes in prices due to new information are serially uncorrelated and are uncorrelated with lagged or leading values of the price change due to the spread. Then

---

31 Roll (1984) also models the bid-ask spread estimator for financial securities. Moreover, Bhardwaj and Moore (1998) modify the Roll's (1984) model by using spread estimator developed directly for a correlated value innovation process. We do not describe Roll's (1984) model in this thesis since we use Stoll's (1989) model.

$$\mathrm{Cov}\,(\Delta V_t, \Delta V_{t+1}) = \mathrm{cov}\,(\Delta P_t, \Delta P_{t+1}) \tag{4.3}$$

Under the assumption of constant spread, the possible price changes ΔP_t, starting at the bid price (Stoll, 1989), are

$$\Delta P_t = (A_t - B_{t-1}) = (1 - \theta)S \qquad \text{with prob } \pi, \tag{4.4}$$

$$(B_t - B_{t-1}) = -\theta S \qquad \text{with prob } (1 - \pi)$$

Under the assumption of symmetry, the possible price changes starting at the ask prices (Stoll, 1989) are

$$\Delta P_t = (B_t - A_{t-1}) = -(1 - \theta)S \qquad \text{with prob } \pi, \tag{4.5}$$
$$(A_t - A_{t-1}) = \theta S \qquad \text{with prob } (1 - \pi)$$

Transactions at time t-1 are assumed to occur with equal probability at the bid or ask.

The expected price change conditional on a transaction at the bid is

$$E\,(\Delta P_t | B_{t-1}) = \pi(1 - \theta)S + (1 - \pi)(-\theta S) = (\pi - \theta)S \tag{4.6}$$

The expected price change conditional on a transaction at the ask is

$$E\,(\Delta P_t | A_{t-1}) = -(1 - \theta)S\pi + (1 - \pi)\theta S = -(\pi - \theta)S \tag{4.7}$$

The realized spread is the expected price change after a dealer purchase less the expected price change after a dealer sale, that is $2(\pi - \theta)S$. Given an equal probability of a transaction at the ask and the bid, the unconditional expected price change is $E(\Delta P_t) = 0$ (Stoll, p121). The realized spread is the expected revenue on two transactions: a purchase and a sale.

Under pure order-processing cost, the realised spread is equal to quoted spread ($\pi = 0.5$, $\theta = 0$). Under pure adverse information, the realised spread is zero ($\pi = 0.5$, $\theta = 0.5$). Under pure inventory holding cost, the realised spread is positive but less than quoted spread ($\pi > 0.5$, $\theta = 0.5$).

The serial covariance depends on the two-period (three-date) sequence of prices. If a transaction at the bid is followed by another transaction at the bid (a continuation), the price change is $-\theta S$, where $0 < \theta < 1$. If a transaction at the bid is followed by a transaction at the ask, the price change is $(1 - \theta)$ S, a reversal. The probability of a continuation is $(1 - \pi)$, and the probability of a reversal is π. Under the assumption of constant spread, the difference in price changes is always equal to the spread, S.

The serial covariance of transaction price changes is (Stoll, 1989):

$$cov_T = cov(\Delta P_t, \Delta P_{t+1}) = S^2[\theta^2(1 - 2\pi) - \pi^2(1 - 2\theta)] \quad (4.8)$$

The serial covariance of quoted price changes is:

$$Cov_B = cov(\Delta B_t, \Delta B_{t+1}) = \theta^2 S^2(1 - 2\pi) \quad (4.9)$$

$$Cov_A = cov(\Delta A_t, \Delta A_{t+1}) = \theta^2 S^2(1 - 2\pi) \quad (4.10)$$

Equations above can be written in a regression framework as

$$Cov_T = a_0 + a_1 S^2 + u \quad (4.11)$$

$$Cov_Q = b_0 + b_1 S^2 + v, \quad (4.12)$$

where u,v are random errors

$$a_1 = \theta^2(1 - 2\pi) - \pi^2(1 - 2\theta) \quad (4.13)$$

$$b_1 = \theta^2(1 - 2\pi) \quad (4.14)$$

We can explain the decomposition of the quoted spread according to order costs, inventory holding cost, and adverse information cost with the following methodology.

We will use simple regression for estimating the value of covariance transaction price and quoted price. To infer the relative importance of bid-ask spread components, we take several steps as follows:

- After obtaining coefficient a_1 and b_1, we calculate the value of $\pi$and θ. Then we will get the realized spread value by substituting the value of $\pi$and θ into realized spread formula: $2(\pi - \theta)S$.
- As noted before, the adverse information cost has zero realized spread. It means the expected revenue per trade is zero. Thus, the adverse information cost component of the quoted spread is the difference between the quoted spread, and the realized spread. Therefore, the realized spread only consists of the order-processing cost and the inventory holding cost.
- Derivation of the order-processing cost and inventory holding cost components requires a division of the realized spread. We will divide the realized spread using the observed value π and the value θ: 0.5 for inventory holding cost and 0 for the order-processing cost.

Then, the relative importance of bid-ask spread components is obtained. The empirical results are reviewed in the following chapter.

Chapter 5

THE EMPIRICAL DECOMPOSITION OF THE BID-ASK SPREAD FOR EXCHANGE RATES

As mentioned in previous chapter, the serial covariance of transaction price changes is (Stoll, 1989): $cov_T = cov(\Delta P_t, \Delta P_{t+1}) = S^2[\theta^2(1 - 2\pi) - \pi^2(1 - 2\theta)]$, and the serial covariance of quoted price (bid or ask) changes is (Stoll, 1989): $cov_Q = cov(\Delta B_t, \Delta B_{t+1})$ or $cov(\Delta A_t, \Delta A_{t+1}) = \theta^2 S^2(1 - 2\pi)$.

According to Stoll, the values of the serial covariances (transaction and quoted price) are shown below (Stoll, 1989 pp.122):

Table 5.1. The serial covariances of a transaction and a quoted price

Determinant of Quoted Spread	Cov_T	Cov_Q
Order Processing ($\theta = 0, \pi = 0.5$)	$-0.25S^2$	0.0
Adverse Information ($\theta = 0.5, \pi = 0.5$)	0.0	0.0
Inventory Cost ($\theta = 0.5, \pi > 0.5$)	$-0.25S^2 < Cov_T < 0.0$	$-0.25S^2 < Cov_Q < 0.0$

We can see that the value of the covariance is zero if the spread is only determined by an adverse information cost. The value of the covariance is in the range -0.25 to 0 if the spread is only determined by inventory holding cost. For the order processing cost, the value of the covariance is different between covariance transaction and covariance quoted price. The values of cov_T and cov_Q, however, are in the range -0.25 and 0 for the three components of the bid-ask spread. Hence, the Reuters data can be used to estimate the values of the covariances.

The estimation of the values of cov_T and cov_Q is obtained by regression. The next step is to use the point estimator to infer the components of the bid-ask spread. The detailed analysis is discussed in the following sections.

5.1. Sources of Data

The data have been obtained from Reuters, United Kingdom[32]. The data contain a date, time (BST), dealer's code, location's code, bid, and ask rate. The currency used is the Deutschmark (DM) against the US dollar (USD). The date is from 10 April to 30 June 1989 (excluding weekends). Due to the difficulty of obtaining the transaction data, we use two assumptions to proceed with the analysis. The assumptions are:

- The dealers make transactions every time they quote the bid and ask rate. The reason behind this assumption is that theory suggests that after buying or selling, the dealers will change the quotation (Stoll, 1989; Bessembinder, 1994; Wei, 1994). Evans (1998) also suggests "changes in trading activity within the interbank market significantly affect quotes while innovation in quote activity affects transactions" (p.4). Furthermore, an interview by the author with a dealer working in a large bank in Sydney confirmed that the banks (dealers) change the bid-ask quote every time they make transactions.
- The transaction price is the mid-point of the bid and ask rate. The reason is that spreads in the market are inside spreads: the spread resulting from the combination of the lowest quoted ask and highest bid, which dealers are committed to trade (Goodhart and

---

[32] Thanks to Dr. Jiang Xin Wang, University of New South Wales, who kindly provided the data.

Payne, 1996). Moreover, Branch and Echevarria (1995, p.541) suggests that "a substantial number of last reported transactions for stocks trading on the New York Stock Exchange occur inside the quoted closing bid-ask spread." Thus, we use the mid-point of the bid and ask rate since the inside spreads are close to the mid-point value.

5.2. THE EMPIRICAL PROCEDURE

To estimate the relative importance of the key forces believed to be acting on the bid-ask spread, we analyzed the data with the following steps:

- Sort the data according to the dealer's code. The number of dealers is from 1 to 246.
- Calculate the bid-ask spread that is the proportional spread (spread divided by mid-point of a bid and ask rate)
- Calculate the transaction price (the mid-points bid and the ask rate).
- Pick up three last transactions, three last bids and asks from closing time.
- Calculate the difference between the last transaction and the second last (as $\Delta Pt+1$), and the difference between the second last and the third last (as ΔPt) from 10 April to 30 June 1989.
- Apply the same procedure to bid and ask.

Stratified sampling is used here, that is, "the population is first subdivided into subpopulations or strata, then a simple random sample is drawn from each stratum" (Ostle, 1963 pp.47). In our data, samples based on the dealer's code were chosen. We then separated the samples based on the same spread. Before doing so, however, we chose only the dealers who transacted at least five days from 10 April to 30 June 1989 because five days are enough to calculate covariances. Then, the covariances of ΔPt and ΔPt+1, ΔBt and ΔBt+1, ΔAt and ΔAt+1 were calculated.

Simple regressions of these formulae, $cov_T = a_0 + a_1 S^2 + u$ and $cov_Q = b_0 + b_1 S^2 + v$, were then estimated, using a zero constant[33], where cov_T is the covariance of transaction price; cov_Q is the covariance of a bid or ask; S^2 is the squared value of the average proportional spread at a closing time.

5.3. Results

First, we used data from all the dealers that is from dealer 1 to 246. We removed three outliers. The reason is that the dealer 146 and dealer 179 had extremely high standard residuals which were far above the average of standard residuals of the others' outliers. Moreover, we excluded the dealer 93 because the dealer was not represented internationally, whereas the other outliers (dealers) had branches in several locations. Dealer 93 did not represent a segment of the sample. Thus, we deleted it to ensure generalisability to the entire sample.

The results are shown in Table below. The theoretical range -0.25 and 0[34] lies in the estimated interval. Furthermore, the three coefficients are in the range -0.25 and 0. Thus, the empirical finding is consistent with the theory.

Table 5.2. (All dealers) The regression result

Dependent variable	Coefficient	Standard Error	Confidence Interval (95%)
Cov_T	-.137	0.524	$-1.168 \le \beta \le 0.893$
Cov_B	-.137	0.528	$-1.176 \le \beta \le 0.902$
Cov_A	-0.011	0.537	$-1.068 \le \beta \le 1.045$

[33] This is consistent with the assumption of market efficiency in which the covariance induced by the spread is the only variable that causes the serial covariance price changes. As a check, the author discovered that the intercept is statistically insignificant when the author used intercept-model regression.

[34] The values that are predicted by theory.

The observation by Bollerslev and Domowitz (1993) concludes that small banks only quote during the regular business hours of their regional markets. Thus, they potentially have a stronger inventory effect than larger banks, and so have more concern about their inventory positions at a closing time. Moreover, smaller banks have less information based on retail order flow at the open time than larger banks that operate continuously. In the sample (Reuters), the small banks (in term of quotation) aggregate the majority of market participants and most of them are located in Europe (Bollerslev and Domowitz, 1993, p.1430).

Based on the observation above, we divided the sample into Asia, Europe, and North-America. Then we compared the results with those using all dealers. We conjecture that the subsamples (Europe dealers) have a stronger inventory effect since most of them are small banks. The regression results for Asia, Europe, and North-America dealers are shown below.

The tables show, again, that the empirical findings are consistent with theory, i.e., the range -0.25 and 0 are included in the estimated interval. Moreover, all three point estimators are in the range -0.25 and 0, except Cov_A (Asia), and Cov_T (North-America).

Table 5.3. (Asia) The regression result

Dependent variable	Coefficients	Standard Error	Confidence Interval (95%)
Cov_T	-0.154	0.504	$-1.151 \leq \beta \leq 0.842$
Cov_B	-0.011	0.496	$-0.992 \leq \beta \leq 0.970$
Cov_A	-0.289	0.512	$-1.303 \leq \beta \leq 0.725$

Table 5.4. (Europe) The regression result

Dependent variable	Coefficients	Standard Error	Confidence Interval (95%)
Cov_T	-0.195	0.685	$-1.550 \leq \beta \leq 1.150$
Cov_B	-0.011	0.762	$-1.518 \leq \beta \leq 1.495$
Cov_A	-0.151	0.672	$-1.479 \leq \beta \leq 1.176$

Table 5.5. (North-America) The regression result

Dependent variable	Coefficients	Standard Error	Confidence Interval (95%)
Cov_T	0.533	2.452	$-4.374 \leq \beta \leq 5.439$
Cov_B	-0.122	2.535	$-5.195 \leq \beta \leq 4.951$
Cov_A	-0.005	2.380	$-4.769 \leq \beta \leq 4.759$

However, the estimates of North-American dealers are not useful for inferring the components of bid-ask spreads as we show below. It may be due to the sample size. To confirm this guess, we used the same sample size of North-American dealers to Asian and European dealers. The result was that we were not able to apply the Asian and European dealers' estimates to infer the components of the bid-ask spreads. Thus, the lack of usefulness of North-American dealers' estimates seems to arise from the small sample size.

From the results above (Table 5.3 and 5.4), we conclude that we can usefully estimate the three components of the bid-ask spread for the foreign exchange market. Before examining the bid-ask spread components in detail, we reviewed the assumptions of the method of least squares, the method that we used. Violations of the assumptions may mean the estimator is not the best linear unbiased estimator. We wished to obtain an unbiased estimator so that on average it captures a "true" value for the parameter. We could then establish the confidence interval to investigate whether the range of the value of the theory is included in the estimated interval. The results of the tests are given in Appendix 3. The overall conclusion is that we obtain an unbiased estimator since the assumptions of the underlying least square are not violated.

We now turn to examine the relative importance of bid-ask spread components.

5.4. THE COMPONENTS OF THE BID-ASK SPREAD

First, we analyzed the relative importance of the bid-ask spread components using estimates for all dealers. From the regression of Cov_T, we obtained a_1 = -0.137. From the regression of Cov_B and Cov_A, we obtained b_1 = -0.137 and -0.011. Because we have two values of b_1 (from Cov_B and Cov_A), we averaged them to give b_1 = -0.074. We then calculated θ (price continuation) and π (the probability of price reversal) with the two equations:

$$a_1 = \theta^2(1 - 2\pi) - \pi^2(1 - 2\theta) \quad (5.1)$$

$$b_1 = \theta^2(1 - 2\pi) \quad (5.2)$$

Using our estimates for a_1 and b_1, we obtained $\pi = 0.6956$ and $\theta = 0.4349$.

As explained in Chapter 4, the realized spread, $2\ (\pi - \theta)$, is the expected profit per trade, while the realized spread comprises order processing costs and inventory holding costs. The realized spread is zero when the quoted spread is determined by adverse information (Stoll, 1989). Following Stoll, we derive the proportions of spread components by:

- $1 - 2\ (\pi - \theta)$ = adverse selection cost. Substituting 0.6956 and 0.4349 in the equation, we get 0.4786 or 48%.
- $2\ (\pi - 0.5)$ = inventory holding cost. Substituting 0.6956 in the equation, we obtain 0.3912 or 39%.
- $1 - 2\theta$ = order processing cost. Substituting 0.4349 in the equation, the result is 0.1302 or 13%.

In summary, the components of bid-ask spread in the foreign exchange market are calculated to be 48% adverse selection, 39% inventory holding cost and 13% order processing cost.

The smallest component of the bid-ask spread in the foreign exchange market appears to be the order-processing cost (13%). It is not a surprising finding because the foreign exchange market is a very competitive market (Flood, 1991; Goodhart and Figliuoli, 1991). Dealers seem to be mainly concerned with inventory cost and adverse selection cost.

The second significant component is inventory holding cost (39%). This finding is relevant to the theory: because of the high volatility in the market, the inventory holding cost demands opportunity costs and the risk of changes in inventory value (Bessembinder, 1994).

Finally, adverse selection cost is 48% of the bid-ask spreads. This finding is supported by Ito et al. (1998) who finds evidence of private information in the foreign exchange market.

Next, we investigated the relative importance of components of spread using Europe and Asia estimates. As we noted before, European dealers (most of them are small banks) are expected to show a strong inventory effect. From the regression of Cov_T, Cov_B and Cov_A of European dealers, we obtain a_1 = -0.195, b_1 = -0.151 and -0.011, and the average of b_1's values is -0.081. We can then deduce $\pi = 0.7535$ and $\theta = 0.3996$.

Using the values of π and θ above, we can derive the proportions of spread.

- 1 - 2 (0.7535 - 0.3996) = adverse selection cost, that is 0.2922or 29%.
- 2 (0.7535 - 0.5) = inventory holding cost, that is 0.5070 or 51%.
- 1 - 2(0.3996) = order processing cost, that is 0.2008 or 20%.

The results above are as we expected, i.e., higher inventory cost.

Further, we reviewed the Asian dealers' estimate. From the Cov_T, Cov_B, and Cov_A of the Asian dealers, we obtain a_1 = -0.154, b_1 = -0.289 and -0.011, and the average of b_1's value is -0.1565. Then, we can conclude $\pi = 0.8037$ and $\theta = 0.4969$.

Following the same procedure, we can decompose the spread components.

- 1 - 2(0.8037 - 0.4969) = 0.3864 or 39%, that is adverse selection cost.
- 2(0.8037 - 0.5) = 0.6074 or 60%, that is inventory holding cost.
- 1 - 2(0.4969) = 0.0062 or 1%, that is order processing cost.

The results above are similar to those from the Europe dealers, i.e., high inventory cost. The comparisons of the proportions of spread are shown in the table below.

Table 5.6. The proportions of components of a spread

Components of spreads	All dealers	Europe	Asia
Adverse selection cost	48%	29%	39%
Inventory holding cost	39%	51%	60%
Order-processing cost	13%	20%	1%

For all groups, order processing costs are least important. The inventory holding cost is the largest component of Europe and Asia. The large inventory holding cost for Europe (small banks) conforms to the view of Bollerslev and Domowitz: the inventory effect is likely to be stronger for small banks since they do not conduct the quotation continuously, i.e., the small banks quote only during business hours of their regional markets. Thus, they are more sensitive to their inventory positions at the closing time. However, the Asian dealers also have a large inventory cost. The reason is that both markets have the same market activity. The patterns are bimodally distributed around the lunch hour, i.e., the activity occurs as flurries surrounding the open and the close of the market, with the moderate trading in between (Bollerslev and Domowitz, p.1426).

Moreover, the inventory holding cost and the adverse selection cost for all dealers are approximately the same proportion of total spread. Nevertheless, the inventory holding cost is considered high compared to order-processing cost. Overall, our findings of high inventory cost and adverse selection cost in foreign exchange market strengthen Lyons's notion of a strong information effect and a strong inventory-control effect in the spot foreign exchange market (Lyons, 1993).

Motivated by Bessembinder's (1994) view that the significance of inventory-cost in foreign exchange markets contrasts with the lack evidence of inventory-cost effects obtained in studies conducted in equity markets, we then compared the components of spread in the foreign exchange market with the components of spread in the equity market.

In the equity market, the relative importance of the components of spread depends on the trading mechanism. Graves et al. (1994) examined the effect of differences in the organization of trading on the components of spread. They compared two major systems for trading common stocks: the New York Stock Exchange (auction market) and NASDAQ (the competitive dealer market). The table below presents the comparisons of the elements of spread in the equity market (Graves et al., 1994) and in the foreign exchange market (our study).

Table 5.7. The components of spread in the equity market and foreign exchange market

Components of spread	Forex (Europe)	Forex (Asia)	Stoll (NASDAQ)[35]	NYSE/AMEX
Adverse selection	29%	39%	43%	50%
Inventory holding	51%	60%	10%	48%
Order-processing	20%	1%	47%	1%

From the table above we can see that there is a similarity of order-processing cost for the foreign exchange market and the NYSE/AMEX. The trading system of the foreign exchange market, however, is comparable with NASDAQ, i.e., the competitive dealers market. According to Graves, et al. (1994) the competitive dealers market has a fragmented structure which requires much dealer participation. Thus, it leads to a high order processing cost. By contrast, an auction-based exchange trading structure (NYSE/AMEX) facilitates the matching of buy

[35] The sample is National Market System (NMS) on NASDAQ.

and sell orders without requiring as much dealer participation as in the fragmented dealers market. Moreover, there is a much higher direct interaction of public orders on the exchange floor. Therefore, a low order-processing cost is anticipated.

The notion of high order-processing cost for competitive dealers market is consistent with the NASDAQ sample. However, the high order processing cost is not true for the foreign exchange market. The small order-processing cost of the foreign exchange market is due to price competition. The price competition appears to outweigh the fragmentation of order-flow. As Stoll (1989, p.123) noted, the dynamic interaction of competing dealers causes market bid-ask quotes and transaction prices to behave as if there were one dealer who prices competitively.

An observed high inventory holding cost for the NYSE/AMEX conforms with the theory. The specialist has to absorb a given amount of order imbalance. Thus, it is more expensive for the specialist than for a group of competing market makers with heterogeneously distributed inventory positions (Graves et al., 1994). In contrast, NASDAQ has low inventory holding cost because multiple dealers can reduce the inventory risk exposure by trading away the inventory imbalances across market makers.

In the highly competitive and closely integrated foreign exchange market, the quotation of an individual dealer depends on the price quotes of others, and it narrows the spread. Moreover, a dealer can easily unload the imbalance position by calling another market maker, or he can make a tiny price adjustment to attract orders from other dealers (Suvanto, 1996). The inventory holding cost in the foreign exchange market is much higher than it is in the equity market (NASDAQ). This finding is supported by Hsieh and Kleidon (1996). They observe that standard information models cannot explain higher spread at the closing time, "the inventory management by market makers in the closing market appears to be the most likely explanation" (p.43). The reason is that although the dealer can easily trade away the unwanted inventory among traders during the most of the day, it is not true before the closing time. "Dealers who are already satisfied with their positions do not want new orders. Widening the spread decreases the likelihood of new orders. There may be unwanted open positions that do not find buyers until the spread is sufficiently large to make the price attractive to somebody, or sufficiently unattractive to the seller until either of them is willing to carry an open overnight position" (Suvanto, 1996, p.69).

The overlapping time zones overcome this problem since the dealers in the closing time zone can trade away the unbalanced inventory to the dealers in open time zones (p.69). However, the levels of trading activity around hour 24 are very low (Bollerslev and Domowitz, 1993). The low trading activity decreases the ability to unload the imbalances across market makers. Thus, it increases the risk of changes in inventory value.

For smaller banks, there is an additional factor that contributes to a higher inventory holding cost. It is their lesser ability to trade away the imbalances across market makers since they operate mainly within regional markets with well-defined market openings and closings (Bollerslev and Domowitz, 1993). Hsieh and Kleidon (1996, p.61) verify this opinion, noting that the smaller regional banks, who start and end the day with flat positions, have significant inventory problems as the close of trading approaches.

The adverse selection cost is approximately the same across the two markets. Nonetheless, the cost is smaller in the foreign exchange market than in the equity market. In the foreign exchange market, it is impossible for traders to have a better knowledge of the future behavior of the macroeconomy of a country or an international financial system (Lyons, 1993). However, it is possible for traders to have some inside information about the future government policy. Thus, adverse selection in the foreign exchange market is the "secret" government intervention, i.e., when the Federal Reserve intervenes in the market secretly through specific financial institutions rather than wholesale trading in the open market (Dominguez, 1993). According to Dominguez, the Federal Reserve conducts the secret intervention for only 20% of all intervention operations when the foreign exchange market is volatile (Dominguez, 1993). However, Hung (1997) suggests that Federal Reserve secret intervention is approximately 40% of all intervention. It means the dealers have a less potential loss from informed traders, and this observation supports Bessembinder's suggestion that adverse selection exists in foreign exchange market even though the potential loss from informed traders is less than it is in the equity market.

In conclusion, the order-processing cost is the least important component of spread since the foreign exchange market is a very competitive market. The largest proportion of the inventory holding cost in the spread component is due to holding currency as inventory imposes the opportunity costs and the risk of changes in inventory value in the high volatility market. Although the adverse selection cost is high in foreign exchange markets, this cost is less important than it is in equity markets. The reason is that in the foreign exchange market, the Federal Reserve is seldom conducting a secret intervention. Otherwise, traders will have the same information about the government policy or the behavior of the macroeconomy of a country.

5.5. Reverse Tick Test as an Alternative to Transaction Prices

In the previous analysis, we used the mid-point of the bid-ask spread as a transaction price. To check whether using another technique confirms the results above, we used a reverse tick test as an alternative and indirect method to a transaction test. Before we proceed with the analysis, we explain the tick test and reverse tick test in detail.

The tick test and reverse tick test are used to distinguish whether a trade (transaction price) is a buy order or a sell order. The tick test is a technique which infers the direction of trade by comparing its price with the price of the preceding trades. There are four categories: an uptick (buy), a downtick (sell), a zero-uptick (buy), and a zero-downtick (sell). A trade is an uptick (buy) if the price is higher than the price of the previous trade. On the other hand, a trade is a downtick (sell) if the price is lower than the price of the previous trade. A zero-uptick (buy) occurs when the price is the same as the previous trade, and the last price change was in uptick; a zero-downtick (sell) is when the price is the same as the previous trade, and the last price change was in down-tick (Lee and Ready, 1991).

The reverse tick test classifies trades by comparing the trade price to prices of trades immediately after the current trade. If the current trade is followed by trade with a higher price, the current trade is classed as a sell. In contrast, if the current trade is followed by trade with a lower price, the current trade is a buy. The tick test and the reverse tick test have the same classification if the current trade is followed by a price reversal (opposite trade), but the classification using both methods are contradicted if the current trade is followed by a price continuation (same trade). Hasbrouck (1988) used the reverse tick test to classify trades at the mid-point of the bid-ask spread. Following Hasbrouck (1988), we used the reverse tick test since we assume a transaction price is at the mid-point of the bid-ask spread.

5.5.1. The Empirical Procedure

We analyzed the data with the same procedure as in section 5.2 above, except for the calculation of the transaction price. We modified the technique of determining a transaction price using the reverse tick test. The procedure is as follows:

- Calculate the mid-points of the bid and ask prices (assume as a transaction price)
- Pick up the three last mid-points from closing price, compare the third last price (assume as a current trade) to second last price (assume as a following trade); if the second last price is higher (lower) than the third one, classify the third one as an ask (bid), and we use the ask (bid) price as a transaction price. However, if the second last price is the same as the third one, use the mid-point as a transaction price. We repeated the same technique to classify the second and the last transaction price (mid-points) as ask, bid or mid-point.

- Calculate the difference between the last transaction and the second last as ΔPt+1 and the difference between the second last and the third last as ΔPt

We used the same value of Cov_Q (Cov bid and Cov ask) as in the previous analysis since we merely modified the assumption of a transaction price.

5.5.2. Results

Repeating the analysis above (section 5.3), we examined all dealers first. Then, we divided the data into three: European dealers, Asian dealers, and North-American dealers. The results are shown in the table below.

Table 5.8. (All dealers) The regression result

Dependent variable	Coefficient	Standard Error	Confidence Interval (95%)
Cov_T	1.061	0.494	$0.088 \leq \beta \leq 2.033$
Cov_B	-0.137	0.528	$-1.176 \leq \beta \leq 0.902$
Cov_A	-0.011	0.537	$-1.068 \leq \beta \leq 1.045$

Table 5.9. (Asia) The regression result

Dependent variable	Coefficients	Standard Error	Confidence Interval (95%)
Cov_T	1.017	0.439	$0.149 \leq \beta \leq 1.885$
Cov_B	-0.011	0.496	$-0.992 \leq \beta \leq 0.970$
Cov_A	-0.289	0.512	$-1.303 \leq \beta \leq 0.725$

Table 5.10. (Europe) The regression result

Dependent variable	Coefficients	Standard Error	Confidence Interval (95%)
Cov_T	0.792	0.708	$-0.609 \leq \beta \leq 2.192$
Cov_B	-0.011	0.762	$-1.518 \leq \beta \leq 1.495$
Cov_A	-0.151	0.672	$-1.479 \leq \beta \leq 1.176$

Table 5.11. (North-America) The regression result

Dependent variable	Coefficients	Standard Error	Confidence Interval(95%)
Cov_T	3.196	2.241	$-1.286 \leq \beta \leq 7.677$
Cov_B	-0.122	2.535	$-5.195 \leq \beta \leq 4.951$
Cov_A	-0.005	2.380	$-4.769 \leq \beta \leq 4.759$

From the table above, we notice that the value of Cov_T for all dealers, European, North-American and Asian dealers are not in the range -0.25 and 0. Moreover, the range -0.25 and 0 are not in the estimated interval for all dealers and Asian dealers. Consequently, we conclude that we do not apply the values of Cov_T for inferring the relative importance of bid-ask spread components.

Using the reverse tick test as an alternative technique to determine a transaction price apparently may not be useful for deriving the proportions of the components of the bid-ask spread. This finding is supported by Branch and Echevarria (1995). They find that there are large numbers of stocks closing inside the spreads on two successive days which means the "models purporting to explain the components of the bid-ask spread may be incorrectly relying on the assumption that transactions occur (exclusively) at the bid or the ask" (p. 555). On the other hand, using the mid-point of spreads (so the value is close to the inside spread) as a transaction cost can explain the components of spreads as we discussed in the previous section (4.2.5). Moreover, Branch and Echevarria (1995) note that "actual stock price changes should be less than predicted in the binomial models" (p.555)[36]. Again, it occurs in our samples (all value of Cov_T are less than 0.25 in absolute value) when we used the mid-point of spread as a transaction price.

[36] Binomial model is the theoretical probability of a price reversal is 0.50 or a 50 percent chance that a transaction at the bid (ask) is followed by a transaction at the ask (bid). Concurrent with the price reversal probability, the magnitude of the expected price change is one-half of the bid-ask spread (0.5S), accordingly, the variance of the expected price change is $0.25S^2$ (Branch and Echevarria, 1995). It is similar to Stoll's model.

5.6. Huang and Stoll's General Approach for the Components of the Bid-Ask Spread

Huang and Stoll (1997) develop a basic trade indicator model of spread components which reconciles the various existing models. The characteristic of the model is that it is driven solely by the direction of trade: whether incoming orders are purchases or sales. Covariance models also depend on the probabilities of changes in trade direction. Following Huang and Stoll we extend the models to separate inventory holding cost and adverse selection cost. First, the extension relies on the serial correlation in trade flows. Second, the extension relies on the contemporaneous cross-correlation in trade flows across stocks.

To assure our previous results (section 5.4) based on Stoll's model (1989), we tried to apply our data to Huang and Stoll's basic trade indicator model. We used the first extension of the basic trade indicator model because we did not have "trade volume" data. Moreover, because of the difficulty of obtaining the transaction price data, we again used the assumption of the mid-point as a transaction data and used the reverse tick test (Lee and Ready, 1991) to distinguish the direction of the trade.

5.6.1. The Model

Following Huang and Stoll (1997) we build three separate and sequential events. They are as follows:

- V_t is the unobservable fundamental value of the stock in the absence of transaction costs which is determined just prior to the posting of the bid and ask quotes at time t
- M_t is the quote mid-point which is calculated from the bid-ask quotes that prevail just before a transaction
- P_t is the price of the transaction at time t

- Q_t is buy-sell-trade indicator variable for the transaction price (P_t): it equals +1 if the transaction is buyer-initiated and occurs above the mid-point, -1 if the transaction is seller-initiated and occurs below the mid-point, and 0 if the transaction occurs at the mid-point.

Unobservable V_t is as follows:

$$V_t = V_{t-1} + \alpha \frac{S}{2} Q_{t-1} + \varepsilon_t \quad (5.3)$$

S is the constant spread
α is the percentage of the half-spread which refers to adverse selection
ε_t is the serially uncorrelated public information shock

Thus, the change in V_t reflects the private information revealed by the last trade and the public information component.

Huang and Stoll (1997) argue that the mid-point of spread consists of the fundamental stock value and the inventory cost since liquidity suppliers adjust the quote mid-point relative to the fundamental value by accumulated inventory to induce inventory equilibrating trades. Assuming that past trades are of normal size of one, the mid-point is as follows:

$$M_t = V_t + \beta \frac{S}{2} \sum_{i=1}^{t-1} Q_i \quad (5.4)$$

β is the proportion of the half spread which refers to inventory holding costs, where $\sum_{i=1}^{t-1} Q_i$ is the cumulated inventory from the market open until time t-1, and Q_1 is the initial inventory for the day.

The combination of the first difference between the mid-point and unobservable V_t implies that quotes are adjusted to the information revealed by the last trade and the inventory cost of the last trade:

$$\Delta M = (\alpha + \beta) \frac{S}{2} Q_{t-1} + \varepsilon_t \quad (5.5)$$

Then,

$$P_t = M_t + \frac{S}{2}Q_1 + \eta_t \tag{5.6}$$

η_t is the deviation of the observed half-spread, P_t - M_t, from the constant half-spread, and is assumed to be white noise.

The basic trade indicator model is the combination of the two last equations (Huang and Stoll, 1997):

$$\Delta P = \frac{S}{2}(Q_t - Q_{t-1}) + \lambda\frac{S}{2}Q_{t-1} + e_t \tag{5.7}$$

$\lambda = \alpha + \beta$, and $e_t = \varepsilon_t + \Delta\eta_t$. This model can not separate the adverse selection cost (α) and inventory holding cost (β). Nevertheless, the model can estimate the order-processing cost, $1 - \lambda$. For this reason, Huang and Stoll (1997) extend the model which relies on the serial correlation in trade flows[37].

The conditional expectation of trade indicator at time t-1, given Q_{t-2} is:

$$E(Q_{t-1} \mid Q_{t-2}) = (1 - 2\pi)Q_{t-2} \tag{5.8}$$

The equation above is calculated from:

$Q_{t-1} = Q_{t-2}$ with probability $(1 - \pi)$

$Q_{t-1} = -Q_{t-2}$ with probability π,

Then,

$$E(Q_{t-1} \mid Q_{t-2}) = Q_{t-2}(1 - \pi) - Q_{t-2}\pi \tag{5.9}$$

$\Leftrightarrow E(Q_{t-1} \mid Q_{t-2}) = (1 - 2\pi)Q_{t-2}$, π is the probability that the trade at t is opposite in sign to the trade at t-1.

[37] We only present one of the two extensions models since we only use the first one.

Assuming that the market knows (5.6), the change in the fundamental value:

$$\Delta V_t = \alpha \frac{S}{2} Q_{t-1} - \alpha \frac{S}{2}(1 - 2\pi) Q_{t-2} + \varepsilon_t \tag{5.10}$$

By combining (5.7) and (5.2), the result is as follows:

$$\Delta M_t = (\alpha + \beta) \frac{S}{2} Q_{t-1} - \alpha \frac{S}{2}(1 - 2\pi) Q_{t-2} + \varepsilon_t \tag{5.11}$$

Then, the extension of the basic trade indicator model is the combination of (5.8) and (5.4):

$$\Delta P_t = \frac{S}{2} Q_t + (\alpha + \beta - 1) \frac{S}{2} Q_{t-1} - \alpha \frac{S}{2}(1 - 2\pi) Q_{t-2} + \varepsilon_t \tag{5.12}$$

Estimation of traded spread (S), the three components of the spread (α,β,1-α-β), and the probability of a trade reversal (π) can be calculated using (5.9) and (5.6) together. However, for our purpose (estimating the proportions of bid-ask spread only, not estimating traded spread), we can use (5.6 and 5.8). Moreover, Huang and Stoll (1997) suggest that the constantly traded spreads in (5.8) are replaced with observed posted spreads. Thus, the equation is:

$$\Delta M_t = (\alpha + \beta) \frac{S_{t-1}}{2} Q_{t-1} + \alpha \frac{S_{t-2}}{2}(1 - 2\pi) Q_{t-2} + \varepsilon_t \tag{5.13}$$

5.6.2. The Empirical Procedure

We used the same data as these for inferring the components of spreads, Reuters DM/$US quotes from 10 April to 30 June 1989 (excluding weekends). However, to keep the modeling tractable we chose 28 dealers who were located in New York, London, and Hong Kong to represent North-American, European, and Asian dealers respectively. The dealers consisted of small and large banks, enough to represent all dealers.

As mentioned above, the data were not transactions data, so we performed the following steps:

- Assume the dealers' trade every time they quote the bid and ask rate
- Assume the mid-point of the spread is a good approximation to the transaction price
- Reverse tick test is employed to indicate the trade, whether it is at the ask or bid or mid-point. I compared the mid-point at t-1 to mid-point at t: if t is higher (lower) than t-1, we classified the t-1 as ask (bid); therefore the trade at t-1 is defined as $Q_t = +1$ ($Q_t = -1$); then I repeated for the following quotation until the closing time. However, if t was the same as t-1, we treated the trade at t-1 as occurring at mid-point, then we defined it as $Q_t = 0$.

After carrying out the steps above, we had all the variables (mid-point, spread, and trade indicator) that we needed to perform the analysis. We used the Generalized Method of Moments procedure to estimate the components of spread. We used the heteroscedasticity and autocorrelation consistent (HAC) approach to take account of the correlations among the disturbances. Thus, GMM yielded results that were robust to heteroscedasticity and serial correlation (E-Views user's guide, 1995).

From the GMM equation (in Appendix 5), we can see that the Durbin-Watson statistic is around two which indicates no first-order autocorrelation. Moreover, the adjusted R-squared is in the range of 10% - 20%, nine out of 28 dealers are above 20%, and only two dealers are below 10%. However, most of the t-statistics are not significant. It is of less concern since the purpose of the regression is to obtain an estimator for inferring the components of spreads.

5.6.3. The Results

As mentioned above, we took 28 dealers in Hong Kong, New York, and London to represent the Asian, North American, and European dealers. The values of π (probability of price reversal), β (inventory holding cost), and αn (adverse selection cost) shown below.

Table 5.12. Hong Kong Dealers

Dealers numbers	Number of observations	π	β	α
22	2284	0.52	7.94	-2.26
52	2074	0.50	63.90	-62
30	1676	0.51	7.76	-4.32
32	1827	0.50	2.82	-0.24
35	9076	0.52	5.12	-2.20
36	2846	0.53	2.84	-0.82
40	594	0.52	7.02	-2.2
41	2450	0.54	2.344	-0.014
47	3234	0.49	6.41	8.42
55	1779	0.52	3.96	-2.54
Average	2784	0.52	11.01	-6.82

Table 5.13. London Dealers

Dealers numbers	Number of observations	π	β	α
122	428	0.48	-3	7.53
109	1737	0.52	4.5	-2.06
107	1412	0.52	4.5	-2.06
98	865	0.50	62.54	-58
94	2931	0.49	8.26	-5.43
103	490	0.49	21.25	-15.03
125	142	0.49	63	-56.92
126	148	0.45	-2.18	16.72
291	291	0.55	4.63	1.85
171	61	0.51	3.37	14.153
Average	850	0.55	16.68	-9.92

Table 5.14. New York Dealers

Dealers numbers	Number of observations	π	β	α
142	8081	0.51	2.16	3.96
146	131	0.57	1.94	17.94
147	3082	0.51	2.44	0.26
148	287	0.48	15.36	-23.40
156	466	0.51	0.62	6.64
159	4585	0.53	1.84	0.098
170	386	0.51	6.59	0.014
179	133	0.51	22.32	34.72
Average	2143	0.52	6.66	5.03

From the table above, we notice that the probability of price reversal is around 50%. However, the value of inventory holding cost is more than 100%, and the value of adverse selection cost is negative for Hong Kong and London dealers, and it is more than 100% for New York dealers. According to the theory, those values are impossible.

Thus, we conclude that using the mid-point of spread and employing "reverse tick test" as an indicator is not useful in allowing us to infer the relative importance of the components of bid-ask spread under Huang and Stoll's (1997) model. We consequently maintain the values estimated by our earlier direct method.

So far, we have looked into the impact of an intervention on the inventory control mechanism and the relative importance of inventory cost compared with the other two costs. However, we have not yet examined whether intervention also influences the size of the spread. We analyze the topic in more detail in the coming chapter.

Chapter 6

GOVERNMENT INTERVENTION ON THE SPREAD

In Chapter 3 we discussed the impact of an intervention on the dealers' behavior in controlling their inventory by shifting the quotes. Then, we turned to an analysis of how important is the inventory cost as a component of bid-ask spreads (in Chapter 5). Now, in this chapter, we wish to determine whether the intervention affects spread.[38] Since intervention not only influences the level of the exchange rate but also influences the volatility of the exchange rate, which will widen or narrow the spread.

We use three approaches to look into the impact of an intervention on spread: using the dummy variables, using the size of the intervention, and using the event study. Furthermore, we use the same data as in a discussion of an inventory-control mechanism (Chapter 3): the G-3 currencies and intervention by the Fed from 1985 to 1987.

Before running the regression, firstly, we tested the stationarity of the Deutsche mark-dollar and the Japanese yen-dollar series since the

---

[38] The number of exchange listings is one of the variables that influence the spread (Chung and Charoenwong, 1998). This variable represents the number of the stocks being traded. It is already implied in the series (the Deutsche mark-dollar and Japanese yen-dollar) that we use, i.e., they are heavily traded in the market.

empirical work based on time series data assumes that the underlying time series is stationary.

6.1. Stationarity Testing

First, we tested the stationarity of the time series data using the standard approach of the unit root test, i.e., Augmented Dickey-Fuller and Phillips-Perron unit root test. The results are shown below.

The Augmented Dicky Fuller and Phillips-Perron test statistics are significant at 1%, 5%, and 10% critical values for both the Deutsche mark-dollar and the Japanese yen-dollar. It means we can reject the hypothesis of a unit root: the time series are stationary. However, the trend variables are significant[39]. It means that the series is trend stationary.

Table 6.1. Augmented Dickey-Fuller Unit Root test (Deutsche mark-dollar)

ADF Test Statistic		-7.901850		
1% Critical Value*		-3.9755		
5% Critical Value		-3.4183		
10% Critical Value		-3.1313		
*MacKinnon critical values for rejection of the hypothesis of a unit root.				
Variable	Coefficient	Std. Error	t-Statistic	Prob.
LGSPREAD(-1)	-0.468735	0.059320	-7.901850	0.0000
D(LGSPREAD(-1))	-0.403761	0.058785	-6.868443	0.0000
D(LGSPREAD(-2))	-0.271272	0.054927	-4.938779	0.0000
D(LGSPREAD(-3))	-0.231970	0.048608	-4.772274	0.0000
D(LGSPREAD(-4))	-0.111147	0.037239	-2.984724	0.0029
C	-1.276146	0.161860	-7.884269	0.0000
@TREND(1)		-0.000299	4.38E-05	-6.827850

[39] "Data involving economic time series often tend to move in the same direction because of a trend that is common to all of them" (Gujarati, 1995, p.722).

Table 6.2. Phillips-Perron Unit Root test (Deutsche mark-dollar)

PP Test Statistic	-23.06109	1% Critical Value*		-3.9750
		5% Critical Value		-3.4180
		10% Critical Value		-3.1311
*MacKinnon critical values for rejection of the hypothesis of a unit root.				
Lag truncation for Bartlett kernel: 6		(Newey-West suggests: 6)		
Residual variance with no correction				0.018824
Residual variance with correction				0.025900
Phillips-Perron Test Equation				
Dependent Variable: D(LGSPREAD)				
Method: Least Squares				
Variable	Coefficient	Std. Error	t-Statistic	Prob.
LGSPREAD(-1)	-0.777361	0.035211	-22.07694	0.0000
C	-2.108133	0.096107	-21.93523	0.0000
@TREND(1)	-0.000482	3.16E-05	-15.24004	0.0000

Table 6.3. Augmented Dicky-FullerUnit Root test (Japanese yen-dollar)

ADF Test Statistic		-9.288957		
1% Critical Value*		-3.9750		
5% Critical Value		-3.4180		
10% Critical Value		-3.1311		
*MacKinnon critical values for rejection of the hypothesis of a unit root.				
Variable	Coefficient	Std. Error	t-Statistic	Prob.
LGSPREAD(-1)	-0.578454	0.062273	-9.288957	0.0000
D(LGSPREAD(-1))	-0.294205	0.060625	-4.852901	0.0000
D(LGSPREAD(-2))	-0.215455	0.056067	-3.842805	0.0001
D(LGSPREAD(-3))	-0.120926	0.048543	-2.491088	0.0130
D(LGSPREAD(-4))	0.011201	0.036684	0.305353	0.7602
C	-0.529505	0.057724	-9.173035	0.0000
@TREND(1)	-0.000205	3.07E-05	-6.680880	0.0000

Table 6.4. Phillips-Perron Unit Root test (Japanese yen-dollar)

PP Test Statistic	-23.94942	1% Critical Value*		-3.9750
		5% Critical Value		-3.4180
		10% Critical Value		-3.1311
*MacKinnon critical values for rejection of the hypothesis of a unit root.				
Lag truncation for Bartlett kernel: 6		(Newey-West suggests: 6)		
Residual variance with no correction				0.016385
Residual variance with correction				0.022121
Phillips-Perron Test Equation				
Dependent Variable: D(LGSPREAD)				
Method: Least Squares				
Variable	Coefficient	Std. Error	t-Statistic	Prob.
LGSPREAD(-1)	-0.827709	0.035804	-23.11793	0.0000
C	-0.758664	0.034175	-22.19921	0.0000
@TREND(1)	-0.000291	2.49E-05	-11.71584	0.0000

The exchange rate series are generally volatile. To check to see if this volatility arises from structural breaks in the Deutsche mark-dollar and the Japanese yen-dollar, we tested a modified alternative hypothesis of trend stationarity with a break (Zivot and Andrews, 1992). There are three models (A, B, and C) that Zivot and Andrews (1992) use to test for a unit root.

Model A:

$$y_t = \hat{\mu}^A + \hat{\theta}^A DU_t\left(\hat{\lambda}\right) + \hat{\beta}^A t + \hat{\alpha}^A y_{t-1} + \sum_{j=1}^{k} \hat{c}_j^A \Delta y_{t-j} + \hat{e}_t \tag{6.1}$$

Model B:

$$y_t = \hat{\mu}^B + \hat{\gamma}^B DT_t^*\left(\hat{\lambda}\right) + \hat{\beta}^B t + \hat{\alpha}^B y_{t-1} + \sum_{j=1}^{k} \hat{c}_j^B \Delta y_{t-j} + \hat{e}_t \tag{6.2}$$

Model C:

$$y_t = \hat{\mu}^C + \hat{\gamma}^C DT_t^*\left(\hat{\lambda}\right) + \hat{\theta}^C DU_t\left(\hat{\lambda}\right) + \hat{\beta}^C t + \hat{\alpha}^C y_{t-1} + \sum_{j=1}^{k} \hat{c}_j^C \Delta y_{t-j} + \hat{e}_t \tag{6.3}$$

where $DU_t() = 1$ if $t > T$, 0 otherwise; $DT^*{}_t() = t - T$ if $t > T$, 0 otherwise.

They consider the following statistics computed from models A - C:

$$t_{\hat{\alpha}^i}\left(\hat{\lambda}^i_{\inf}\right) = \inf_{\lambda \in \wedge} t_{\hat{\alpha}^i}(\lambda), \quad i = A, B, C \tag{6.4}$$

where is a specified closed subset of (0,1), and t represents the standard t statistic for testing $^i = 1$[40]. These statistics depend on the location of the breakpoint = T_B/T[41]. The rejection of the null hypothesis of a unit root means the series is trend stationary.

We choose T_B based on events[42] (Plaza Agreement, Tokyo Summit, Louvre Accord, and Stock Crash), months (four months)[43], and the date from Plaza (22 September 1985) to stock crash (late October 1987). Thus we have three s: =4/754, =80/754, and =530/754. The number k of extra regressors is determined by $N^{1/3}$, where N is a number of samples (Insukindro, 1994). The tables below present the results of the regressions model A, B, and C.

The tables below show that we reject the null hypothesis of a unit root for both series. Thus, we conclude that the Deutsche mark-dollar and the Japanese yen-dollar series are trend stationary. The first approach of the impact on the spread (using dummy variable) is discussed next.

---

[40] We use Zivot critical value since we follow his model.

[41] T_B is time break, and T is time (the whole period/sample).

[42] There are four significant events during 1985 to 1987.

[43] We assume that the length of the period of each event is a month. A week is five working days; thus, four months are 80 days.

Table 6.5. Unit Root Test (T_B=4)[44]
(Deutsche mark-dollar)

Model	t-statistics	Zivot critical value (5%)	Accept or Reject H_0
A	7.21	-4.80	Reject H_0
B	6.65	-4.42	Reject H_0
C	6.69	-5.08	Reject H_0

Table 6.6. Unit Root Test (T_B=80)
(Deutsche mark-dollar)

Model	t-statistics	Zivot critical value (5%)	Accept or Reject H_0
A	9.04	-4.80	Reject H_0
B	7.23	-4.42	Reject H_0
C	6.26	-5.08	Reject H_0

Table 6.7. Unit Root Test (T_B=530)
(Deutsche mark-dollar)

Model	t-statistics	Zivot critical value (5%)	Accept or Reject H_0
A	9.13	-4.80	Reject H_0
B	9.20	-4.42	Reject H_0
C	9.08	-5.08	Reject H_0

Table 6.8. Unit Root Test (T_B=4)[45]
(Japanese yen-dollar)

Model	t-statistics	Zivot critical value (5%)	Accept or Reject H_0
A	6.37	-4.80	Reject H_0
B	5.56	-4.42	Reject H_0
C	5.54	-5.08	Reject H_0

---

[44] The number of lagged difference terms are 2 for model A, and 1 for model B and C. The reason for not including all lagged difference terms (9) is that there is near singular matrix.

[45] The number of lagged difference terms is 2 for model A, and 1 for model B, and C. The reason is the same as in DM T_B=4.

Table 6.9. Unit Root Test (T_B=80)
(Japanese yen-dollar)

Model	t-statistics	Zivot critical value (5%)	Accept or Reject H_0
A	6.36	-4.80	Reject H_0
B	5.90	-4.42	Reject H_0
C	5.85	-5.08	Reject H_0

Table 6.10. Unit Root Test (T_B=530)
(Japanese yen-dollar)

Model	t-statistics	Zivot critical value (5%)	Accept or Reject H_0
A	6.38	-4.80	Reject H_0
B	6.45	-4.42	Reject H_0
C	5.12	-5.08	Reject H_0

6.2. DUMMY VARIABLE

We split the data into two dummy variables, i.e., a dummy to represent purchases of US dollar and a dummy to represent sales of US dollar. The regression equation is as follows:

$$\text{Spread} = + {}_1\text{DPrch} + {}_2\text{DSls} + + \varepsilon \qquad (6.5)$$

where:

DPrch = dummy variable for government purchases of US dollar (1=purchases, 0=no intervention)

DSls = dummy variable for government sales of US dollar (1=sale, 0=no intervention)

= error term

To make easy the interpretation of the result, we transformed the dependent variable by taking logarithms. Thus, we obtain the relative change of dependent variable (spread) instead of the absolute change of spread: the slope coefficient measures the relative change independent variable (spread) for a given absolute change in the value of an independent variable (government intervention) (Ramanathan, 1995).

As noted in section 6.1, the time series is trend stationary, then, the variable trend (T) is included as one of the regressors to avoid spurious correlation. In other words, the trend variable in the regression has the effect of detrending, which is removing the influence of trend (Gujarati, 1995, p.722). Restating the regression (6.1):

$$LgSpread = + {}_1DPrch + {}_2DSls + {}_3T + \varepsilon \qquad (6.6),$$

where T = trend variable.

The results of the regressions for the Deutsche mark-dollar and the Japanese yen-dollar are presented in the tables below.

Table 6.11. Regression result (Deutsche mark-dollar)

LS // Dependent Variable is LgSpread				
Variable	Coefficient	Std. Error	t-Statistic	Prob.
Constant	-2.724369	0.010385	-262.3403	0.0000
DPrch	0.069985	0.028062	2.494000	0.0129
DSls	0.009221	0.027151	0.339598	0.7343
T	-0.000639	2.53E-05	-25.24422	0.0000
R-squared	0.484619		Adjusted R-squared	0.482466.
S.E. of regression	0.134689		Schwarz criterion	-3.978663
F-statistic	225.0484		Durbin-Watson stat	1.592490
Prob(F-statistic)	0.000000			

Before interpreting the results above, we checked the violations of underlying assumptions of OLS, namely serial correlation, heteroscedasticity, and non-normality. These are given in Appendix 9.

After checking the violations of underlying OLS, the null hypothesis is tested with including the autoregressive moving average component and Newey-West correction. The coefficients of the regression are presented in the tables below. The Adjusted-R Square is significant and large, i.e., 0.54

and 0.31 for the Deutsche mark-dollar and the Japanese yen-dollar respectively. Durbin-Watson is close to 2, which indicates there is no first-order autocorrelation.

Table 6.12. Regression result (Japanese yen-dollar)

LS // Dependent Variable is LgSpread				
Variable	Coefficient	Std. Error	t-Statistic	Prob.
Constant	-0.928763	0.009731	-95.44612	0.0000
DPrch	-0.024083	0.021507	-1.119800	0.2632
DSls	0.125909	0.028915	4.354501	0.0000
T	-0.000326	2.29E-05	-14.25749	0.0000
R-squared	0.270932	Adjusted R-squared		0.268016
S.E. of regression	0.129255	Schwarz criterion		-4.062101
F-statistic	92.90369	Durbin-Watson stat		1.676787
Prob(F-statistic)		0.000000		

Table 6.13. Regression result after Newey-West correction (Deutsche mark-dollar)

LS // Dependent Variable is LgSpread				
Convergence achieved after 8 iterations				
Newey-West HAC Standard Errors & Covariance (lag truncation=6)				
Variable	Coefficient	Std. Error	t-Statistic	Prob.
Constant	-2.698208	0.031730	-85.03750	0.0000
DPrch	0.037802	0.024766	1.526401	0.1274
DSls	0.023775	0.033799	0.703410	0.4820
T	-0.000686	8.26E-05	-8.300519	0.0000
AR(1)	0.954103	0.020626	46.25708	0.0000
MA(1)	-0.865099	0.032344	-26.74660	0.0000
R-squared	0.547853	Adjusted R-squared		0.544691
S.E. of regression	0.126415	Schwarz criterion		-4.089967
F-statistic	173.2685	Durbin-Watson stat		1.978779
Prob(F-statistic)		0.000000		
Inverted AR Roots		.95		
Inverted MA Roots		.87		

Table 6.14. Regression result after Newey-West correction (Japanese yen-dollar)

LS // Dependent Variable is LgSpread				
Convergence achieved after 9 iterations				
Newey-West HAC Standard Errors & Covariance (lag truncation=6)				
Variable	Coefficient	Std. Error	t-Statistic	Prob.
Constant	-0.913501	0.024091	-37.91834	0.0000
DPrch	-0.020781	0.033237	-0.625244	0.5320
DSls	0.110891	0.044187	2.509588	0.0123
T	-0.000349	6.14E-05	-5.679951	0.0000
AR(1)	0.961293	0.017849	53.85768	0.0000
MA(1)	-0.894173	0.032180	-27.78619	0.0000
R-squared	0.322690	Adjusted R-squared	0.318156	
S.E. of regression	0.124603	Schwarz criterion	-4.120462	
F-statistic	71.17839	Durbin-Watson stat	1.927104	
Prob(F-statistic)		0.000000		
Inverted AR Roots		.96		
Inverted MA Roots		.89		

From the tables above we notice that only one out of four of the coefficients of government intervention is significant with the positive sign that is the sales of US dollar against the Japanese yen. Moreover, the trend variable is significant and negative for both series. It means over the period (1985 – 1987), on average, the spread decreased at the rate of 0.07 percent and 0.04 percent per day for the Deutsche mark-dollar and the Japanese yen-dollar respectively. Thus, over the period 1985 – 1987, there was a downward trend in a spread.

We can conclude that only the sales of US dollar against the Japanese yen widened the spread in the period 1985 to 1987. Otherwise, there is no impact of government intervention on a spread.

6.3. Size of Intervention Variable

The second approach is to use the size of the intervention. We define the intervention as net daily purchases[46] of US dollar against the Deutsche mark and the Japanese yen. The regression equation is as follow.

$$LgSpread = + {}_1Intervention + {}_2T + + \varepsilon \qquad (6.7),$$

where:

Intervention = net daily purchases of US dollar against the Deutsche mark or the Japanese yen

T = trend

= error term

Table 6.15 and Table 6.16 below present the results of the regressions without the correction for autoregressive moving average components.

Table 6.15. Regression result
(Deutsche mark-dollar)

Dependent Variable: LgSpread				
Method: Least Squares				
Variable	Coefficient	Std. Error	t-Statistic	Prob.
Constant	-2.714530	0.010520	-258.0325	0.0000
INTERVENTION	3.24E-05	0.000112	0.290764	0.7713
T	-0.000613	2.42E-05	-25.30349	0.0000
R-squared	0.467019	Schwarzcriterion		-1.035088
Adjusted R-squared	0.465600	F-statistic		329.0286
S.E. of regression	0.142606	Prob(F-statistic)		0.000000
Durbin-Watson stat	1.531829			

[46] It means purchases minus sales.

Table 6.16. Regression result (Japanese yen-dollar)

Dependent Variable: LgSpread				
Method: Least Squares				
Variable	Coefficient	Std. Error	t-Statistic	Prob.
Constant	-0.918757	0.009607	-95.63110	0.0000
INTERVENTION	-1.99E-05	9.33E-05	-0.212983	0.8314
T	-0.000347	2.23E-05	-15.52258	0.0000
R-squared	0.251327	Schwarz criterion		-1.206633
Adjusted R-squared	0.249334	F-statistic		126.0544
S.E. of regression	0.130884	Prob(F-statistic)		0.000000
Durbin-Watson stat	1.644025			

We perform the same check procedure on the appropriateness of OLS as in the previous section before interpreting the results above. The results of these checks are given in Appendix 9.

Appendix 9 shows the need for an autoregressive moving average and the Newey-West corrections.

Table 6.17. Regression result after Newey-West correction (Deutsche mark-dollar)

Dependent Variable: LgSpread				
Method: Least Squares				
Convergence achieved after 7 iterations				
Newey-West HAC Standard Errors & Covariance (lag truncation=6)				
Backcast: 1				
Variable	Coefficient	Std. Error	t-Statistic	Prob.
Constant	-2.677682	0.031546	-84.88286	0.0000
INTERVENTION	-3.58E-05	9.45E-05	-0.378841	0.7049
T	-0.000679	7.63E-05	-8.901585	0.0000
AR(1)	0.959797	0.018173	52.81588	0.0000
MA(1)	-0.883179	0.032090	-27.52176	0.0000
R-squared	0.540191	Schwarz criterion		-1.168225
Adjusted R-squared	0.537733	F-statistic		219.6910
S.E. of regression	0.132429	Prob(F-statistic)		0.000000
Durbin-Watson stat	1.915859			

Table 6.18. Regression result after Newey-West correction (Japanese yen-dollar)

Dependent Variable: LgSpread				
Method: Least Squares				
Convergence achieved after 8 iterations				
Newey-West HAC Standard Errors & Covariance (lag truncation=6)				
Backcast: 1				
Variable	Coefficient	Std. Error	t-Statistic	Prob.
Constant	-0.901403	0.026324	-34.24236	0.0000
INTERVENTION	0.000156	8.49E-05	1.837313	0.0666
T	-0.000379	6.46E-05	-5.858698	0.0000
AR(1)	0.957707	0.017741	53.98213	0.0000
MA(1)	-0.877684	0.031921	-27.49583	0.0000
R-squared	0.314983	Schwarz criterion		-1.280225
Adjusted R-squared	0.311320	F-statistic		85.98603
S.E. of regression	0.125216	Prob(F-statistic)		0.000000
Durbin-Watson stat	1.933772			
Inverted AR Roots	.96			
Inverted MA Roots	.88			

We can see in the tables above that we do not reject the null hypothesis for the Deutsche mark-dollar, but we reject the null hypothesis for the Japanese mark dollar at 10% significance value. It means that the net purchases of US dollar against the Deutsche mark did not have any effect on a spread in the period of 1985 to 1987. On the other hand, the spread widened around 0.02 percent when there were net purchases of US dollar against the Japanese yen in the period of 1985 to 1987. Moreover, over the period there was a downward trend in a spread for both series. Thus, the spread, on average, decreased 0.07 and 0.04 percent for the Deutsche mark-dollar and the Japanese yen-dollar respectively.

6.4. Event Study

This method is designed to examine whether there are significant changes in spreads on the intervention day. The abnormal spread is defined as a spread on the event period (intervention period) minus the average of spread before and after the event period. Put them in the equation:

$$AS_t = Spread_t - \sigma \tag{6.8}$$

where:

AS_t = abnormal spread

$Spread_t$ = the spread on the intervention day, i.e., t = 0

= the average of spread before and after the intervention day, i.e., one week before and one week after[47].

Then, we test the null hypothesis of no difference in the spread between non-intervention day and the intervention day. In other words, we can state the null hypothesis and the alternative hypothesis as:

H_0: $AS_t = 0$

H_1: AS_t 0

The tables below present the average abnormal spreads, the level of significant of a normal distribution, the confidence intervals and the hypothesis results for the Deutsche mark-dollar and the Japanese yen-dollar respectively.

Table 6.19. Spread behavior around intervention day (Deutsche mark-dollar)

Average Abnormal Spread: 0.0001547		
	Confidence Interval	Reject or Accept H_0
1%	$-0.00001 < AS_t < 0.000418$	Accept H_0
5%	$-0.00004 < AS_t < 0.000352$	Accept H_0
10%	$-0.00001 < AS_t < 0.00032$	Accept H_0

[47] We suppose that the average of spread one week before and one week after the intervention day is enough to represent the normal spread during non-intervention day.

Table 6.20. Spread behavior around intervention day (Japanese yen-dollar)

Average Abnormal Spread: 0.016033		
	Confidence Interval	Reject or Accept H_0
1%	$0.002195 < AS_t < 0.029871$	Reject H_0
5%	$0.005615 < AS_t < 0.026451$	Reject H_0
10%	$0.007327 < AS_t < 0.024739$	Reject H_0

It is clear that there were no significant changes in spreads on the intervention day for the Deutsche mark-dollar. However, we reject the null hypothesis for the Japanese yen-dollar. The average abnormal spread for both currencies is positive. It means the spread widened during the intervention day in the period of 1985 to 1987.

CONCLUSION

The three approaches that we use to test whether an intervention has any impact on spread reach the same conclusion, i.e., the intervention in the Japanese yen widened the spread and the intervention in the Deutsche mark did not have any influence on spread during 1985 to 1987. Furthermore, the spread, on average, decreased over that period. Several events may explain the result.

There is evidence of a relation between the spread and price volatility; the more volatile the exchange rate, the wider the spread (Boothe, 1988; Bessembinder, 1994; Glassman, 1987). Conforming to our finding, during 1985–1991 Federal Reserve intervention either increased yen/US dollar or had no impact on the volatility of DM/US dollar (Neal and Tanner, 1996).

Regarding volatility, De Grauwe (1996) suggests that in flexible exchange rate system the volatility is determined by the expectations agents to hold about the future. Fundamental variables and irrelevant variables influence the agent's expectations. We know that intervention signals to the market the future exchange rate as long as monetary policy supports it. The results above may relate to the objective of intervention.

Intervention has many objectives, but two are of most interest to our analysis (Belongia, 1992):

- a change in the level of the US dollar exchange rate
- a reduction in the volatility of the US dollar value around some level.

As we discussed in the previous section, central banks intervened in the market to change the level of exchange rates in the sample period. Dominguez (1993) supports this view: throughout the period January 1985 to mid-February 1987 the central banks' stated intention was to affect the level rather than reduce the variance of the exchange rate.

However, beginning in March was a time that might be considered one of the mixed central bank signals. In that period traders reported that the Bank of Japan had unilaterally begun a reverse intervention to slow the appreciation of the yen. On the other hand, the United States was accused by other G-3 countries of "talking down" the dollar (Dominguez, 1990). These mixed signals increased the volatility of Japanese yen-dollar rate, which leads to a widened spread.

In conclusion, the intervention in the Japanese yen-dollar widened the spread since the Fed intervention increased the volatility of the yen/US dollar rate. Moreover, the objective[48] of the intervention during that period may be the reason for the insignificant result on the Deutsche mark-dollar.

---

[48] A change in the level of the US dollar exchange rate.

Chapter 7

FINDINGS: FOREIGN EXCHANGE INTERVENTION EFFECTIVENESS

7.1. FOREIGN EXCHANGE INTERVENTION ISSUES

Studies by other authors of the effectiveness of government intervention utilizing fundamental models of the determination of exchange rates can explain the behavior of the exchange rate for the first part of the floating regime after 1973, but not the later part of the regime. Moreover, they cannot explain the movements of the exchange rate in the short and medium term horizon. These difficulties have motivated researchers to use at market microstructure to explain the impact of government intervention on the movements of exchange rates over these time horizons.

The research objectives of this book were defined in Chapter 1 as the follwoing:

- To understand, through the use of microstructure analysis based on information asymmetry and information economics perspective, how intervention by authorities in foreign exchange markets affects the quotation of foreign exchange rates, in particular, the setting of bid-ask prices from 1985 to 1987 (during Plaza Agreement to Louvre Accord).

- To survey the relative importance of the inventory cost in the components of the bid-ask spread.
- To comprehend whether the intervention does not only affect the quotation of bid-ask prices but also influences the spread.

7.2. THE EMPIRICAL RESULTS AND THE IMPLICATIONS FOR INTERVENTION

We found that government intervention by sales of US dollar was insignificant during the period 1985 – 1987, despite a major change in government policy toward the concept of intervention. It meant the dealers do not believe the signal which is given by the government through coordinated government intervention.

The intervention by a purchase of the US dollar was significant with a positive sign, but this sign was the reverse of that expected. The positive sign meant that the dealers shifted down the quote to discourage their customers from selling the US dollars (buy DM and Yen) and to encourage them to buy the US dollars (sell DM and Yen) as they anticipated the dollar would depreciate. A purchase of dollar signaled to the market that the government had an intention to appreciate the dollars in the future. Thus, the dealers reacted in the opposite direction of the government's intention[49].

We concluded that this reaction was due to the lack of credibility of the government intervention. Moreover, the large scale of G-3 (Japan, Germany and USA) intervention supporting the dollar (purchasing dollars against DM) after the stock market crash of October 1987 was perceived by market participants as a commitment of the US to preventing a post-

---

[49] The dealers' behavior is conforming to the fact that the dollars kept depreciating at that time, although the Fed bought US$ in large amount.

crash liquidity crisis rather than a commitment to supporting the dollar (Dominguez, 1990, p.139).

In summary, the government intervention during the period of Plaza agreement to Louvre accord was not an effective influence on the dealers' behavior in controlling inventory position by shifting the quote (up or down). It may have been due to the lack of commitment of G-5 to policy coordination (Funabashi, 1988).

Different school of thoughts may give different theoretical explanations for this finding. For example, the proponents of information economics may argue this finding in terms of the information asymmetry, agency theory, moral hazard, adverse selection and other related multi-agent game theoretic issues. Transaction cost economics has different views and provides transaction cost as a major factor for this phenomenon. (see Kreps, 1990 for different shcools of thoughts).

As a preamble to evaluating intervention effect on foreign exchange bid-ask spreads, we turned to an analysis of how important is the inventory cost as a component of the bid-ask spreads. Our research showed that the components of bid-ask spread in foreign exchange market could be ranked, in order from most to least importance, as inventory holding cost, adverse selection, and order processing cost. High inventory holding cost is related to the impact of opportunity costs and the risk of changes in inventory values. Moreover, we found that the small banks have less ability to unload the inventory imbalances since they do not operate continuously.

The less important adverse selection cost is consistent with the fact that the government is believed to have intervened secretly for about 40 percent of all intervention operations in our sample period. Our finding of lesser importance for the adverse selection cost in the foreign exchange market than in the equity market conforms to evidence that the potential loss from an informed trader is lower in the foreign exchange market. Highly competitive trading (price competition) in the foreign exchange market leads to a very small order processing cost.

We recognized above that the intervention was not credible in the period of Plaza agreements to Louvre accord. The next question was whether the intervention affected spread through the components of the spread. We found that intervention in the Japanese yen widened the spread and the intervention in the Deutsche mark did not have any influence on spread during 1985 to 1987. This finding is supported by Neal and Tanner (1996): Federal Reserve intervention either increased the volatility of yen/US dollar or had no impact on the volatility of DM/US dollar during the period 1985-1991[50].

7.3. Major Contributions of Book

By developing an interesting perspective of foreign exchange market interventions based on microstructure theory, this book makes the following contributions:

- The effect of an intervention on the behavior of dealers in controlling their inventory position.

To date, little attention has been paid to the particular microstructure of the foreign intervention of exchange rates. Now researchers are beginning to use market microstructure as an explanation for the effectiveness of the intervention on the movement of exchange rates in short and medium-term horizon. This is happening because the market microstructure perspective is an improved perspective for analyzing the issues of market operation and coordination since this framework is based on the resolution of the moral hazard, adverse selection, information asymmetry, agency theory and other related game theoretic issues.

This book examined the impact of an intervention on the inventory-control theory particularly. We looked into the behavior of the foreign exchange dealers in controlling their inventory when there is government intervention. We found that the commitment of the government to the intervention played the major role in influencing the dealers' behavior. It

---

[50] There is evidence of a relationship between the spread and price volatility (Boothe, 1988; Bessembinder, 1994; Glassman, 1987).

was particularly true for the period of changing perceptions about intervention by the US, 1985 to 1987.

The contribution of our book here has been to throw light on the mechanism of controlling the inventory position by dealers when the markets believe that the government fully commits to its policy.

- The decomposition of the determinants of the bid-ask spread

Our research confirmed that the components of the bid-ask spread—inventory holding cost, adverse selection, and transaction cost — noted for equity markets, can be measured for the foreign exchange market. Interestingly, it appears that adverse selection in the foreign exchange market is less than in equity markets. Foreign exchange market studies have not traditionally focused on an analysis of the relative importance of those three components.

Therefore, a further contribution of our book has been to identify the relative importance of the components of the foreign exchange bid-ask spread.

In addition, we have examined the impact of an intervention on the bid-ask spread and recognized that the intervention works mainly through the inventory component.

These are important findings in the area of the working of the foreign exchange market and the role of policy interventions in managing the foreign market in the developed economies.

APPENDICES

APPENDIX 1. DERIVATION OF SERIAL COVARIANCES (STOLL, 1989)

A. Serial covariances of transaction price changes

Initial Trade at Bid			Initial Trade at Ask		
$-\partial S(BB)$		$(1-\partial)S(BA)$	$\partial S(AA)$	$-(1-\partial)S(AB)$	
ΔPt	$-\partial S(BB)$	$(1-\pi)2$	0	0	$\pi(1-\pi)$
	$(1-\partial)S(BA)$	$\pi(1-\pi)$	0	0	$\pi 2$
$\Delta Pt+1$	$\partial S(AA)$	0	$\pi(1-\pi)$	$(1-\pi)2$	0
	$-(1-\partial)S(AB)$	0	$\pi 2$	$\pi(1-\pi)$	0

$$COVT \equiv COV\ (\Delta Pt,\ \Delta Pt+1) = (1-\pi)2\partial 2S2 - \partial S(1-\partial)S\pi(1-\pi) + \partial S(1-\partial)S\pi(1-\pi) - (1-\partial)2S2\pi 2$$

$$COVT = S2[\theta 2(1 - 2\pi) - \pi 2(1 - 2\theta)]$$

Serial covariances of quoted price changes

ΔBt

Initial Trade at Bid	Initial Trade at Ask		
	$-\partial S$		∂S
Next trade at Bid	$-\partial S$	$1-\pi$	π
$\Delta Bt+1$ Next trade at Ask	∂S	π	$1-\pi$

$$COVB \equiv COV\ (\Delta Bt, \Delta Bt+1) = (1-\pi)2\partial 2S2 - \pi\partial 2S2$$
$$COVB = \theta 2\ S2(1 - 2\pi)$$

Under the assumption of symmetry and constant spread

$$COVA \equiv COV\ (\Delta At, \Delta At+1) = (1-\pi)2\partial 2S2 - \pi\partial 2S2$$
$$COVA = \theta 2\ S2(1 - 2\pi)$$
$$COVQ = COV\ (\Delta Qt, \Delta Qt+1) = \theta 2\ S2(1 - 2\pi) \qquad Q=A,B$$

Appendix 2. Sterilized and Nonsterilized Intervention (Humpage, 1989)

Monetary Authority's Balance Sheet (a stylised balance sheet)

Assets	Liabilities
Net Foreign Assets Gold Foreign exchange SDR Net position in IMF	Monetary Base Currency held by the public Reserves
Domestic Assets Government securities Loans to depository institutions Other	Net Worth

Net foreign assets + Domestic Assets = Monetary Base

For example: If a central bank intervenes in the foreign exchange market to support the domestic currency, it buys foreign asset (not gold) in exchange for its domestic currency. The transaction increases the nation's monetary base. It leads to an expansion of money supply. It is called nonsterilized intervention.

The central bank can sterilize the intervention by selling the government securities in the open market, thus it leaves the monetary base not changes. The money supply is constant.

APPENDIX 3. DECOMPOSITION OF DETERMINANTS OF BID-ASK SPREAD: THE ASSUMPTIONS UNDERLYING THE METHOD OF LEAST SQUARES

According to Gujarati (1995), ten assumptions are usually made to derive and apply the method of least squares. However, we focus on just four of them, which are most important for the simple regression we are using. These are linearity, homoscedasticity, independence of error, and normality. We examined all samples (all dealers) and subsamples (Asia and Europe) for the violations of the assumptions of OLS.

Linearity

According to Norusis (1993), a convenient method to check for violations of linearity and homogeneity of variance is to plot the residuals against the predicted value. If there is a violation, systematic patterns between the predicted values and the residuals exist, such as U-shape (quadratic) or S-shape (cubic).

From the graphs below, we observe that there are no certain patterns, i.e., quadratic or cubic. They appear to be clustered around zero or randomly distributed residuals.

All Dealers

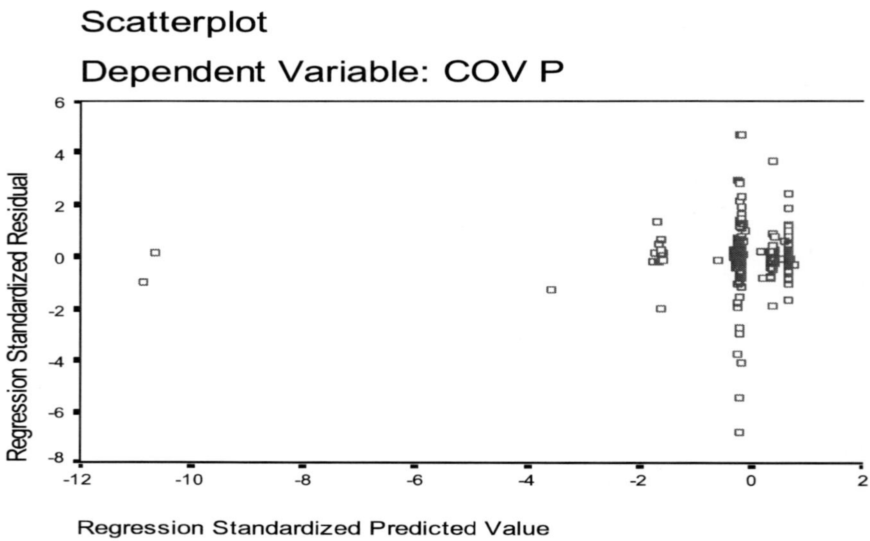

Graph 1.

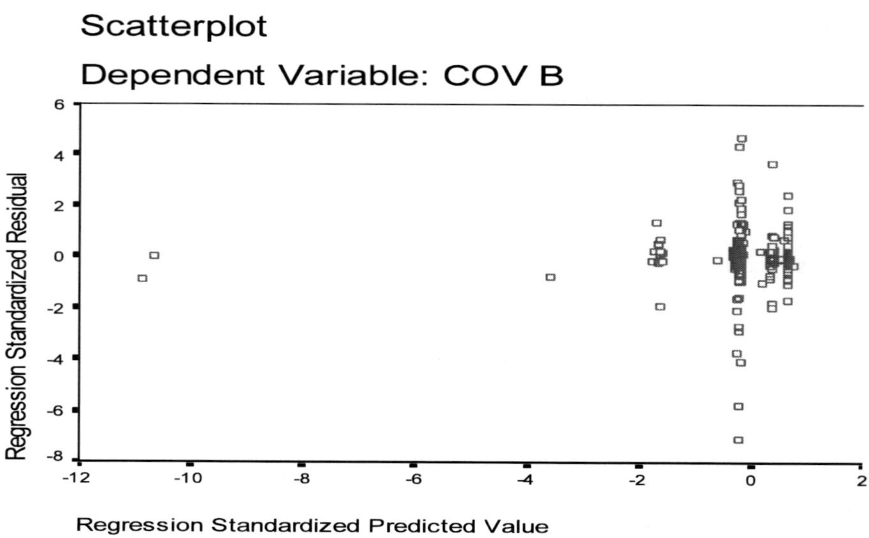

Graph 2.

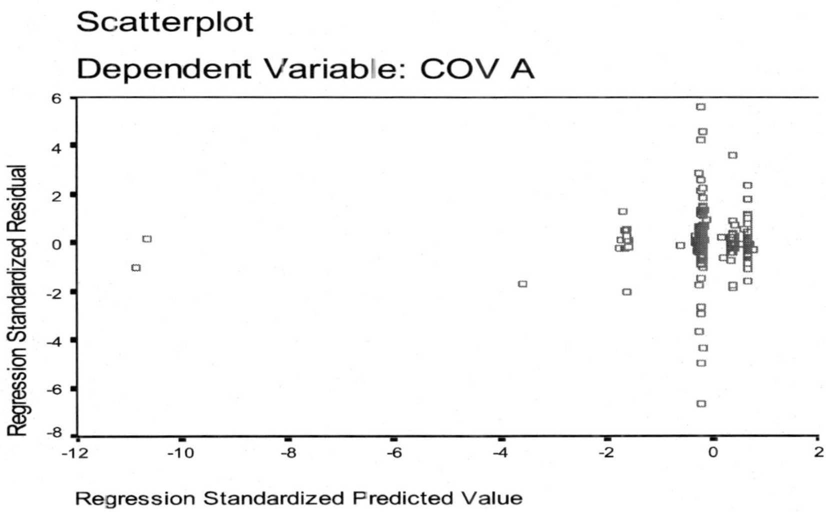

Graph 3.

Asia

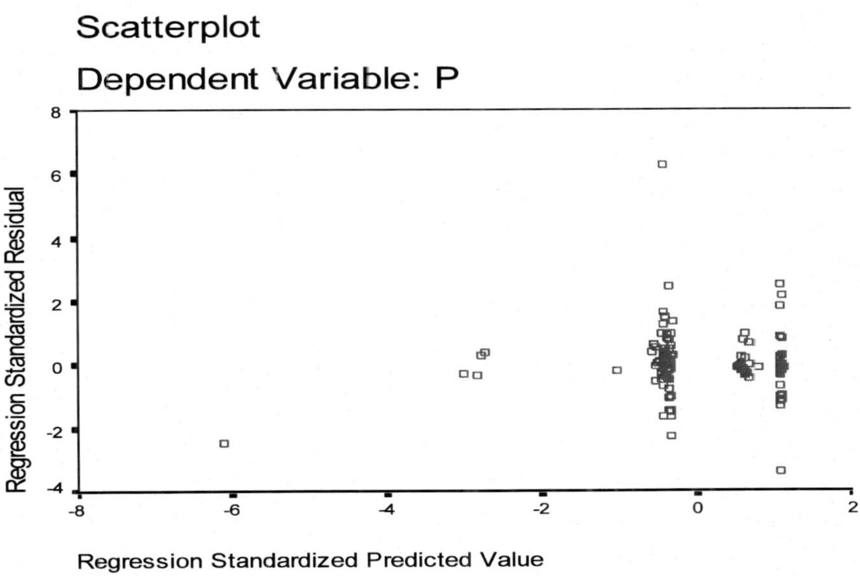

Graph 4.

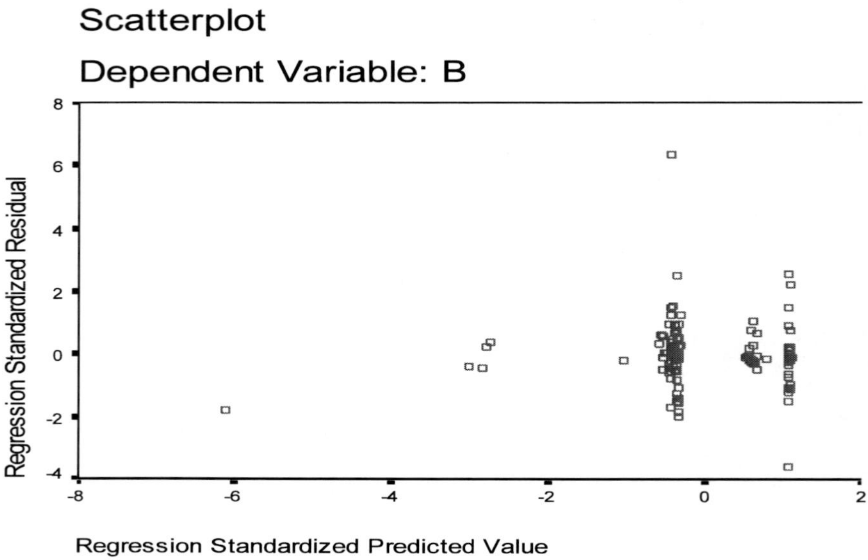

Graph 5.

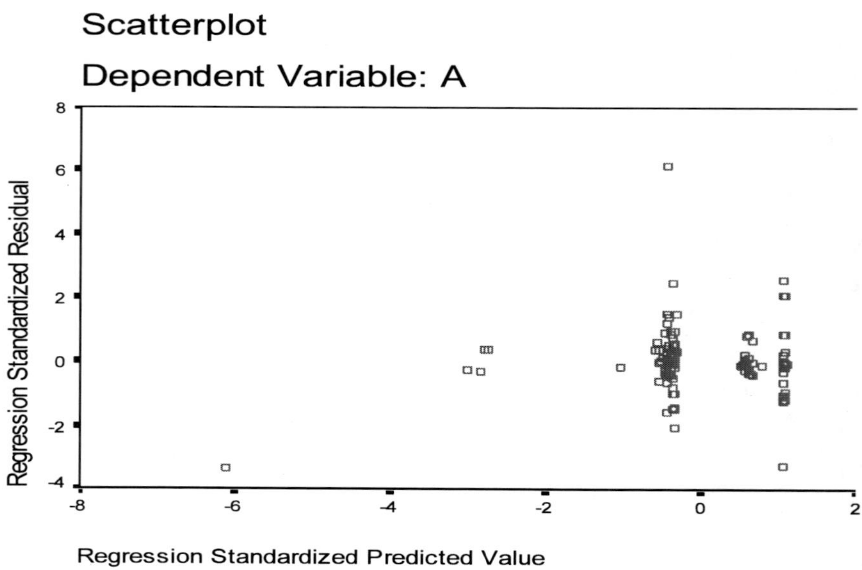

Graph 6.

Europe

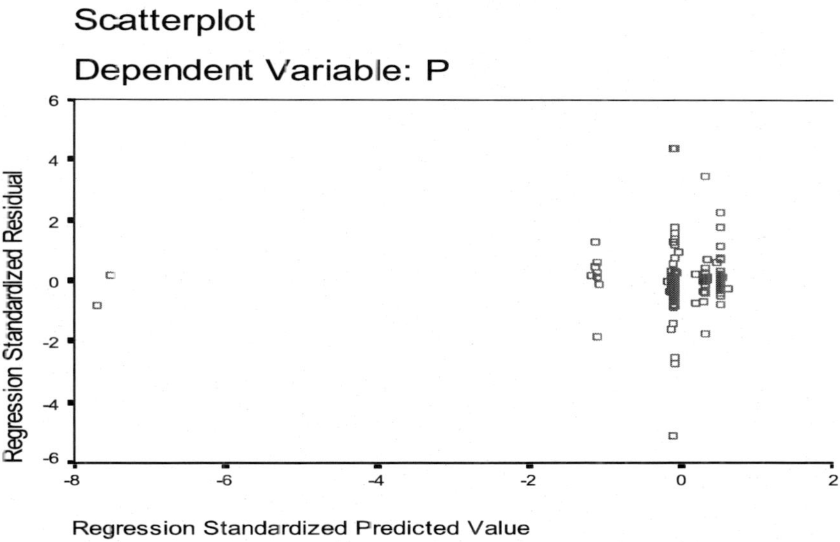

Graph 7.

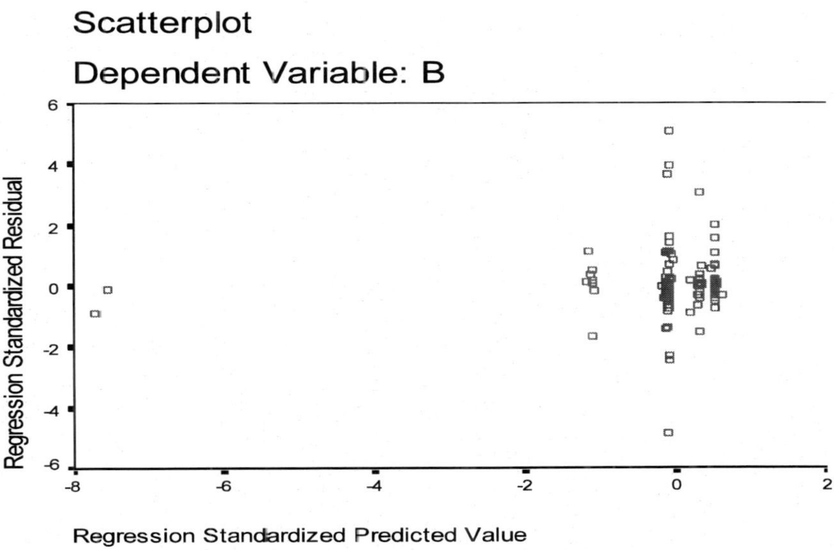

Graph 8.

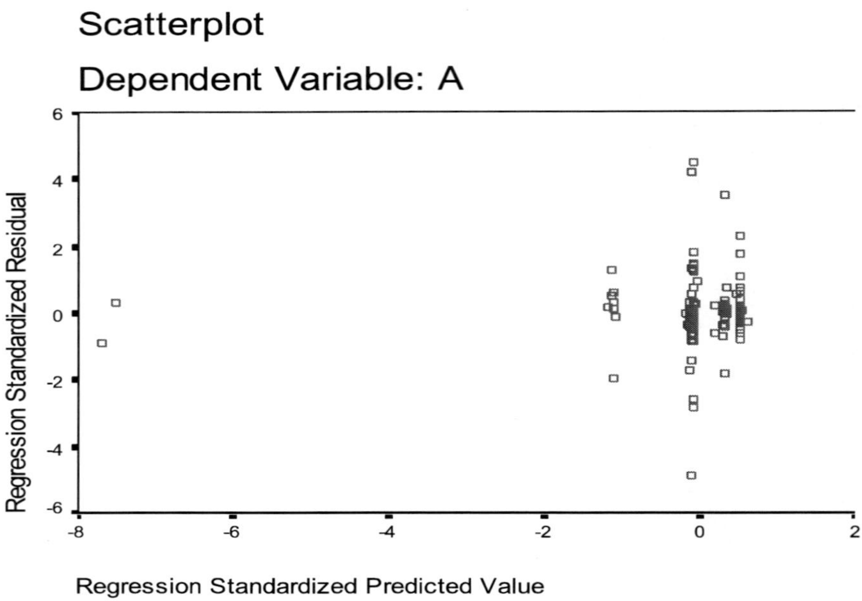

Graph 9.

Equality of Variance (Homoscedasticity)

Homoscedasticity means "given the value of X, the variance of disturbances (u) is the same for all observations." If this assumption is violated, the parameter is not efficient or does not have minimum variance: heteroscedasticity will be present. There are many ways to detect the heteroscedasticity. One of them is to plot the Studentized residuals (weighted estimated residuals) against the standardised predicted values (Norusis, 1993 pp.327). The studentized residual is defined as $e_i^* \equiv \frac{e_i}{s(i)\sqrt{1-h_i}}$, "it provides a better way to examine the information in the residuals, both because they have equal variances and because they are easily related to t-distribution in many situations" (Belsley, David. A, et al., 1980, p.20).

All Dealers

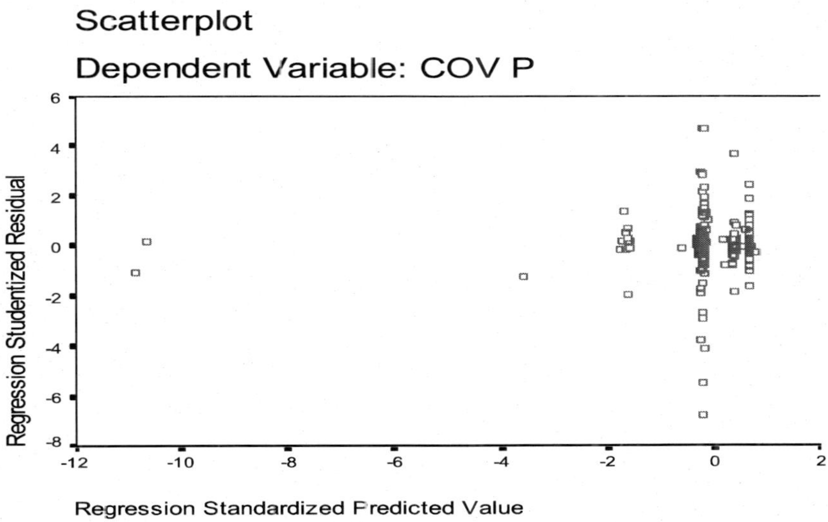

Graph 10.

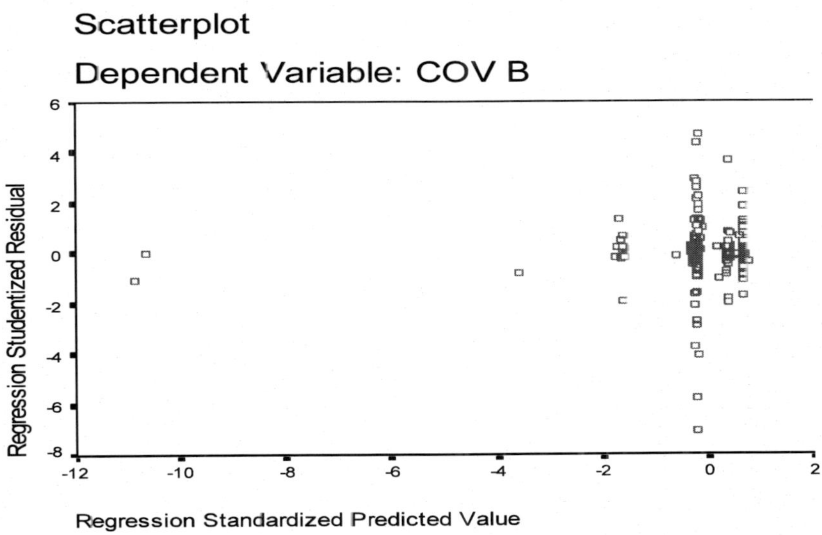

Graph 11.

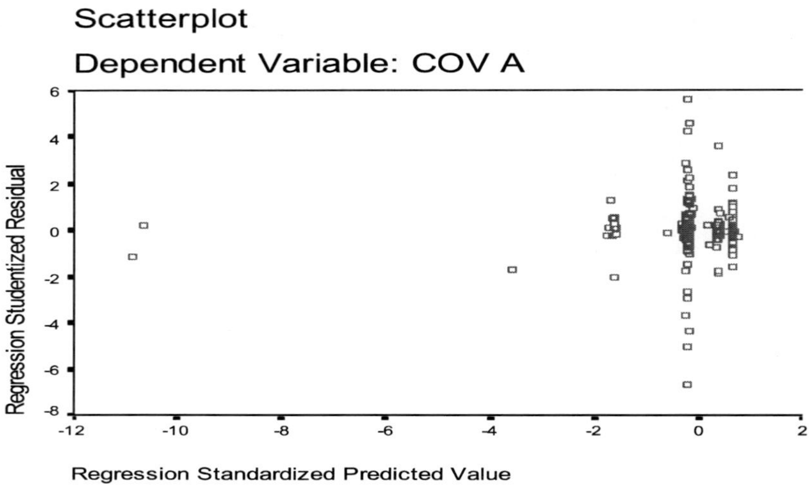

Graph 12.

Asia

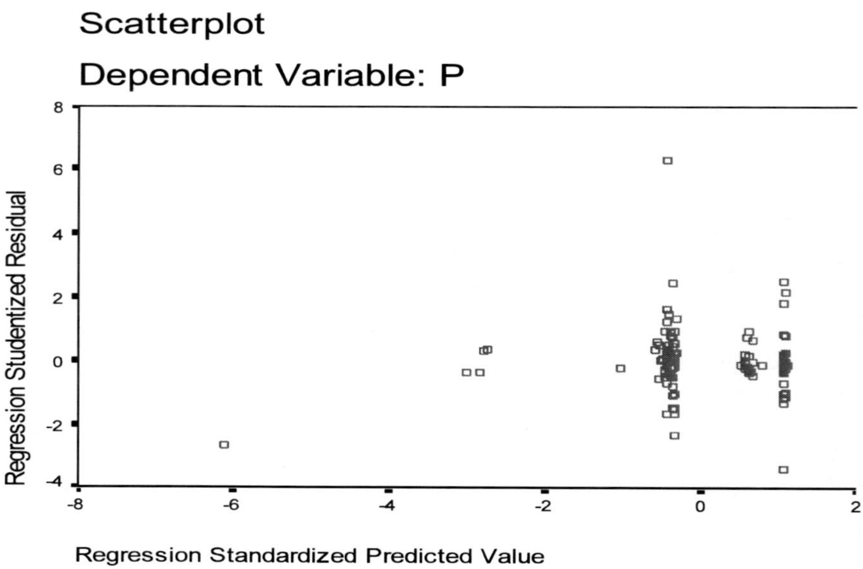

Graph 2.

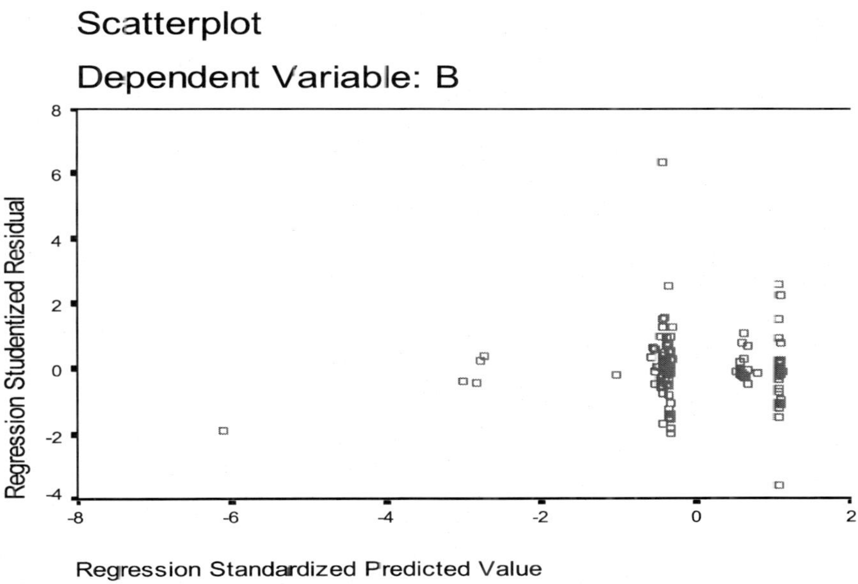

Graph 3.

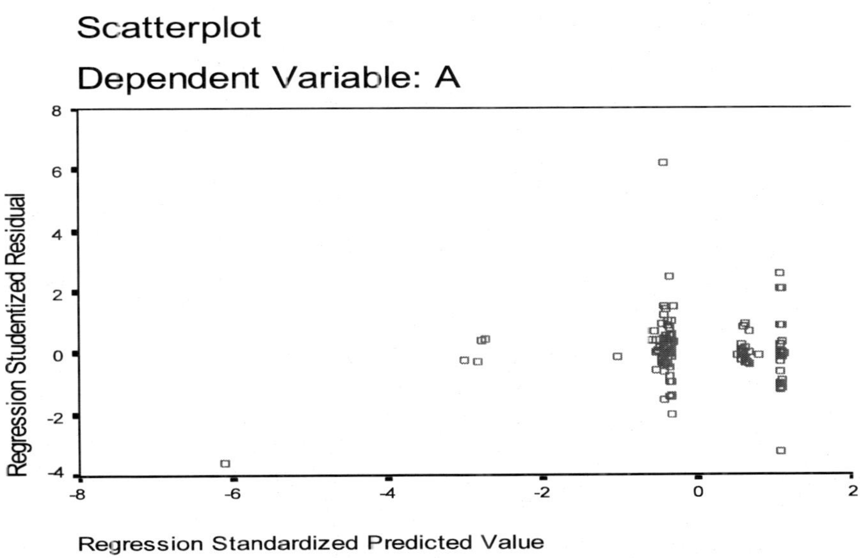

Graph 4.

The runs test is a test of randomness. That is, given a sequence of observations, the runs test examines whether the value of one observation influences the values for later observations. If there is no influence (the observations are independent), the sequence is considered random (Norusis, 1993 pp.382). The null hypothesis test (here) is that the residuals are independent. The runs test tables of Cov T, Cov B, and Cov A are presented below.

All Dealers

Table 1. (Cov A) Run test

Cut Point[51]	Number of Runs	Z-value	Sig (2-tailed)
Median	160	-0.983	0.325
Mean	154	-1.126	0.260
Mode	144	-0.699	0.484

Table 2. (Cov B) Run test

Cut Point	Number of Runs	Z-value	Sig (2-tailed)
Median	166	-0.328	0.743
Mean	162	-0.486	0.627
Mode	91	-0.906	0.365

Table 3. (Cov T) Run test

Cut Point	Number of Runs	Z-value	Sig (2-tailed)
Median	162	-.765	0.444
Mean	164	-0.340	0.734
Mode	162	-0.675	0.500

[51] Assigns cases with values less than the cut point to one group and cases with values equal to or greater than the cut point to the other group (Norusis, 1993 pp.395).

Asia

Table 4. (Cov A) Run test

Cut Point[52]	Number of Runs	Z-value	Sig (2-tailed)
Median	55	-1.775	0.076
Mean	59	-0.690	0.490
Mode	48	-1.045	0.296

Table 5. (Cov B) Run test

Cut Point	Number of Runs	Z-value	Sig (2-tailed)
Median	59	-1.065	0.287
Mean	57	-1.220	0.223
Mode	31	-0.820	0.412

Table 6. (Cov T) Run test

Cut Point	Number of Runs	Z-value	Sig (2-tailed)
Median	59	-1.065	0.287
Mean	57	-1.058	0.290
Mode	49	-2.018	0.044

Europe

Table 7. (Cov A) Run test

Cut Point	Number of Runs	Z-value	Sig (2-tailed)
Median	67	-0.842	0.400
Mean	65	-1.003	0.316
Mode	65	-0.146	0.884

[52] Assigns cases with values less than the cut point to one group and cases with values equal to or greater than the cut point to the other group (Norusis, 1993 pp.395).

Table 8. (Cov T) Run test

Cut Point	Number of Runs	Z-value	Sig (2-tailed)
Median	67	-0.842	0.400
Mean	61	-1.605	0.109
Mode	29	-0.779	0.436

Table 9. (Cov B) Run test

Cut Point	Number of Runs	Z-value	Sig (2-tailed)
Median	67	-0.923	0.356
Mean	65	-0.655	0.513
Mode	29	-2.252	0.024

From the table above, we can see that only Cov B (Europe) with mode cut point is significant at 5% (2-tailed). However, the rest of variables are not significant at 5% (2-tailed). Overall the null hypothesis is not rejected, i.e., it suggests that the first-order autocorrelation is not present.

Normality

This assumption says that the stochastic disturbance is normally distributed. We can detect normality most simply by a cumulative probability plot of residuals or in formal way, such as the chi-square goodness of fit test and the Jarque-Bera (JB) test. We will use the cumulative probability plot of residuals. As Gujarati (1993 pp.143) states "very often such a visual picture is a good way of learning informally about the likely shape of the probability distribution of a random variable."

Apparently the distributions of residuals for all dealers, Asia and Europe are not normal, according to graphs below. The observed residuals are not at the "normal" line (the straight line). Nevertheless, Gujarati cites: "This assumption is not essential if our objective is estimation only...the OLS estimators are BLUE regardless of whether the "u" are normally distributed or not" (Gujarati, 1995 pp.316). As mentioned before we use the regression only for estimation of the values of the serial covariance.

All Dealers

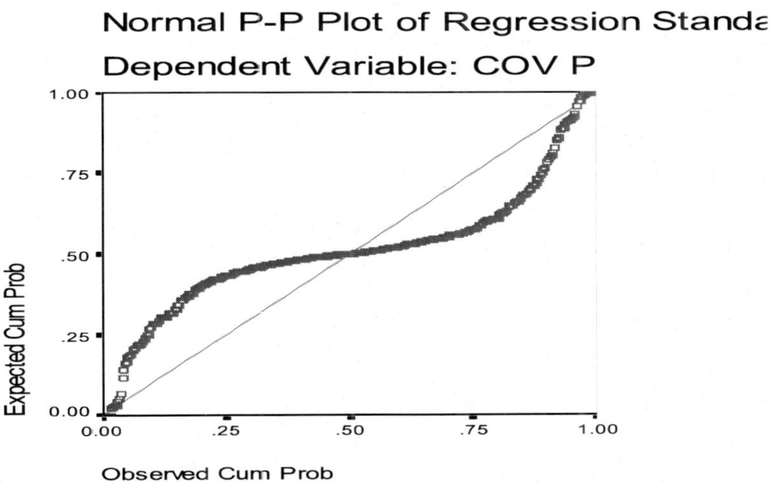

Graph 8.

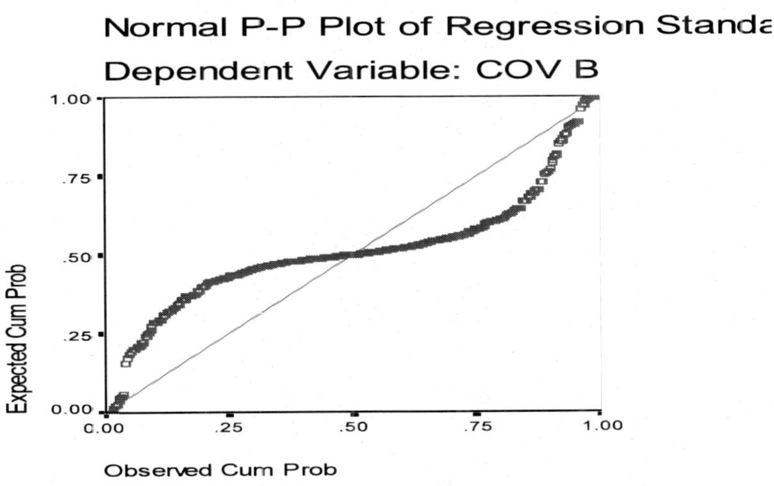

Graph 9.

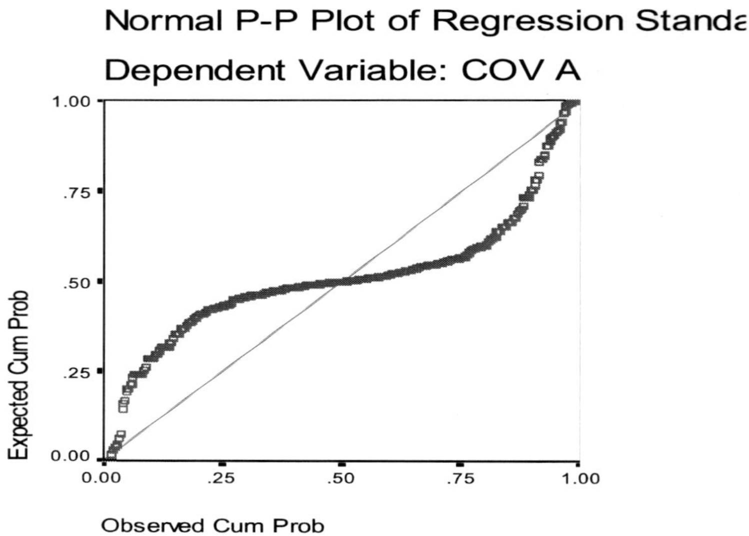

Graph 10.

Asia

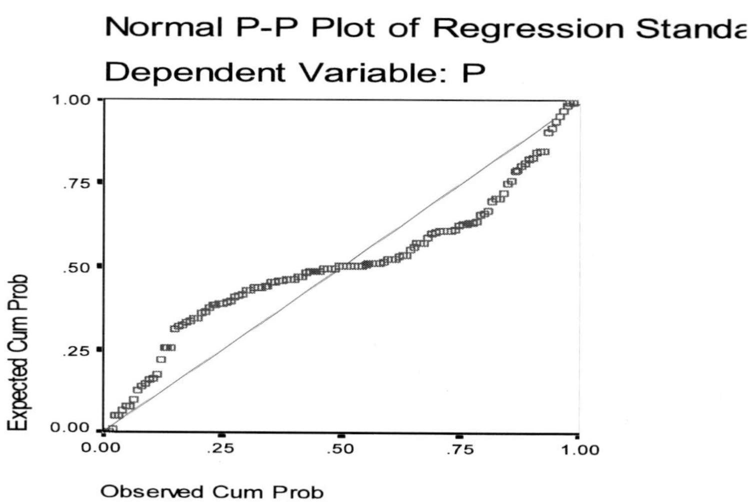

Graph 11.

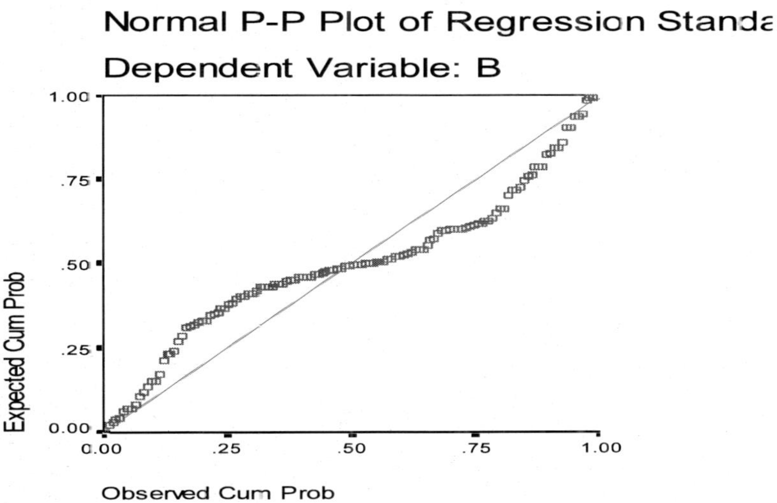

Graph 12.

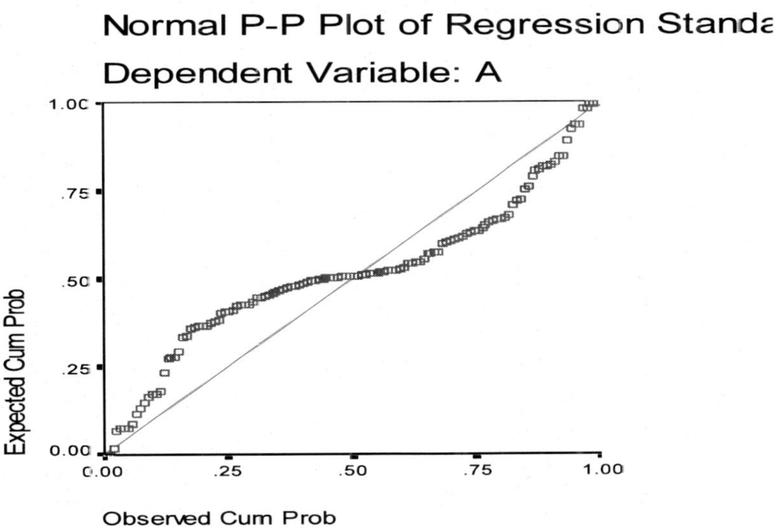

Graph 13.

Europe

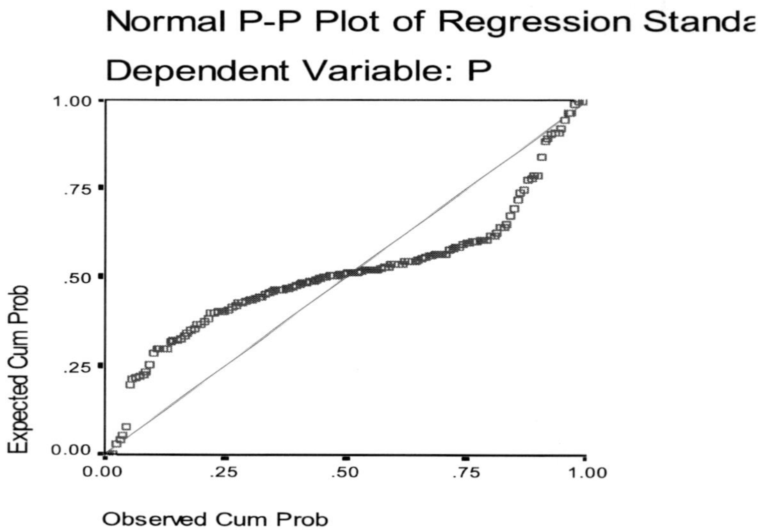

Graph 14.

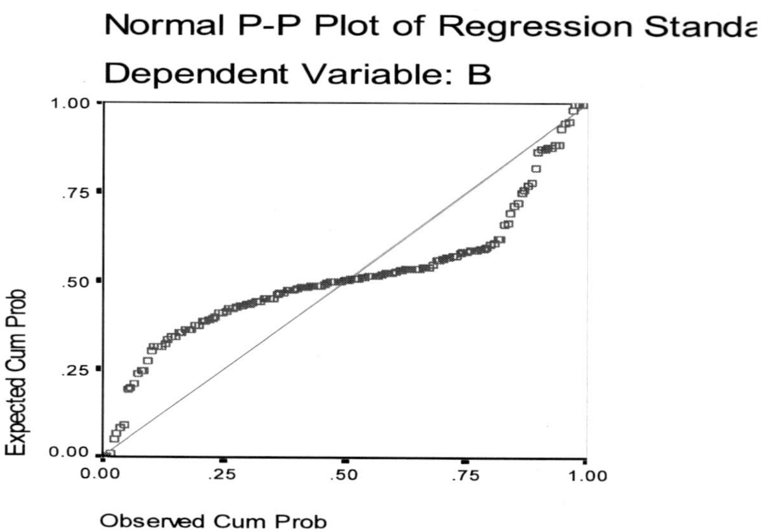

Graph 15.

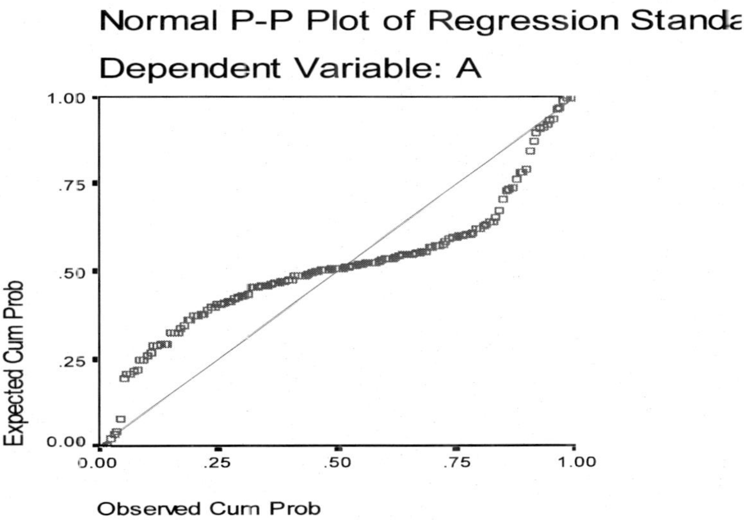

Graph 16.

APPENDIX 4. CALCULATION OF PRICE REVERSAL (μ), INVENTORY HOLDING COST (β), AND ADVERSE SELECTION COST (α)

$$E(Qt\text{-}1 \mid Qt\text{-}2) = (1 - 2\pi)Qt\text{-}2 \quad (A1)$$

$$\Delta M_t = (\alpha + \beta)\frac{S_{t-1}}{2}Q_{t-1} + \alpha(1-2\pi)\frac{S_{t-2}}{2}Q_{t-2} + e_t \quad (A2)$$

Based on the equations above, the system equation (GMM) to estimate μ, β, and α are as follows:

QT1 = C(1) + C(2)*QT2 @ QT2
M = C(3) + C(4)*QT1*ST1 + C(5)*C(2)*QT2*ST2 @ QT1 ST1 QT2 ST2

which:

C(1) and C(3) are constant

$C(2) = 1 - 2\mu$

$C(4) = (\alpha + \beta)/2$

$C(5) = -\alpha/2$

Appendix 5. GMM Results for Banks Located in London, New York, and Hongkong

London

Westpac bank (103)

System: SYS103

Estimation Method: Generalized Method of Moments

Prewhitening

Bandwidth: Fixed (5)

Kernel: Bartlett

Convergence achieved after 5 iterations

	Coefficient	Std. Error	t-Statistic	Prob.
C(1)	0.026291	0.041780	0.629267	0.5293
C(2)	0.018537	0.038518	0.481263	0.6304
C(3)	9.39E-05	0.000168	0.558721	0.5765
C(4)	3.111118	0.320700	9.701025	0.0000
C(5)	7.517501	20.51142	0.366503	0.7141

Equation: QT1 = C(1) + C(2)*QT2 @ QT2

Observations: 488

R-squared	0.000071	Mean dependent var	0.030738
Adjusted R-squared	-0.001987	S.D. dependent var	0.995409
S.E. of regression	0.996398	Sum squared resid	482.5048
Durbin-Watson stat	2.003765		

Equation: M = C(3) + C(4)*QT1*ST1 + C(5)*C(2)*QT2*ST2 @ QT1 ST1 QT2 ST2

Observations: 488

R-squared	0.194027	Mean dependent var	.000184
Adjusted R-squared	0.189032	S.D. dependent var	0.005153
S.E. of regression	0.004641	Sum squared resid	0.010424
Durbin-Watson stat	2.036070		

Danske bank (107)

System: SYS107

Estimation Method: Generalized Method of Moments

Prewhitening

Bandwidth: Fixed (7)

Kernel: Bartlett

Convergence achieved after 4 iterations

	Coefficient	Std. Error	t-Statistic	Prob.
C(1)	0.039875	0.025494	1.564077	0.1179
C(2)	-0.042355	0.026042	-1.626373	0.1040
C(3)	-1.39E-05	7.19E-05	-0.193582	0.8465
C(4)	1.720658	0.113325	15.18340	0.0000
C(5)	1.531755	2.419286	0.633143	0.5267

Equation: QT1 = C(1) + C(2)*QT2 @ QT2

Observations: 1410

R-squared	0.001767	Mean dependent var	0.038298
Adjusted R-squared	0.001058	S.D. dependent var	0.972997
S.E. of regression	0.972482	Sum squared resid	1331.575
Durbin-Watson stat	1.997645		

Equation: M = C(3) + C(4)*QT1*ST1 + C(5)*C(2)*QT2*ST2 @ QT1 ST1 QT2 ST2

Observations: 1410

R-squared	0.149864	Mean dependent var	4.55E-05
Adjusted R-squared	0.148050	S.D. dependent var	0.003463
S.E. of regression	0.003196	Sum squared resid	0.014365
Durbin-Watson stat	1.961691		

Shearson bank (109)

System: SYS109

Estimation Method: Generalized Method of Moments

Prewhitening

Bandwidth: Fixed (7)

Kernel: Bartlett

Convergence achieved after 4 iterations

	Coefficient	Std. Error	t-Statistic	Prob.
C(1)	0.039875	0.025494	1.564077	0.1179
C(2)	-0.042355	0.026042	-1.626373	0.1040
C(3)	-1.39E-05	7.19E-05	-0.193582	0.8465
C(4)	1.720658	0.113325	15.18340	0.0000
C(5)	1.531755	2.419286	0.633143	0.5267

Equation: QT1 = C(1) + C(2)*QT2 @ QT2

Observations: 1410

R-squared	0.001767	Mean dependent var	0.038298
Adjusted R-squared	0.001058	S.D. dependent var	0.972997
S.E. of regression	0.972482	Sum squared resid	1331.575
Durbin-Watson stat	1.997645		

Equation: M = C(3) + C(4)*QT1*ST1 + C(5)*C(2)*QT2*ST2 @ QT1 ST1 QT2 ST2

Observations: 1410

R-squared	0.149864	Mean dependent var	4.55E-05
Adjusted R-squared	0.148050	S.D. dependent var	0.003463
S.E. of regression	0.003196	Sum squared resid	0.014365
Durbin-Watson stat	1.961691		

Amex bank (122)

System: SYS122

Estimation Method: Generalized Method of Moments

Prewhitening

Bandwidth: Fixed (5)

Kernel: Bartlett

Convergence achieved after 5 iterations

	Coefficient	Std. Error	t-Statistic	Prob.
C(1)	0.053611	0.042984	1.247237	0.2127
C(2)	0.043070	0.042450	1.014611	0.3106
C(3)	2.47E-05	0.000269	0.091671	0.9270
C(4)	2.298822	0.379341	6.060039	0.0000
C(5)	-3.766004	6.721943	-0.560255	0.5755

Equation: QT1 = C(1) + C(2)*QT2 @ QT2

Observations: 426

R-squared	0.001415	Mean dependent var	0.058685
Adjusted R-squared	-0.000940	S.D. dependent var	0.976829
S.E. of regression	0.977288	Sum squared resid	404.9591
Durbin-Watson stat	2.005632		

Equation: M = C(3) + C(4)*QT1*ST1 + C(5)*C(2)*QT2*ST2 @ QT1 ST1 QT2 ST2

Observations: 426

R-squared	0.106602	Mean dependent var	0.000173
Adjusted R-squared	0.100250	S.D. dependent var	0.005234
S.E. of regression	0.004964	Sum squared resid	0.010400
Durbin-Watson stat	1.663210		

Barclays bank (94)

System: SYS94

Estimation Method: Generalized Method of Moments

Prewhitening

Bandwidth: Fixed (8)

Kernel: Bartlett

Convergence achieved after 5 iterations

	Coefficient	Std. Error	t-Statistic	Prob.
C(1)	-0.005961	0.016772	-0.355391	0.7223
C(2)	0.016898	0.018434	0.916667	0.3594
C(3)	2.38E-05	2.49E-05	0.955405	0.3394
C(4)	1.420531	0.052411	27.10383	0.0000
C(5)	2.713718	3.885820	0.698364	0.4850

Equation: QT1 = C(1) + C(2)*QT2 @ QT2

Observations: 2929

R-squared	0.000255	Mean dependent var	-0.006487
Adjusted R-squared	-0.000087	S.D. dependent var	0.979098
S.E. of regression	0.979141	Sum squared resid	2806.162
Durbin-Watson stat	1.999961		

Equation: M = C(3) + C(4)*QT1*ST1 + C(5)*C(2)*QT2*ST2 @ QT1 ST1 QT2 ST2

Observations: 2929

R-squared	0.282367	Mean dependent var	2.55E-05
Adjusted R-squared	0.281631	S.D. dependent var	0.002211
S.E. of regression	0.001874	Sum squared resid	0.010268
Durbin-Watson stat	1.987369		

BNP bank (98)

System: SYS98

Estimation Method: Generalized Method of Moments

Prewhitening

Bandwidth: Fixed (6)

Kernel: Bartlett

Convergence achieved after 5 iterations

	Coefficient	Std. Error	t-Statistic	Prob.
C(1)	0.009257	0.032892	0.281427	0.7784
C(2)	0.007258	0.030525	0.237773	0.8121
C(3)	8.27E-06	0.000108	0.076777	0.9388
C(4)	2.276993	0.167006	13.63417	0.0000
C(5)	29.76277	126.1022	0.236021	0.8134

Equation: QT1 = C(1) + C(2)*QT2 @ QT2

Observations: 861

R-squared	0.000106	Mean dependent var	0.012776
Adjusted R-squared	-0.001058	S.D. dependent var	0.987633
S.E. of regression	0.988155	Sum squared resid	838.7706

Durbin-Watson stat 1.990011

Equation: M = C(3) + C(4)*QT1*ST1 + C(5)*C(2)*QT2*ST2 @ QT1 ST1 QT2 ST2

Observations: 861

R-squared	0.237724	Mean dependent var	8.37E-05
Adjusted R-squared	0.235055	S.D. dependent var	0.004170
S.E. of regression	0.003648	Sum squared resid	0.011402
Durbin-Watson stat	1.715947		

Sumitomo bank (171)

System: SYS171

Estimation Method: Generalized Method of Moments

Prewhitening

Bandwidth: Fixed (3)

Kernel: Bartlett

Convergence achieved after 8 iterations

	Coefficient	Std. Error	t-Statistic	Prob.
C(1)	0.121913	0.120039	1.015613	0.3120
C(2)	-0.022980	0.108136	-0.212511	0.8321
C(3)	0.001274	0.001037	1.228826	0.2217
C(4)	8.764385	1.613389	5.432284	0.0000
C(5)	-7.153142	58.90802	-0.121429	0.9036

Equation: QT1 = C(1) + C(2)*QT2 @ QT2

Observations: 59

R-squared	0.000628	Mean dependent var	0.101695
Adjusted R-squared	-0.016905	S.D. dependent var	0.994726
S.E. of regression	1.003099	Sum squared resid	57.35379
Durbin-Watson stat	2.007970		

Equation: M = C(3) + C(4)*QT1*ST1 + C(5)*C(2)*QT2*ST2 @ QT1 ST1 QT2 ST2

Observations: 59

R-squared	0.211602	Mean dependent var	0.001310
Adjusted R-squared	0.168599	S.D. dependent var	0.015202
S.E. of regression	0.013861	Sum squared resid	0.010567
Durbin-Watson stat	2.107744		

Bank of Tokyo (130)

System: SYS130

Estimation Method: Generalized Method of Moments

Prewhitening

Bandwidth: Fixed (5)

Kernel: Bartlett

Convergence achieved after 3 iterations

	Coefficient	Std. Error	t-Statistic	Prob.
C(1)	0.022369	0.059288	0.377301	0.7061
C(2)	-0.100100	0.065400	-1.530574	0.1264
C(3)	0.000237	0.000259	0.916369	0.3599
C(4)	3.242760	0.791294	4.098047	0.0000
C(5)	-0.924164	4.934721	-0.187278	0.8515

Equation: QT1 = C(1) + C(2)*QT2 @ QT2

Observations: 289

R-squared	0.009975	Mean dependent var	0.020761
Adjusted R-squared	0.006525	S.D. dependent var	0.989310
S.E. of regression	0.986077	Sum squared resid	279.0638
Durbin-Watson stat	1.977648		

Equation: M = C(3) + C(4)*QT1*ST1 + C(5)*C(2)*QT2*ST2 @ QT1 ST1 QT2 ST2

Observations: 289

R-squared	0.137392	Mean dependent var	0.000218
Adjusted R-squared	0.128312	S.D. dependent var	0.006080
S.E. of regression	0.005677	Sum squared resid	0.009185
Durbin-Watson stat	2.112741		

DG bank (125)

System: SYS125

Estimation Method: Generalized Method of Moments

Prewhitening

Bandwidth: Fixed (4)

Kernel: Bartlett

Convergence achieved after 8 iterations

	Coefficient	Std. Error	t-Statistic	Prob.
C(1)	0.071635	0.080158	0.893670	0.3723
C(2)	0.025140	0.067933	0.370064	0.7116
C(3)	0.000690	0.000702	0.982675	0.3266
C(4)	3.046255	0.855164	3.562189	0.0004
C(5)	28.46304	82.97014	0.343052	0.7318

Equation: QT1 = C(1) + C(2)*QT2 @ QT2
Observations: 140

R-squared	0.001140	Mean dependent var	0.092857
Adjusted R-squared	-0.006098	S.D. dependent var	0.981090
S.E. of regression	0.984077	Sum squared resid	133.6403
Durbin-Watson stat	1.966044		

Equation: M = C(3) + C(4)*QT1*ST1 + C(5)*C(2)*QT2*ST2 @ QT1 ST1 QT2 ST2
Observations: 140

R-squared	0.084209	Mean dependent var	0.000478
Adjusted R-squared	0.064008	S.D. dependent var	0.010556
S.E. of regression	0.010213	Sum squared resid	0.014185
Durbin-Watson stat	2.224600		

Dresdner bank (126)
System: SYS126
Estimation Method: Generalized Method of Moments
Prewhitening
Bandwidth: Fixed (4)
Kernel: Bartlett
Convergence achieved after 5 iterations

	Coefficient	Std. Error	t-Statistic	Prob.
C(1)	-0.006902	0.078374	-0.088070	0.9299
C(2)	0.112983	0.075307	1.500299	0.1346
C(3)	0.000793	0.000622	1.273481	0.2039
C(4)	7.271418	1.600561	4.543043	0.0000
C(5)	-8.364848	15.09221	-0.554249	0.5798

Equation: QT1 = C(1) + C(2)*QT2 @ QT2
Observations: 146

R-squared	0.011631	Mean dependent var	-0.006849
Adjusted R-squared	0.004768	S.D. dependent var	0.979068
S.E. of regression	0.976731	Sum squared resid	137.3765
Durbin-Watson stat	1.975186		

Equation: M = C(3) + C(4)*QT1*ST1 + C(5)*C(2)*QT2*ST2 @ QT1 ST1 QT2 ST2

Observations: 146

R-squared	0.251021	Mean dependent var	0.000452
Adjusted R-squared	0.235198	S.D. dependent var	0.010036
S.E. of regression	0.008776	Sum squared resid	0.010933
Durbin-Watson stat	2.286613		

New York

Barclays bank (179)

System: SYS179

Estimation Method: Generalized Method of Moments

Prewhitening

Bandwidth: Fixed (4)

Kernel: Bartlett

Convergence achieved after 6 iterations

	Coefficient	Std. Error	t-Statistic	Prob.
C(1)	-0.001604	0.078888	-0.020335	0.9838
C(2)	-0.023419	0.068117	-0.343810	0.7313
C(3)	0.000438	0.000649	0.675291	0.5001
C(4)	6.199258	0.788919	7.857914	0.0000
C(5)	-17.36181	53.67217	-0.323479	0.7466

Equation: QT1 = C(1) + C(2)*QT2 @ QT2

Observations: 131

R-squared	0.000556	Mean dependent var	-0.007634
Adjusted R-squared	-0.007192	S.D. dependent var	0.972674
S.E. of regression	0.976166	Sum squared resid	122.9240
Durbin-Watson stat	1.977860		

Equation: M = C(3) + C(4)*QT1*ST1 + C(5)*C(2)*QT2*ST2 @ QT1 ST1 QT2 ST2

Observations: 131

R-squared	0.396355	Mean dependent var	0.000618
Adjusted R-squared	0.382095	S.D. dependent var	0.010224
S.E. of regression	0.008037	Sum squared resid	0.008203
Durbin-Watson stat	2.145410		

BNP bank (170)

System: SYS170

Estimation Method: Generalized Method of Moments

Prewhitening

Bandwidth: Fixed (5)

Kernel: Bartlett

Convergence achieved after 11 iterations

	Coefficient	Std. Error	t-Statistic	Prob.
C(1)	0.053033	0.050684	1.046330	0.2957
C(2)	0.014719	0.052663	0.279499	0.7799
C(3)	1.88E-05	0.000278	0.067700	0.9460
C(4)	3.300933	0.327020	10.09398	0.0000
C(5)	-0.007530	0.030062	-0.250480	0.8023

Equation: QT1 = C(1) + C(2)*QT2 @ QT2

Observations: 384

R-squared	0.000295	Mean dependent var	0.057292
Adjusted R-squared	-0.002322	S.D. dependent var	0.994423
S.E. of regression	0.995576	Sum squared resid	378.6277
Durbin-Watson stat	1.983465		

Equation: M = C(3) + C(4)*QT1*ST1 + C(5)*C(2)*QT2*ST2 @ QT1 ST1 QT2 ST2

Observations: 384

R-squared	0.193187	Mean dependent var	0.000206
Adjusted R-squared	0.186817	S.D. dependent var	0.005817
S.E. of regression	0.005245	Sum squared resid	0.010456
Durbin-Watson stat	1.952415		

Citibank (159)

System: SYS159

Estimation Method: Generalized Method of Moments

Prewhitening

Bandwidth: Fixed (9)

Kernel: Bartlett

Convergence achieved after 5 iterations

	Coefficient	Std. Error	t-Statistic	Prob.
C(1)	0.017315	0.013680	1.265771	0.2056
C(2)	-0.059781	0.014761	-4.049825	0.0001
C(3)	9.47E-07	2.03E-05	0.046608	0.9628
C(4)	0.971643	0.024152	40.23040	0.0000
C(5)	-0.049678	0.327238	-0.151811	0.8793

Equation: QT1 = C(1) + C(2)*QT2 @ QT2

Observations: 4583

R-squared	0.003494	Mean dependent var	0.016801
Adjusted R-squared	0.003276	S.D. dependent var	0.968931
S.E. of regression	0.967342	Sum squared resid	4286.677
Durbin-Watson stat	2.000333		

Equation: M = C(3) + C(4)*QT1*ST1 + C(5)*C(2)*QT2*ST2 @ QT1 ST1 QT2 ST2

Observations: 4583

R-squared	0.332716	Mean dependent var	1.90E-05
Adjusted R-squared	0.332279	S.D. dependent var	0.001679
S.E. of regression	0.001372	Sum squared resid	0.008617
Durbin-Watson stat	2.032328		

Soc. Gen. Bank (156)

System: SYS156

Estimation Method: Generalized Method of Moments

Prewhitening

Bandwidth: Fixed (5)

Kernel: Bartlett

Convergence achieved after 4 iterations

	Coefficient	Std. Error	t-Statistic	Prob.
C(1)	0.009321	0.042691	0.218341	0.8272
C(2)	0.028087	0.046027	0.610219	0.5419
C(3)	0.000224	0.000202	1.110322	0.2671
C(4)	3.630533	0.435073	8.344654	0.0000
C(5)	-3.322365	13.08175	-0.253969	0.7996

Equation: QT1 = C(1) + C(2)*QT2 @ QT2

Observations: 464

R-squared	0.000959	Mean dependent var	0.008621
Adjusted R-squared	-0.001203	S.D. dependent var	0.983630
S.E. of regression	0.984222	Sum squared resid	447.5359
Durbin-Watson stat	1.983557		

Equation: M = C(3) + C(4)*QT1*ST1 + C(5)*C(2)*QT2*ST2 @ QT1 ST1 QT2 ST2

Observations: 464

R-squared	0.171039	Mean dependent var	0.000186
Adjusted R-squared	0.165633	S.D. dependent var	0.005611
S.E. of regression	0.005125	Sum squared resid	0.012084
Durbin-Watson stat	2.007231		

Royal bank (148)

System: SYS148

Estimation Method: Generalized Method of Moments

Prewhitening

Bandwidth: Fixed (5)

Kernel: Bartlett

Convergence achieved after 4 iterations

	Coefficient	Std. Error	t-Statistic	Prob.
C(1)	0.008157	0.055870	0.145991	0.8840
C(2)	0.035133	0.060571	0.580032	0.5621
C(3)	0.000188	0.000452	0.416436	0.6772
C(4)	4.026094	0.603349	6.672908	0.0000
C(5)	11.76900	26.88561	0.437743	0.6617

Equation: QT1 = C(1) + C(2)*QT2 @ QT2

Observations: 285

R-squared	0.000991	Mean dependent var	0.024561
Adjusted R-squared	-0.002539	S.D. dependent var	0.990853
S.E. of regression	0.992110	Sum squared resid	278.5516
Durbin-Watson stat	1.984021		

Equation: M = C(3) + C(4)*QT1*ST1 + C(5)*C(2)*QT2*ST2 @ QT1 ST1 QT2 ST2

Observations: 285

R-squared	0.132815	Mean dependent var	0.000298
Adjusted R-squared	0.123557	S.D. dependent var	0.008191
S.E. of regression	0.007668	Sum squared resid	0.016522
Durbin-Watson stat	1.870044		

Deutsche (147)

System: SYS147

Estimation Method: Generalized Method of Moments

Prewhitening

Bandwidth: Fixed (8)

Kernel: Bartlett

Convergence achieved after 5 iterations

	Coefficient	Std. Error	t-Statistic	Prob.
C(1)	0.004359	0.017443	0.249926	0.8027
C(2)	-0.014478	0.017820	-0.812430	0.4166
C(3)	2.08E-05	3.05E-05	0.683658	0.4942
C(4)	1.354990	0.045970	29.47526	0.0000
C(5)	-0.139351	2.703436	-0.051546	0.9589

Equation: QT1 = C(1) + C(2)*QT2 @ QT2

Observations: 3080

R-squared	0.000193	Mean dependent var	0.006494
Adjusted R-squared	-0.000132	S.D. dependent var	0.985749
S.E. of regression	0.985814	Sum squared resid	2991.292
Durbin-Watson stat	1.999049		

Equation: M = C(3) + C(4)*QT1*ST1 + C(5)*C(2)*QT2*ST2 @ QT1 ST1 QT2 ST2

Observations: 3080

R-squared	0.286247	Mean dependent var	2.73E-05
Adjusted R-squared	0.285551	S.D. dependent var	0.002063
S.E. of regression	0.001743	Sum squared resid	0.009350
Durbin-Watson stat	1.940797		

Nat Comm bank (146)

System: SYS146

Estimation Method: Generalized Method of Moments

Prewhitening

Bandwidth: Fixed (4)

Kernel: Bartlett

Convergence achieved after 5 iterations

	Coefficient	Std. Error	t-Statistic	Prob.
C(1)	0.135672	0.076428	1.775161	0.0771
C(2)	-0.141788	0.076306	-1.858151	0.0643
C(3)	-0.000291	0.000570	-0.509994	0.6105
C(4)	8.038074	1.333269	6.028845	0.0000
C(5)	-8.970187	7.236777	-1.239528	0.2163

Equation: QT1 = C(1) + C(2)*QT2 @ QT2
Observations: 129

R-squared	0.021971	Mean dependent var	0.124031
Adjusted R-squared	0.014270	S.D. dependent var	0.992218
S.E. of regression	0.985113	Sum squared resid	123.2469
Durbin-Watson stat	2.010561		

Equation: M = C(3) + C(4)*QT1*ST1 + C(5)*C(2)*QT2*ST2 @ QT1 ST1 QT2 ST2
Observations: 129

R-squared	0.264550	Mean dependent var	0.000717
Adjusted R-squared	0.246899	S.D. dependent var	0.008847
S.E. of regression	0.007677	Sum squared resid	0.007368
Durbin-Watson stat	2.070214		

Morgan (142)
System: SYS142
Estimation Method: Iterative Three-Stage Least Squares
Convergence achieved after 2 iterations

	Coefficient	Std. Error	t-Statistic	Prob.
C(1)	0.007782	0.010957	0.710250	0.4776
C(2)	-0.014096	0.011124	-1.267098	0.2051
C(3)	4.88E-06	1.17E-05	0.415447	0.6778
C(4)	0.903813	0.015804	57.18946	0.0000
C(5)	-1.987179	1.928056	-1.030665	0.3027

Equation: QT1 = C(1) + C(2)*QT2 @ QT2
Observations: 8079

R-squared	0.000199	Mean dependent var	0.007674
Adjusted R-squared	0.000075	S.D. dependent var	0.985003
S.E. of regression	0.984966	Sum squared resid	7835.967
Durbin-Watson stat	2.000425		

Equation: M = C(3) + C(4)*QT1*ST1 + C(5)*C(2)*QT2*ST2 @ QT1 ST1 QT2 ST2

Observations: 8079

R-squared	0.309694	Mean dependent var	1.06E-05
Adjusted R-squared	0.309438	S.D. dependent var	0.001271
S.E. of regression	0.001056	Sum squared resid	0.009004
Durbin-Watson stat	1.931619		

Hongkong

Dresdner bank (55)

System: SYS55

Estimation Method: Generalized Method of Moments

Prewhitening

Bandwidth: Fixed (7)

Kernel: Bartlett

Convergence achieved after 6 iterations

	Coefficient	Std. Error	t-Statistic	Prob.
C(1)	0.039821	0.022057	1.805336	0.0711
C(2)	0.044798	0.024804	1.806034	0.0710
C(3)	-1.86E-05	1.86E-05	-1.002128	0.3164
C(4)	0.718221	0.020237	35.49135	0.0000
C(5)	1.278529	0.804219	1.589777	0.1120

Equation: QT1 = C(1) + C(2)*QT2 @ QT2

Observations: 1777

R-squared	0.002119	Mean dependent var	0.045582
Adjusted R-squared	0.001557	S.D. dependent var	0.957812
S.E. of regression	0.957066	Sum squared resid	1625.855
Durbin-Watson stat	1.996302		

Equation: M = C(3) + C(4)*QT1*ST1 + C(5)*C(2)*QT2*ST2 @ QT1 ST1 QT2 ST2

Observations: 1665

R-squared	0.539511	Mean dependent var	1.41E-05
Adjusted R-squared	0.538679	S.D. dependent var	0.001100
S.E. of regression	0.000747	Sum squared resid	0.000927
Durbin-Watson stat	1.876585		

Soc. Gen. Bank (52)

System: SYS52

Estimation Method: Generalized Method of Moments

Prewhitening

Bandwidth: Fixed (7)

Kernel: Bartlett

Convergence achieved after 5 iterations

	Coefficient	Std. Error	t-Statistic	Prob.
C(1)	0.024702	0.020563	1.201328	0.2297
C(2)	-0.004112	0.021925	-0.187559	0.8512
C(3)	2.08E-05	5.48E-05	0.379451	0.7044
C(4)	0.954345	0.075617	12.62077	0.0000
C(5)	31.07567	166.4019	0.186751	0.8519

Equation: QT1 = C(1) + C(2)*QT2 @ QT2

Observations: 2072

R-squared	0.000024	Mean dependent var	0.025097
Adjusted R-squared	-0.000459	S.D. dependent var	0.946338
S.E. of regression	0.946555	Sum squared resid	1854.651
Durbin-Watson stat	2.000847		

Equation: M = C(3) + C(4)*QT1*ST1 + C(5)*C(2)*QT2*ST2 @ QT1 ST1 QT2 ST2

Observations: 2072

R-squared	0.108615	Mean dependent var	3.96E-05
Adjusted R-squared	0.107322	S.D. dependent var	0.002775
S.E. of regression	0.002622	Sum squared resid	0.014215
Durbin-Watson stat	2.044372		

Amex (47)
System: SYS47
Estimation Method: Generalized Method of Moments
Prewhitening
Bandwidth: Fixed (8)
Kernel: Bartlett
Convergence achieved after 4 iterations

	Coefficient	Std. Error	t-Statistic	Prob.
C(1)	0.018070	0.016745	1.079162	0.2806
C(2)	0.015188	0.016966	0.895207	0.3707
C(3)	2.22E-05	3.13E-05	0.708777	0.4785
C(4)	1.008193	0.073648	13.68926	0.0000
C(5)	-4.215958	6.080753	-0.693328	0.4881

Equation: QT1 = C(1) + C(2)*QT2 @ QT2
Observations: 3232

R-squared	0.000217	Mean dependent var	0.018255
Adjusted R-squared	-0.000092	S.D. dependent var	0.982030
S.E. of regression	0.982076	Sum squared resid	3115.246
Durbin-Watson stat	1.998263		

Equation: M = C(3) + C(4)*QT1*ST1 + C(5)*C(2)*QT2*ST2 @ QT1 ST1 QT2 ST2
Observations: 3232

R-squared	0.081893	Mean dependent var	2.50E-05
Adjusted R-squared	0.081039	S.D. dependent var	0.002314
S.E. of regression	0.002218	Sum squared resid	0.015878
Durbin-Watson stat	2.027374		

Manhantan bank (41)
System: SYS41
Estimation Method: Generalized Method of Moments
Prewhitening

Bandwidth: Fixed (8)
Kernel: Bartlett
Convergence achieved after 4 iterations

Coefficient	Std. Error	t-Statistic	Prob.	Coefficient
C(1)	0.044920	0.019036	2.359770	0.0183
C(2)	-0.077120	0.020108	-3.835269	0.0001
C(3)	-1.54E-05	5.18E-05	-0.297557	0.7661
C(4)	1.165442	0.059550	19.57089	0.0000
C(5)	0.007882	0.625792	0.012596	0.9900

Equation: QT1 = C(1) + C(2)*QT2 @ QT2
Observations: 2448

R-squared	0.006115	Mean dependent var	0.043301
Adjusted R-squared	0.005709	S.D. dependent var	0.971059
S.E. of regression	0.968283	Sum squared resid	2293.299
Durbin-Watson stat	2.002084		

Equation: M = C(3) + C(4)*QT1*ST1 + C(5)*C(2)*QT2*ST2 @ QT1 ST1 QT2 ST2
Observations: 2448

R-squared	0.154289	Mean dependent var	3.35E-05
Adjusted R-squared	0.153251	S.D. dependent var	0.002865
S.E. of regression	0.002637	Sum squared resid	0.016990

Durbin-Watson stat 2.055012
Deutsche (40)
System: SYS40
Estimation Method: Generalized Method of Moments
Prewhitening
Bandwidth: Fixed (5)
Kernel: Bartlett
Convergence achieved after 4 iterations

	Coefficient	Std. Error	t-Statistic	Prob.
C(1)	0.026837	0.036507	0.735138	0.4624
C(2)	-0.037531	0.040435	-0.928173	0.3535
C(3)	9.03E-05	0.000188	0.480231	0.6312
C(4)	2.414565	0.201086	12.00764	0.0000
C(5)	1.100601	5.299832	0.207667	0.8355

Equation: QT1 = C(1) + C(2)*QT2 @ QT2
Observations: 592

R-squared	0.001230	Mean dependent var	0.023649
Adjusted R-squared	-0.000463	S.D. dependent var	0.986944
S.E. of regression	0.987173	Sum squared resid	574.9609
Durbin-Watson stat	1.994855		

Equation: M = C(3) + C(4)*QT1*ST1 + C(5)*C(2)*QT2*ST2 @ QT1 ST1 QT2 ST2
Observations: 592

R-squared	0.196878	Mean dependent var	0.000137
Adjusted R-squared	0.192780	S.D. dependent var	0.005387
S.E. of regression	0.004840	Sum squared resid	0.013776
Durbin-Watson stat	2.095875		

Bank of Tokyo (36)
System: SYS36
Estimation Method: Generalized Method of Moments
Prewhitening
Bandwidth: Fixed (8)
Kernel: Bartlett
Convergence achieved after 4 iterations

	Coefficient	Std. Error	t-Statistic	Prob.
C(1)	0.024127	0.017628	1.368676	0.1712
C(2)	-0.053407	0.018512	-2.884948	0.0039
C(3)	5.67E-05	2.70E-05	2.099558	0.0358
C(4)	1.012097	0.059453	17.02345	0.0000
C(5)	0.410118	1.024738	0.400217	0.6890

Equation: QT1 = C(1) + C(2)*QT2 @ QT2
Observations: 2844

R-squared	0.002495	Mean dependent var	0.023207
Adjusted R-squared	0.002144	S.D. dependent var	0.968819
S.E. of regression	0.967780	Sum squared resid	2661.812
Durbin-Watson stat	1.992780		

Equation: M = C(3) + C(4)*QT1*ST1 + C(5)*C(2)*QT2*ST2 @ QT1 ST1 QT2 ST2
Observations: 2844

R-squared	0.126369	Mean dependent var	2.78E-05
Adjusted R-squared	0.125447	S.D. dependent var	0.002604
S.E. of regression	0.002435	Sum squared resid	0.016838
Durbin-Watson stat	1.977773		

Morgan bank (35)
System: SYS35
Estimation Method: Iterative Three-Stage Least Squares
Convergence achieved after 2 iterations

	Coefficient	Std. Error	t-Statistic	Prob.
C(1)	0.009812	0.010040	0.977257	0.3285
C(2)	-0.035240	0.010491	-3.358954	0.0008
C(3)	5.62E-06	1.31E-05	0.428511	0.6683
C(4)	1.462239	0.034008	42.99655	0.0000
C(5)	1.101622	1.019346	1.080715	0.2798

Equation: QT1 = C(1) + C(2)*QT2 @ QT2
Observations: 9074

R-squared	0.001242	Mean dependent var	0.009478
Adjusted R-squared	0.001132	S.D. dependent var	0.956982
S.E. of regression	0.956440	Sum squared resid	8298.866
Durbin-Watson stat	2.004530		

Equation: M = C(3) + C(4)*QT1*ST1 + C(5)*C(2)*QT2*ST2 @ QT1 ST1 QT2 ST2

Observations: 9074

R-squared	0.188998	Mean dependent var	8.94E-06
Adjusted R-squared	0.188730	S.D. dependent var	0.001386
S.E. of regression	0.001249	Sum squared resid	0.014144
Durbin-Watson stat	2.014311		

Citibank (32)

System: SYS32

Estimation Method: Generalized Method of Moments

Prewhitening

Bandwidth: Fixed (7)

Kernel: Bartlett

Convergence achieved after 4 iterations

	Coefficient	Std. Error	t-Statistic	Prob.
C(1)	-0.008274	0.023363	-0.354144	0.7233
C(2)	-0.004369	0.023317	-0.187370	0.8514
C(3)	8.04E-05	5.54E-05	1.452234	0.1465
C(4)	1.297603	0.089284	14.53346	0.0000
C(5)	0.120231	15.65218	0.007681	0.9939

Equation: QT1 = C(1) + C(2)*QT2 @ QT2

Observations: 1825

R-squared	0.000014	Mean dependent var	-0.009863
Adjusted R-squared	-0.000534	S.D. dependent var	0.976652
S.E. of regression	0.976913	Sum squared resid	1739.798
Durbin-Watson stat	1.999569		

Equation: M = C(3) + C(4)*QT1*ST1 + C(5)*C(2)*QT2*ST2 @ QT1 ST1 QT2 ST2

Observations: 1825

R-squared	0.137652	Mean dependent var	4.42E-05
Adjusted R-squared	0.136231	S.D. dependent var	0.002969
S.E. of regression	0.002759	Sum squared resid	0.013862
Durbin-Watson stat	1.953309		

DG bank (30)

System: SYS30

Estimation Method: Generalized Method of Moments

Prewhitening

Bandwidth: Fixed (7)

Kernel: Bartlett

Convergence achieved after 4 iterations

	Coefficient	Std. Error	t-Statistic	Prob.
C(1)	0.005933	0.023211	0.255623	0.7983
C(2)	-0.031762	0.022742	-1.396637	0.1626
C(3)	5.28E-05	7.04E-05	0.750718	0.4529
C(4)	1.720649	0.117523	14.64096	0.0000
C(5)	2.163355	3.547585	0.609811	0.5420

Equation: QT1 = C(1) + C(2)*QT2 @ QT2

Observations: 1674

R-squared	0.000990	Mean dependent var	0.008961
Adjusted R-squared	0.000392	S.D. dependent var	0.973303
S.E. of regression	0.973113	Sum squared resid	1583.297
Durbin-Watson stat	2.000312		

Equation: M = C(3) + C(4)*QT1*ST1 + C(5)*C(2)*QT2*ST2 @ QT1 ST1 QT2 ST2

Observations: 1674

R-squared	0.133780	Mean dependent var	4.93E-05
Adjusted R-squared	0.132224	S.D. dependent var	0.003222
S.E. of regression	0.003002	Sum squared resid	0.015049
Durbin-Watson stat	1.972033		

Chase bank (22)

System: SYS22

Estimation Method: Generalized Method of Moments

Prewhitening

Bandwidth: Fixed (8)

Kernel: Bartlett

Convergence achieved after 4 iterations

	Coefficient	Std. Error	t-Statistic	Prob.
C(1)	0.026637	0.019323	1.378482	0.1681
C(2)	-0.046290	0.019803	-2.337549	0.0195
C(3)	4.28E-05	4.43E-05	0.965691	0.3343
C(4)	2.844063	0.149806	18.98493	0.0000
C(5)	1.635204	3.217365	0.508243	0.6113

Equation: QT1 = C(1) + C(2)*QT2 @ QT2

Observations: 2282

R-squared	0.002132	Mean dependent var	0.024540
Adjusted R-squared	0.001694	S.D. dependent var	0.985788
S.E. of regression	0.984953	Sum squared resid	2211.900
Durbin-Watson stat	2.004479		

Equation: M = C(3) + C(4)*QT1*ST1 + C(5)*C(2)*QT2*ST2 @ QT1 ST1QT2 ST2

Observations: 2282

R-squared	0.139685	Mean dependent var	3.52E-05
Adjusted R-squared	0.138552	S.D. dependent var	0.002757
S.E. of regression	0.002558	Sum squared resid	0.014911
Durbin-Watson stat	1.970754		

APPENDIX 6. ZIVOT AND ANDREW'S UNIT ROOTS TEST RESULT

Model A:

$$y_t = \hat{\mu}^A + \hat{\theta}^A DU_t\left(\hat{\lambda}\right) + \hat{\beta}^A t + \hat{\alpha}^A y_{t-1} + \sum_{j=1}^{k} \hat{c}_j^A \Delta y_{t-j} + \hat{e}_t$$

Model B:

$$y_t = \hat{\mu}^B + \hat{\gamma}^B DT_t^*\left(\hat{\lambda}\right) + \hat{\beta}^B t + \hat{\alpha}^B y_{t-1} + \sum_{j=1}^{k} \hat{c}_j^B \Delta y_{t-j} + \hat{e}_t$$

Model C:

$$y_t = \hat{\mu}^C + \hat{\gamma}^C DT_t^*\left(\hat{\lambda}\right) - \hat{\theta}^C DU_t\left(\hat{\lambda}\right) + \hat{\beta}^C t + \hat{\alpha}^C y_{t-1} + \sum_{j=1}^{k} \hat{c}_j^C \Delta y_{t-j} + \hat{e}_t$$

where DUt(λ) = 1 if t > Tλ, 0 otherwise; DT* t(λ) = t - Tλ if t > Tλ, 0 otherwise.

They consider the following statistics computed from models A - C:

$$t_{\hat{\alpha}^i}\left(\hat{\lambda}^i_{\inf}\right) = \inf_{\lambda \in \Lambda} t_{\hat{\alpha}^i}(\lambda), \quad i = A, B, C$$

where Λ is a specified closed subset of (0,1), and t represents the standard t statistic for testing αi = 1 These statistics depend on the location of the break point λ = TB/T. The rejection of null hypothesis of a unit root means the series are trend stationary.

Deutsche mark-dollar series

Time Break = 4 (Plaza agreements, Tokyo summit, Louvre accord, and Stock crash market)

Model A

Dependent Variable: LGSPREAD				
Method: Least Squares				
Date: 07/08/99 Time: 15:42				
Sample(adjusted): 4 754				
Included observations: 751 after adjusting endpoints				
LGSPREAD=C(1)+C(2)*DU+C(3)*T+C(4)*LAGY+C(5)*D(LAGY)+C(6)*D(LAGY,2)				
	Coefficient	Std. Error	t-Statistic	Prob.
C(1)	-1.544202	0.210689	-7.329283	0.0000
C(2)	-0.150722	0.138088	-1.091491	0.2754
C(3)	-0.000391	3.96E-05	-9.885410	0.0000
C(4)	0.374327	0.051851	7.219288	0.0000
C(5)	-0.298164	0.074993	-3.975874	0.0001
C(6)	0.100503	0.036362	2.763955	0.0059
R-squared	0.517611	Mean dependent var		-2.945422
Adjusted R-squared	0.514374	S.D. dependent var		0.195015
S.E. of regression	0.135900	Akaike info criterion		-1.145839
Sum squared resid	13.75924	Schwarz criterion		-1.108917
Log likelihood	436.2626	Durbin-Watson stat		2.018419

Model B

Dependent Variable: LGSPREAD				
Method: Least Squares				
Date: 07/08/99 Time: 15:43				
Sample(adjusted): 3 754				
Included observations: 752 after adjusting endpoints				
LGSPREAD=C(1)+C(2)*DT+C(3)*T+C(4)*LAGY+C(5)*D(LAGY)				
	Coefficient	Std. Error	t-Statistic	Prob.
C(1)	-2.561528	0.583944	-4.386599	0.0000
C(2)	-0.167662	0.138523	-1.210357	0.2265
C(3)	0.167225	0.138517	1.207252	0.2277
C(4)	0.301845	0.045367	6.653464	0.0000
C(5)	-0.114991	0.036250	-3.172218	0.0016
R-squared	0.512366	Mean dependent var		-2.945495
Adjusted R-squared	0.509755	S.D. dependent var		0.194895
S.E. of regression	0.136461	Akaike info criterion		-1.138931
Sum squared resid	13.91031	Schwarz criterion		-1.108195
Log likelihood	433.2380	Durbin-Watson stat		2.016630

Model C

Dependent Variable: LGSPREAD				
Method: Least Squares				
Date: 07/08/99 Time: 15:46				
Sample(adjusted): 3 754				
Included observations: 752 after adjusting endpoints				
LGSPREAD=C(1)+C(2)*DU+C(3)*T+C(4)*DT+C(5)*LAGY+C(6)				
*D(LAGY)				
	Coefficient	Std. Error	t-Statistic	Prob.
C(1)	-2.847505	0.702804	-4.051633	0.0001
C(2)	-0.100618	0.137501	-0.731758	0.4645
C(3)	0.265909	0.193354	1.375244	0.1695
C(4)	-0.266343	0.193355	-1.377479	0.1688
C(5)	0.305044	0.045591	6.690913	0.0000
C(6)	-0.116581	0.036326	-3.209312	0.0014
R-squared	0.512716	Mean dependent var		-2.945495
Adjusted R-squared	0.509450	S.D. dependent var		0.194895
S.E. of regression	0.136503	Akaike info criterion		-1.136989
Sum squared resid	13.90033	Schwarz criterion		-1.100105
Log likelihood	433.5078	Durbin-Watson stat		2.016454

Time Break = 80 (a month for each event)

Model A

Dependent Variable: LGSPREAD				
Method: Least Squares				
Date: 07/08/99 Time: 15:09				
Sample(adjusted): 11 754				
Included observations: 744 after adjusting endpoints				
LGSPREAD=C(1)+C(2)*DU+C(3)*T+C(4)*LAGY+C(5)*D(LAGY)+C(6)				
*D(LAGY,2)+C(7)*D(LAGY,3)+C(8)*D(LAGY,4)+C(9)*D(LAGY,5)				
+C(10)*D(LAGY,6)+C(11)*D(LAGY,7)+C(12)*D(LAGY,8)+C(13)				
*D(LAGY,9)				
	Coefficient	Std. Error	t-Statistic	Prob.
C(1)	-0.985361	0.194406	-5.068584	0.0000
C(2)	0.007839	0.019800	0.395890	0.6923
C(3)	-0.000242	5.42E-05	-4.458263	0.0000

Model A. (Continued)

	Coefficient	Std. Error	t-Statistic	Prob.
C(4)	0.636939	0.070463	9.039379	0.0000
C(5)	-2.717325	0.447453	-6.072873	0.0000
C(6)	8.081271	1.585761	5.096146	0.0000
C(7)	-16.16483	3.429575	-4.713363	0.0000
C(8)	22.15956	4.880330	4.540586	0.0000
C(9)	-20.73423	4.706946	-4.405028	0.0000
C(10)	13.01235	3.068434	4.240715	0.0000
C(11)	-5.263015	1.301301	-4.044424	0.0001
C(12)	1.250216	0.325384	3.842283	0.0001
C(13)	-0.133931	0.036536	-3.665706	0.0003
R-squared	0.555211	Mean dependent var		-2.946260
Adjusted R-squared	0.547909	S.D. dependent var		0.195497
S.E. of regression	0.131448	Akaike info criterion		-1.203093
Sum squared resid	12.63063	Schwarz criterion		-1.122506
Log likelihood	460.5507	Durbin-Watson stat		2.001307

Model B

Dependent Variable: LGSPREAD				
Method: Least Squares				
Date: 07/08/99 Time: 15:13				
Sample(adjusted): 11 754				
Included observations: 744 after adjusting endpoints				
LGSPREAD=C(1)+C(2)*DT+C(3)*T+C(4)*LAGY+C(5)*D(LAGY)+C(6)				
*D(LAGY,2)+C(7)*D(LAGY,3)+C(8)*D(LAGY,4)+C(9)*D(LAGY,5)				
+C(10)*D(LAGY,6)+C(11)*D(LAGY,7)+C(12)*D(LAGY,8)+C(13)				
*D(LAGY,9)				
	Coefficient	Std. Error	t-Statistic	Prob.
C(1)	-1.221387	0.234217	-5.214767	0.0000
C(2)	-0.000952	0.000529	-1.799641	0.0723
C(3)	0.000651	0.000493	1.320518	0.1871
C(4)	0.571523	0.079071	7.227959	0.0000
C(5)	-2.394992	0.479870	-4.990921	0.0000
C(6)	7.155554	1.660371	4.309611	0.0000
C(7)	-14.44936	3.546406	-4.074368	0.0001
C(8)	20.00819	5.007144	3.995929	0.0001

	Coefficient	Std. Error	t-Statistic	Prob
C(9)	-18.87772	4.802648	-3.930691	0.0001
C(10)	11.92040	3.117820	3.823313	0.0001
C(11)	-4.843221	1.317944	-3.674830	0.0003
C(12)	1.154833	0.328684	3.513505	0.0005
C(13)	-0.124194	0.036828	-3.372266	0.0008
R-squared	0.557078	Mean dependent var		-2.946260
Adjusted R-squared	0.549807	S.D. dependent var		0.195497
S.E. of regression	0.131172	Akaike info criterion		-1.207300
Sum squared resid	12.57761	Schwarz criterion		-1.125713
Log likelihood	462.1154	Durbin-Watson stat		1.998018

Model C

Dependent Variable: LGSPREAD				
Method: Least Squares				
Date: 07/08/99 Time: 15:16				
Sample(adjusted): 11 754				
Included observations: 744 after adjusting endpoints				
LGSPREAD=C(1)+C(2)*DU+C(3)*T+C(4)*DT+C(5)*LAGY+C(6)				
*D(LAGY)+C(7)*D(LAGY,2)+C(8)*D(LAGY,3)+C(9)*D(LAGY,4)				
+C(10)*D(LAGY,5)+C(11)*D(LAGY,6)+C(12)*D(LAGY,7)+C(13)				
*D(LAGY,8)+C(14)*D(LAGY,9)				
	Coefficient	Std. Error	t-Statistic	Prob.
C(1)	-1.411470	0.254667	-5.542404	0.0000
C(2)	-0.064788	0.034404	-1.883178	0.0601
C(3)	0.002050	0.000891	2.300496	0.0217
C(4)	-0.002373	0.000921	-2.576511	0.0102
C(5)	0.521237	0.083328	6.255218	0.0000
C(6)	-2.171513	0.493516	-4.400084	0.0000
C(7)	6.532505	1.690185	3.864965	0.0001
C(8)	-13.31128	3.591458	-3.706370	0.0002
C(9)	18.60124	5.053973	3.680518	0.0002
C(10)	-17.68447	4.835996	-3.656840	0.0003
C(11)	11.23202	3.133796	3.584159	0.0004
C(12)	-4.583698	1.322853	-3.465010	0.0006
C(13)	1.096929	0.329551	3.328561	0.0009
C(14)	-0.118376	0.036893	-3.208596	0.0014
R-squared	0.559219	Mean dependent var		-2.946260

Model C. (Continued)

	Coefficient	Std. Error	t-Statistic
Adjusted R-squared	0.551369	S.D. dependent var	0.195497
S.E. of regression	0.130944	Akaike info criterion	-1.209458
Sum squared resid	12.51680	Schwarz criterion	-1.122672
Log likelihood	463.9182	Durbin-Watson stat	1.998286

Time Break = 530 (from Plaza agreements to Stock crash market)

Model A

Dependent Variable: LGSPREAD				
Method: Least Squares				
Date: 07/08/99 Time: 14:49				
Sample(adjusted): 11 754				
Included observations: 744 after adjusting endpoints				
LGSPREAD=C(1)+C(2)*DU+C(3)*T+C(4)*LAGY+C(5)*D(LAGY)+C(6)				
*D(LAGY,2)+C(7)*D(LAGY,3)+C(8)*D(LAGY,4)+C(9)*D(LAGY,5)				
+C(10)*D(LAGY,6)+C(11)*D(LAGY,7)+C(12)*D(LAGY,8)+C(13)				
*D(LAGY,9)				
	Coefficient	Std. Error	t-Statistic	Prob.
C(1)	-0.990306	0.186101	-5.321344	0.0000
C(2)	0.021319	0.017525	1.216479	0.2242
C(3)	-0.000277	6.06E-05	-4.563575	0.0000
C(4)	0.630501	0.069039	9.132545	0.0000
C(5)	-2.711013	0.438132	-6.187663	0.0000
C(6)	8.099419	1.560795	5.189292	0.0000
C(7)	-16.23563	3.387142	-4.793312	0.0000
C(8)	22.27741	4.830865	4.611475	0.0000
C(9)	-20.85424	4.666699	-4.468734	0.0000
C(10)	13.09193	3.045902	4.298213	0.0000
C(11)	-5.296685	1.293016	-4.096379	0.0000
C(12)	1.258488	0.323580	3.889265	0.0001
C(13)	-0.134831	0.036360	-3.708237	0.0002
R-squared	0.556014	Mean dependent var		-2.946260
Adjusted R-squared	0.548726	S.D. dependent var		0.195497
S.E. of regression	0.131329	Akaike info criterion		-1.204901
Sum squared resid	12.60781	Schwarz criterion		-1.124314
Log likelihood	461.2232	Durbin-Watson stat		2.002243

Model B

Dependent Variable: LGSPREAD				
Method: Least Squares				
Date: 07/08/99 Time: 14:53				
Sample(adjusted): 11 754				
Included observations: 744 after adjusting endpoints				
LGSPREAD=C(1)+C(2)*DT+C(3)*T+C(4)*LAGY+C(5)*D(LAGY)+C(6)				
*D(LAGY,2)+C(7)*D(LAGY,3)+C(8)*D(LAGY,4)+C(9)*D(LAGY,5)				
+C(10)*D(LAGY,6)+C(11)*D(LAGY,7)+C(12)*D(LAGY,8)+C(13)				
*D(LAGY,9)				
	Coefficient	Std. Error	t-Statistic	Prob.
C(1)	-0.984269	0.185736	-5.299299	0.0000
C(2)	0.000131	0.000117	1.118242	0.2638
C(3)	-0.000267	5.77E-05	-4.632846	0.0000
C(4)	0.633076	0.068849	9.195146	0.0000
C(5)	-2.715263	0.438151	-6.197095	0.0000
C(6)	8.098943	1.561411	5.186937	0.0000
C(7)	-16.22318	3.388454	-4.787782	0.0000
C(8)	22.25562	4.832479	4.605425	0.0000
C(9)	-20.83323	4.668044	-4.462947	0.0000
C(10)	13.07867	3.046680	4.292762	0.0000
C(11)	-5.291144	1.293319	-4.091136	0.0000
C(12)	1.257095	0.323651	3.884108	0.0001
C(13)	-0.134671	0.036367	-3.703082	0.0002
R-squared	0.555875	Mean dependent var		-2.946260
Adjusted R-squared	0.548584	S.D. dependent var		0.195497
S.E. of regression	0.131350	Akaike info criterion		-1.204588
Sum squared resid	12.61176	Schwarz criterion		-1.124001
Log likelihood	461.1067	Durbin-Watson stat		2.002499

Model C

Dependent Variable: LGSPREAD
Method: Least Squares
Date: 07/08/99 Time: 15:01
Sample(adjusted): 11 754
Included observations: 744 after adjusting endpoints
LGSPREAD=C(1)+C(2)*DU+C(3)*T+C(4)*DT+C(5)*LAGY+C(6)

Model C. (Continued)

*D(LAGY)+C(7)*D(LAGY,2)+C(8)*D(LAGY,3)+C(9)*D(LAGY,4)				
+C(10)*D(LAGY,5)+C(11)*D(LAGY,6)+C(12)*D(LAGY,7)+C(13)				
*D(LAGY,8)+C(14)*D(LAGY,9)				
	Coefficient	Std. Error	t-Statistic	Prob.
C(1)	-0.994861	0.186393	-5.337453	0.0000
C(2)	0.015069	0.021157	0.712263	0.4765
C(3)	-0.000284	6.21E-05	-4.567601	0.0000
C(4)	7.46E-05	0.000141	0.527807	0.5978
C(5)	0.628253	0.069204	9.078237	0.0000
C(6)	-2.701163	0.438745	-6.156561	0.0000
C(7)	8.073173	1.562357	5.167304	0.0000
C(8)	-16.19000	3.389916	-4.775930	0.0000
C(9)	22.22389	4.834314	4.597113	0.0000
C(10)	-20.81101	4.669722	-4.456584	0.0000
C(11)	13.06793	3.047745	4.287736	0.0000
C(12)	-5.287845	1.293763	-4.087181	0.0000
C(13)	1.256531	0.323761	3.881048	0.0001
C(14)	-0.134632	0.036380	-3.700762	0.0002
R-squared	0.556183	Mean dependent var		-2.946260
Adjusted R-squared	0.548280	S.D. dependent var		0.195497
S.E. of regression	0.131394	Akaike info criterion		-1.202595
Sum squared resid	12.60300	Schwarz criterion		-1.115809
Log likelihood	461.3652	Durbin-Watson stat		2.002447

Japanese yen-dollar series

Time Break = 4 (Plaza agreements, Tokyo summit, Louvre accord, and Stock crash market)

Model A

Dependent Variable: LGSPREAD
Method: Least Squares
Date: 07/08/99 Time: 13:51
Sample(adjusted): 4 754
Included observations: 751 after adjusting endpoints
LGSPREAD=C(1)+C(2)*DU+C(3)*T+C(4)*LAGY+C(5)*D(LAGY)+C(6)
*D(LAGY,2)

	Coefficient	Std. Error	t-Statistic	Prob.
C(1)	-0.622348	0.140557	-4.427740	0.0000
C(2)	0.020826	0.128175	0.162430	0.8710
C(3)	-0.000233	2.87E-05	-8.113453	0.0000
C(4)	0.342812	0.053853	6.365696	0.0000
C(5)	-0.314937	0.076428	-4.120718	0.0000
C(6)	0.112655	0.036513	3.085314	0.0021
R-squared	0.296964	Mean dependent var		-1.049566
Adjusted R-squared	0.292245	S.D. dependent var		0.151067
S.E. of regression	0.127090	Akaike info criterion		-1.279893
Sum squared resid	12.03305	Schwarz criterion		-1.242971
Log likelihood	486.5997	Durbin-Watson stat		2.027583

Model B

Dependent Variable: LGSPREAD				
Method: Least Squares				
Date: 07/08/99 Time: 13:54				
Sample(adjusted): 3 754				
Included observations: 752 after adjusting endpoints				
LGSPREAD=C(1)+C(2)*DT+C(3)*T+C(4)*LAGY+C(5)*D(LAGY)				
	Coefficient	Std. Error	t-Statistic	Prob.
C(1)	-0.793972	0.520136	-1.526470	0.1273
C(2)	-0.029170	0.128830	-0.226421	0.8209
C(3)	0.028908	0.128827	0.224396	0.8225
C(4)	0.260334	0.046840	5.557897	0.0000
C(5)	-0.107705	0.036440	-2.955657	0.0032
R-squared	0.287862	Mean dependent var		-1.049500
Adjusted R-squared	0.284048	S.D. dependent var		0.150977
S.E. of regression	0.127747	Akaike info criterion		-1.270897
Sum squared resid	12.19059	Schwarz criterion		-1.240161
Log likelihood	482.8573	Durbin-Watson stat		2.022126

Model C

Dependent Variable: LGSPREAD				
Method: Least Squares				
Date: 07/08/99 Time: 13:55				
Sample(adjusted): 3 754				
Included observations: 752 after adjusting endpoints				
LGSPREAD=C(1)+C(2)*DT+C(3)*T+C(4)*DU+C(5)*LAGY+C(6)				
*D(LAGY)				
	Coefficient	Std. Error	t-Statistic	Prob.
C(1)	-0.611094	0.644344	-0.948397	0.3432
C(2)	0.032053	0.181089	0.177003	0.8596
C(3)	-0.032316	0.181088	-0.178452	0.8584
C(4)	0.061713	0.128214	0.481326	0.6304
C(5)	0.259644	0.046886	5.537720	0.0000
C(6)	-0.107361	0.036466	-2.944136	0.0033
R-squared	0.288083	Mean dependent var		-1.049500
Adjusted R-squared	0.283311	S.D. dependent var		0.150977
S.E. of regression	0.127813	Akaike info criterion		-1.268548
Sum squared resid	12.18680	Schwarz criterion		-1.231664
Log likelihood	482.9741	Durbin-Watson stat		2.021985

Time Break = 80 (a month for each event)

Model A

Dependent Variable: LGSPREAD				
Method: Least Squares				
Date: 07/08/99 Time: 14:02				
Sample(adjusted): 11 754				
Included observations: 744 after adjusting endpoints				
LGSPREAD=C(1)+C(2)*DU+C(3)*T+C(4)*LAGY+C(5)*D(LAGY)+C(6)				
*D(LAGY,2)+C(7)*D(LAGY,3)+C(8)*D(LAGY,4)+C(9)*D(LAGY,5)				
+C(10)*D(LAGY,6)+C(11)*D(LAGY,7)+C(12)*D(LAGY,8)+C(13)				
*D(LAGY,9)				
	Coefficient	Std. Error	t-Statistic	Prob.
C(1)	-0.470115	0.075764	-6.205033	0.0000
C(2)	0.021874	0.018753	1.166480	0.2438
C(3)	-0.000195	3.98E-05	-4.896899	0.0000

	Coefficient	Std. Error	t-Statistic	Prob.
C(4)	0.500453	0.078695	6.359368	0.0000
C(5)	-1.504968	0.469769	-3.203633	0.0014
C(6)	3.771775	1.627323	2.317779	0.0207
C(7)	-6.982998	3.502407	-1.993771	0.0465
C(8)	8.917389	4.986443	1.788327	0.0741
C(9)	-7.627297	4.814334	-1.584289	0.1136
C(10)	4.293383	3.137263	1.368512	0.1716
C(11)	-1.516707	1.328324	-1.141820	0.2539
C(12)	0.296117	0.331451	0.893397	0.3719
C(13)	-0.022672	0.037140	-0.610460	0.5417
R-squared	0.321261	Mean dependent var		-1.050032
Adjusted R-squared	0.310118	S.D. dependent var		0.151700
S.E. of regression	0.126000	Akaike info criterion		-1.287746
Sum squared resid	11.60541	Schwarz criterion		-1.207160
Log likelihood	492.0417	Durbin-Watson stat		2.000529

Model B

Dependent Variable: LGSPREAD				
Method: Least Squares				
Date: 07/08/99 Time: 13:21				
Sample(adjusted): 11 754				
Included observations: 744 after adjusting endpoints				
LGSPREAD=C(1)+C(2)*DT+C(3)*T+C(4)*LAGY+C(5)*D(LAGY,1)+C(6)				
*D(LAGY,2)+C(7)*D(LAGY,3)+C(8)*D(LAGY,4)+C(9)*D(LAGY,5)				
+C(10)*D(LAGY,6)+C(11)*D(LAGY,7)+C(12)*D(LAGY,8)+C(13)				
*D(LAGY,9)				
	Coefficient	Std. Error	t-Statistic	Prob.
C(1)	-0.526280	0.089257	-5.896200	0.0000
C(2)	-0.000740	0.000460	-1.609293	0.1080
C(3)	0.000534	0.000441	1.211996	0.2259
C(4)	0.478113	0.081102	5.895236	0.0000
C(5)	-1.393853	0.479630	-2.906102	0.0038
C(6)	3.455730	1.650121	2.094228	0.0366
C(7)	-6.405192	3.537332	-1.810741	0.0706
C(8)	8.202794	5.023247	1.632966	0.1029
C(9)	-7.018762	4.841266	-1.449778	0.1475
C(10)	3.939771	3.150750	1.250423	0.2115

Model B. (Continued)

	Coefficient	Std. Error	t-Statistic	Prob.
C(11)	-1.382173	1.332737	-1.037094	0.3000
C(12)	0.265807	0.332299	0.799903	0.4240
C(13)	-0.019599	0.037212	-0.526693	0.5986
R-squared	0.322398	Mean dependent var		-1.050032
Adjusted R-squared	0.311274	S.D. dependent var		0.151700
S.E. of regression	0.125895	Akaike info criterion		-1.289423
Sum squared resid	11.58596	Schwarz criterion		-1.208837
Log likelihood	492.6655	Durbin-Watson stat		2.000919

Model C

Dependent Variable: LGSPREAD				
Method: Least Squares				
Date: 07/08/99 Time: 14:07				
Sample(adjusted): 11 754				
Included observations: 744 after adjusting endpoints				
LGSPREAD=C(1)+C(2)*DT+C(3)*T+C(4)*DU+C(5)*LAGY+C(6)				
*D(LAGY)+C(7)*D(LAGY,2)+C(8)*D(LAGY,3)+C(9)*D(LAGY,4)				
+C(10)*D(LAGY,5)+C(11)*D(LAGY,6)+C(12)*D(LAGY,7)+C(13)				
*D(LAGY,8)+C(14)*D(LAGY,9)				
	Coefficient	Std. Error	t-Statistic	Prob.
C(1)	-0.532214	0.093680	-5.681175	0.0000
C(2)	-0.000871	0.000773	-1.126656	0.2603
C(3)	0.000665	0.000764	0.870382	0.3844
C(4)	-0.006609	0.031475	-0.209983	0.8337
C(5)	0.476572	0.081486	5.848502	0.0000
C(6)	-1.385957	0.481415	-2.878925	0.0041
C(7)	3.434191	1.654384	2.075813	0.0383
C(8)	-6.368241	3.544019	-1.796898	0.0728
C(9)	8.160293	5.030608	1.622129	0.1052
C(10)	-6.985216	4.847067	-1.441122	0.1500
C(11)	3.921705	3.153986	1.243412	0.2141
C(12)	-1.375787	1.333956	-1.031359	0.3027
C(13)	0.264464	0.332578	0.795193	0.4268
C(14)	-0.019471	0.037241	-0.522838	0.6012

	Coefficient	Std. Error	t-Statistic
R-squared	0.322439	Mean dependent var	-1.050032
Adjusted R-squared	0.310373	S.D. dependent var	0.151700
S.E. of regression	0.125977	Akaike info criterion	-1.286796
Sum squared resid	11.58526	Schwarz criterion	-1.200010
Log likelihood	492.6879	Durbin-Watson stat	2.001206

Time Break = 530 (from Plaza agreements to Stock crash market)

Model A

Dependent Variable: LGSPREAD				
Method: Least Squares				
Date: 07/08/99 Time: 14:49				
Sample(adjusted): 11 754				
Included observations: 744 after adjusting endpoints				
LGSPREAD=C(1)+C(2)*DU–C(3)*T+C(4)*LAGY+C(5)*D(LAGY)+C(6)				
*D(LAGY,2)+C(7)*D(LAGY,3)+C(8)*D(LAGY,4)+C(9)*D(LAGY,5)				
+C(10)*D(LAGY,6)+C(11)*D(LAGY,7)+C(12)*D(LAGY,8)+C(13)				
*D(LAGY,9)				
	Coefficient	Std. Error	t-Statistic	Prob.
C(1)	-0.990306	0.186101	-5.321344	0.0000
C(2)	0.021319	0.017525	1.216479	0.2242
C(3)	-0.000277	6.06E-05	-4.563575	0.0000
C(4)	0.630501	0.069039	9.132545	0.0000
C(5)	-2.711013	0.438132	-6.187663	0.0000
C(6)	8.099419	1.560795	5.189292	0.0000
C(7)	-16.23563	3.387142	-4.793312	0.0000
C(8)	22.27741	4.830865	4.611475	0.0000
C(9)	-20.85424	4.666699	-4.468734	0.0000
C(10)	13.09193	3.045902	4.298213	0.0000
C(11)	-5.296685	1.293016	-4.096379	0.0000
C(12)	1.258488	0.323580	3.889265	0.0001
C(13)	-0.134831	0.036360	-3.708237	0.0002
R-squared	0.556014	Mean dependent var		-2.946260
Adjusted R-squared	0.548726	S.D. dependent var		0.195497
S.E. of regression	0.131329	Akaike info criterion		-1.204901
Sum squared resid	12.60781	Schwarz criterion		-1.124314
Log likelihood	461.2232	Durbin-Watson stat		2.002243

Model B

Dependent Variable: LGSPREAD				
Method: Least Squares				
Date: 07/08/99 Time: 14:53				
Sample(adjusted): 11 754				
Included observations: 744 after adjusting endpoints				
LGSPREAD=C(1)+C(2)*DT+C(3)*T+C(4)*LAGY+C(5)*D(LAGY)+C(6)				
*D(LAGY,2)+C(7)*D(LAGY,3)+C(8)*D(LAGY,4)+C(9)*D(LAGY,5)				
+C(10)*D(LAGY,6)+C(11)*D(LAGY,7)+C(12)*D(LAGY,8)+C(13)				
*D(LAGY,9)				
	Coefficient	Std. Error	t-Statistic	Prob.
C(1)	-0.984269	0.185736	-5.299299	0.0000
C(2)	0.000131	0.000117	1.118242	0.2638
C(3)	-0.000267	5.77E-05	-4.632846	0.0000
C(4)	0.633076	0.068849	9.195146	0.0000
C(5)	-2.715263	0.438151	-6.197095	0.0000
C(6)	8.098943	1.561411	5.186937	0.0000
C(7)	-16.22318	3.388454	-4.787782	0.0000
C(8)	22.25562	4.832479	4.605425	0.0000
C(9)	-20.83323	4.668044	-4.462947	0.0000
C(10)	13.07867	3.046680	4.292762	0.0000
C(11)	-5.291144	1.293319	-4.091136	0.0000
C(12)	1.257095	0.323651	3.884108	0.0001
C(13)	-0.134671	0.036367	-3.703082	0.0002
R-squared	0.555875	Mean dependent var		-2.946260
Adjusted R-squared	0.548584	S.D. dependent var		0.195497
S.E. of regression	0.131350	Akaike info criterion		-1.204588
Sum squared resid	12.61176	Schwarz criterion		-1.124001
Log likelihood	461.1067	Durbin-Watson stat		2.002499

Model C

Dependent Variable: LGSPREAD				
Method: Least Squares				
Date: 07/08/99 Time: 15:01				
Sample(adjusted): 11 754				
Included observations: 744 after adjusting endpoints				
LGSPREAD=C(1)+C(2)*DU+C(3)*T+C(4)*DT+C(5)*LAGY+C(6)				
*D(LAGY)+C(7)*D(LAGY,2)+C(8)*D(LAGY,3)+C(9)*D(LAGY,4)				
+C(10)*D(LAGY,5)+C(11)*D(LAGY,6)+C(12)*D(LAGY,7)+C(13)				
*D(LAGY,8)+C(14)*D(LAGY,9)				
	Coefficient	Std. Error	t-Statistic	Prob.
C(1)	-0.994861	0.186393	-5.337453	0 0000
C(2)	0.015069	0.021157	0.712263	0 4765
C(3)	-0.000284	6.21E-05	-4.567601	0.0000
C(4)	7.46E-05	0.000141	0.527807	0.5978
C(5)	0.628253	0.069204	9.078237	0.0000
C(6)	-2.701163	0.438745	-6.156561	0.0000
C(7)	8.073173	1.562357	5.167304	0.0000
C(8)	-16.19000	3.389916	-4.775930	0.0000
C(9)	22.22389	4.834314	4.597113	0.0000
C(10)	-20.81101	4.669722	-4.456584	0.0000
C(11)	13.06793	3.047745	4.287736	0.0000
C(12)	-5.287845	1.293763	-4.087181	0.0000
C(13)	1.256531	0.323761	3.881048	0.0001
C(14)	-0.134632	0.036380	-3.700762	0.0002
R-squared	0.556183	Mean dependent var		-2.946260
Adjusted R-squared	0.548280	S.D. dependent var		0.195497
S.E. of regression	0.131394	Akaike info criterion		-1 202595
Sum squared resid	12.60300	Schwarz criterion		-1 115809
Log likelihood	461.3652	Durbin-Watson stat		2.002447

Appendix 7. Event Study

Japanese yen-dollar

AS		AS		AS	
Mean	0.016033	Mean	0.016033	Mean	0.016033
Standard Error	0.00522	Standard Error	0.00522	Standard Error	0.00522
Median	0.012131	Median	0.012131	Median	0.012131
Mode	-0.00358	Mode	-0.00358	Mode	-0.00358
Standard Deviation	0.043041	Standard Deviation	0.043041	Standard Deviation	0.043041
Sample Variance	0.001853	Sample Variance	0.001853	Sample Variance	0.001853
Kurtosis	4.479009	Kurtosis	4.479009	Kurtosis	4.479009
Skewness	1.734841	Skewness	1.734841	Skewness	1.734841
Range	0.25	Range	0.25	Range	0.25
Minimum	-0.05356	Minimum	-0.05356	Minimum	-0.05356
Maximum	0.196441	Maximum	0.196441	Maximum	0.196441
Sum	1.090236	Sum	1.090236	Sum	1.090236
Count	68	Count	68	Count	68
Largest (1)	0.196441	Largest (1)	0.196441	Largest (1)	0.196441
Smallest (1)	-0.05356	Smallest (1)	-0.05356	Smallest (1)	-0.05356
Confidence Level (95.0%)	0.010418	Confidence Level (90.0%)	0.008706	Confidence Level (99.0%)	0.013838

Deutsche mark-dollar

AS		AS		AS	
Mean	0.000155	Mean	0.000155	Mean	0.000154713
Standard Error	9.82E-05	Standard Error	9.82E-05	Standard Error	9.82459E-05
Median	0.0001	Median	0.0001	Median	0.0001
Mode	9.29E-05	Mode	9.29E-05	Mode	9.28571E-05
Standard Deviation	0.000688	Standard Deviation	0.000688	Standard Deviation	0.000687721
Sample Variance	4.73E-07	Sample Variance	4.73E-07	Sample Variance	4.72961E-07
Kurtosis	8.678037	Kurtosis	8.678037	Kurtosis	8.678037456
Skewness	2.369978	Skewness	2.369978	Skewness	2.369977586

AS		AS		AS	
Range	0.004143	Range	0.004143	Range	0.004142857
Minimum	-0.00086	Minimum	-0.00086	Minimum	-0.00085714
Maximum	0.003286	Maximum	0.003286	Maximum	0.003285714
Sum	0.007581	Sum	0.007581	Sum	0.007580952
Count	49	Count	49	Count	49
Largest (1)	0.003286	Largest (1)	0.003286	Largest (1)	0.003285714
Smallest (1)	-0.00086	Smallest (1)	-0.00086	Smallest (1)	-0.00085714
Confidence Level (99.0%)	0.000264	Confidence Level (95.0%)	0.000198	Confidence Level (90.0%)	0.00016478

REFERENCES

Almekinders, G. J., *Foreign Exchange Intervention: Theory and Evidence*, Vermont: Edward Elgar Publishing Limited, 1995.

Almekinders, G. J. and S. Eijffinger, "A Friction Model of Daily Bundesbank and Federal Reserve Intervention," *Journal of Banking and Finance*, 1996, 20, 1365- 1380.

Amihud, Y. and H. Mendelson, "Dealership Market, Market Making with Inventory," *Journal of Financial Economics*, 1980, 8, 31-53.

Bagehot, W., "The Only Game in Town," *Financial Analysts Journal*, March/April 1971, 27:12-14, 22 cited in Glassman, Debra."Exchange Rate Risk and Transactions Costs: Evidence from Bid-Ask Spreads," *Journal of International Money and Finance,* 1987, 6, 479-490.

Baillie, T. and Bollerslev, "Intra-Day and Inter-Market Volatility in Foreign Exchange Rates," *Review of Economic Studies*, 1990, 58, 565-585.

Balbach, A., "The Mechanics of Intervention in Exchange Markets," *Federal Reserve Bank of St. Louis Review,* 1978, February, 2-7.

Battacharya, U. and P. Weller, "The advantage to hiding one's hand: Speculation and Central Bank Intervention in the Foreign Exchange Market," *Journal of Monetary Economics*, 1997, 39, 251-277.

Belongia, T., "Foreign Exchange Intervention by the United States: A Review and Assessment of 1985-89," *Federal Reserve Bank of St. Louis*, May/June 1992, 32-48.

Belsley, D., et al., *Regression Diagnostics: Identifying Influential Data and Sources of Collinearity*, New York: John Wiley & Sons, 1980.

Beng, G. W. and W. K Siong, "Exchange Rate Expectations and Risk Premium in the Singapore/US Dollar Exchange Rate: Evidence from Survey Data," *Applied Financial Economics*, 1993, 3, 365-373.

Bessembinder, H., "Bid-ask Spreads in the Interbank Foreign Exchange Markets," *Journal of Financial Economics*, 1994, 35, 317-348.

Bhardwaj, Ravinder K. and W. T Moore, "Bid-Ask Spread Estimation For A Correlated Value Innovation Process," *The Financial Review,* 1998, 33, 35-52.

Black, S., "Transactions Costs and Vehicle Currencies," *Journal of International Money and Finance*, 1991, 10, 512-526.

Bollerslev, T. and I. Domowitz, "Trading Patterns and Prices in the Interbank Foreign Exchange Market," *The Journal of Finance*, September 1993, XLVIII, 1421-1443.

Boothe, P., "Exchange Rate Risk and the Bid-Ask Spread: a Seven Country Comparison," *Economic Inquiry*, July 1988, XXVI, 485-492.

Bossaerts, P. and P. Hillion, "Market Microstructure Effects of Government Intervention in the Foreign Exchange Market," *The Review of Financial Studies*, 1991, 4, 3, p.513-541.

Branch, B. and D. Echevarria, "Market Microstructure Empirical Regulaties: Behaviour of the Bid-Ask Spread and Closing Prices," *Financial Review*, August 1995, 30, 3, 541-565.

Branson, W., "Macroeconomic determinants of real exchange risk," *Managing Foreign Exchange Risk*, Cambridge University Press, Cambridge, cited in Almekinders, G. J., *Foreign Exchange Intervention: Theory and Evidence,* Vermont: Edward Elgar Publishing Limited, 1995.

Branson, W. H., H. Halttunen, and P. Masson, "Exchange Rates in the Short Run – the Dollar-Deutschemark Rate," *European Economic Review,* 1977, 10, 303-324, cited in Almekinders, G. J., *Foreign*

Exchange Intervention: Theory and Evidence, Vermont: Edward Elgar Publishing Limited, 1995.

Broto, Carmen, "The Effectiveness of Forex Interventions in four Latin American Countries." *Emerging Markets Review*, 2013, 17, 224-240.

Chen, S., Chien, C. C., & Chang, M. J., "Order flow, bid–ask spread and trading density in foreign exchange markets," *Journal of Banking and Finance*, (2012), 36(2), 597-612.

Chung, Kee H. and C. Charoenwong, "Insider Trading and the Bid-Ask Spread," *The Financial Review,* 1998, 33, 1-20.

Cohen, J., S. Maier, R. Schwartz, and D. Whitcomb, "Transaction Costs, Order Placement Strategy, and Existence of the Bid-Ask Spread," *Journal of Political Economy,* 1981, 89, 287-305.

De Grauwe, P., *International Money: Post-War Trends and Theories*, New York: Oxford University Press, 1989.

Dominguez, K. M., "Market Responses to Coordinated Central Bank Intervention," *Carniege-Rochester Conference Series On Public Policy,* 1990, 32, 121-164.

Dominguez, K. M., "*Does Central Bank Intervention Increase the Volatility of Foreign Exchange Rates?,"* November 1993, NBER Working Paper No.4532.

Dominguez, K. M., "The Informational Role of Official Foreign Exchange Intervention Operations: An Empirical Investigation," Harvard University, Working Paper, November 1988, cited in Osterberg William P, "Intervention and the Bid-Ask Spread in G-3 Foreign Exchange Rates," *Economic Review,* Federal Reserve Bank of Cleveland, 1992, 28, 2, 2-13.

Dominguez, Kathryn M. E., R. Fatum and P. Vacek. "Do Sales of Foreign Exchange Reserves Lead to Currency Appreciation?" *Journal of Money, Credit and Banking*, 2013, 45(5), 867-890.

Dornbusch, R., "Expectations and Exchange Rate Dynamics," *Journal of Political Economy,* 1976, 84, 1161-1176, cited in Almekinders, G. J., *Foreign Exchange Intervention: Theory and Evidence,* Vermont: Edward Elgar Publishing Limited, 1995.

Du W., Tepper A., Verdelhan A., "Deviations from Covered Interest Rate Parity," *The Journal of Finance,* 2018, 73(3), 915-957.

Evans, Martin D., "*The Microstructure of Foreign Exchange Dynamics,*" mimeo, 1998, Department of Economics, Georgetown University.

Eviews User's Guide, *Quantitative Micro Software*, California: Irvine, 1995.

Federal Reserve Bank of New York Fedpoints 44: *U.S. Foreign Exchange Intervention.* (online). Available: http://www.ny.frb.org/pihome/fedpoint/fed44.html (1996, Nov. 10).

Flood, M., "Microstructure Theory and the Foreign Exchange Market," *Federal Reserve Bank of ST. Louis*, November/December 1991, 52-70.

Flood, M., "Market Structure and Inefficiency in the Foreign Exchange Market," *Journal of International Money and Finance,* 1994, 13, 2, 131-158.

Frankel, J. A., "*A Survey of Empirical Research on Nominal Exchange Rates,*" September 1994, NBER Working Paper No.4865.

Frankel, J. A. and Kenneth A. Froot, "Using Survey data to Test Standard Propositions Regarding Exchange Rate Expectations," *On Exchange Rate,"* Cambridge: MIT Press, 1993.

Frankel, J. A. and K. M. Dominguez, "Foreign Exchange Intervention: An Empirical Assessment," *On Exchange Rate,* Cambridge: MIT Press, 1993.

Frenkel, M., "Exchange Rate Dynamics with Chartists, Fundamentalist, and Rational Speculators in the Foreign Exchange Market," *International Journal of Business,* 1997, 2(1), 1-21.

Froot, Kenneth and Richard Thaler, "Anamolies: Foreign Exchange, *Journal of Economic Perspectives,*" 1990, 4, 179-192.

Funabashi, Y., *Managing the Dollar: From the Plaza to the Louvre,* Washington, DC: Institute for International Economics, 1988.

Garman, M. B., "Market Microstructure," *Journal of Financial Economics,* 1976, 3, 257-275.

George, T. J., G. Kaul and M. Nimalendran, "Estimation of the Bid-Ask Spread and Its Components: a New Approach," *The Review of Financial Studies*, 1991, 4, 4, 623-656.

Glassman, D., "Exchange Rate Risk and Transactions Costs: Evidence from Bid-Ask Spreads," *Journal of International Money and Finance,* 1987, 6, 479-490.

Glosten, L., and P. Milgrom, "Bid, Ask and Transaction Prices in a Specialist Market with heterogenously Informed Traders," *Journal of Financial Economics,* 1985, 14, 71-100.

Glosten, L., "Components of the Bid-Ask Spread and the Statistical Properties of Transaction Prices," *Journal of Finance*, 1987, 42, 5, 1293-1307.

Glosten, L. and L. Harris, "Estimating the Components of the Bid/Ask Spread," *Journal of Financial Economics,* 1988, 21, 123-142.

Goodhart, C., "The Foreign Exchange Market: A Random Walk with a Dragging Anchor," *Economica,* 1988, 55, 437-460.

Goodhart, C. A. E. and R. G. Payne, "Microstructural Dynamics in a Foreign Exchange Electronic Broking System," *Journal of International Money and Finance,* 1996, 15, 6, 829-852.

Goodhart, C. A. E. and L. Figliuoli, "Every Minute Counts in Financial Markets," *Journal of International Money and Finance*, 1991, 10, 23-52.

Goodhart, C. A. E. and T. Hesse, "Central Bank Forex Intervention Assessed in Continuous Time," *Journal of International Money and Finance,* 1993, 12, 368-389.

Gaynor, P. E. and Rickey C. K., *Introduction to Time-Series Modelling and Forecasting in Business and Economics,* Singapore: McGraw-Hill, Inc, 1994.

Graves, J. A., et al., "Trading Mechanism and the Components of the Bid-Ask Spread," *Journal of Finance,* September 1994, 49, 4, 1471-1488.

Griffiths, et al., *Learning and Practicing Econometrics,* Singapore: John Willey and Son, Inc, 1993.

Gujarati, D. N., *Basic Econometrics*, McGraw-Hill, Inc, third edition, 1995.

Hakkio, G. S. and D. K. Pearce, "The Reaction of Exchange Rates to Economic News," *Economic Inquiry,* October 1985, 23, 621-635.

Hallwood, P. and R. Mac Donald, *International Money, Theory, Evidence, and Institutions,* Unwin Hyman, London, cited in Almekinders, G. J, *Foreign Exchange Intervention: Theory and Evidence,* Vermont: Edward Elgar Publishing Limited, 1995.

Harvey, A. C., *Time Series Models,* Great Britain: Harvester Wheatsheaf, second edition, 1993.

Hasbrouck, J., "Trades, Quotes, Inventories, and Information," *Journal of Financial Economics*, 1988, 22, 229-252.

Hasbrouck, J., "Measuring the Information Content of Stock Trades," *The Journal of Finance*, 1991, 46, 1, 179-207.

Hasbrouck, J. and G. Sofianos, "The Trades of Market Makers: an Empirical Analysis of NYSE Specialists," *The Journal of Finance,* 1993, 48, 1565-1593.

Ho, T. and R. Macris, "Dealer Bid-Ask Quotes and Transaction Prices: an Empirical Study of Some AMEX Options," *The Journal of Finance, 1984*, 39, 1, 23-45.

Ho, T. and H. Stoll, "Optimal Dealer Pricing Under Transactions and Return Uncertainty," *Journal of Financial Economics*, 1981, 9, 47-73.

Ho, T. and H. Stoll, "The Dynamics of Dealer Markets Under Competition," *The Journal of Finance*, 1983, 38, 4, 1053-1074.

Hogan, K. C. and M. Melvin, "Sources of Meteor Showers and Heat Waves in the Foreign Exchange Market," *Journal of International Economics,* 1994, 37,239-247.

Holthausen, R., R. Leftwich and D. Mayers, "Large-Block Transactions, the Speed of Response, and Temporary and Permanent Stock-Price Effects," *Journal of Financial Economics*, 1990, 26, 71-95.

Hsieh, D. A., and A. W. Kleidon, "Bid-Ask Spreads in Foreign Exchange Markets Implications for Model of Asymmetric Information," in Frankel, J., Galli, G. and Giovannini Eds. *The Microstructure of Foreign Exchange Market*, NBER, 1996.

Huang, R. D. and H. Stoll, "The Components of the Bid-Ask Spread: A General Approach," *Review of Financial Studies*, Winter 1997, 10, 4, 995 – 1034.

Humpage, O. F., "Central-Bank Intervention: Recent Literature, Continuing Controversy," *Economic Review (Federal Reserve Bank of Cleveland),* 1991, Quarter 2, 12-26.

Humpage, O. F., "Exchange-Market Intervention: The Channels of Influence," *Economic Review: Federal Reserve Bank of Cleveland,* 1986, Quarter 3, 2-13.

Humpage, O. F., "Intervention and the dollar's decline," *Federal Reserve Bank of Cleveland Economic Review,* 1988, Quarter 2, 2-16.

Hung, J. H., "Intervention Strategies and Exchange Rate Volatility: a Noise Trading Perspective," *Journal of International Money and Finance*, 1997, 16, 5, p.779-793.

Hung, J. H., "Noise Trading and the Effectiveness of Sterilized Foreign Exchange Intervention," 1991a, Research Paper, Federal Reserve Bank of New York, no.9118, cited in Almekinders, G. J, *Foreign Exchange Intervention: Theory and Evidence,* Vermont: Edward Elgar Publishing Limited, 1995.

Insukindro, *Ekonomi Uang dan Bank: Teori dan Pengalaman di Indonesia (The Economics of Finance and Banking: Theory and Experience in Indonesia),* Yogyakarta, Indonesia: BPFE, 1994.

Ito, T., "Foreign Exchange Rate Expectations: Micro Survey Data," *The American Economic Review,* June 1990, 80, 2, 131-158.

Ito, T. "The Intradaily Exchange Rate Dynamics and Monetary Policies after the Group of Five Agreement," *Journal of the Japanese and International Economies,* 1987, 1, 275-298.

Ito, T., R. K. Lyons, and M. T. Melvin, "Is There Private Information in the FX Market? The Tokyo Experiment," *Journal of Finance,* 1998, 33, 3, 1111-1130.

Kennedy, P., *A Guide to Econometrics,* Oxford: Basil Blackwell, second edition, 1985.

Klein, M. W., and E. Rosengren, "Foreign Exchange Intervention as a Signal of Monetary Policy," *New England Economic Review,* Federal Reserve Bank of Boston, Jan/Feb 1991, 39-50.

Klein, M. W., "The Accuracy of Reports of Foreign Exchange Intervention," *Journal of International Money and Finance,* 1993, 12. 644-653.

Kreps, D. M., *A Course in Microeconomic Theory*, Princeton, N.J.: Princeton University Press, 1990.

Leach, J. and A. Madhavan, "Intertemporal Price Discovery by Market Makers: Active versus Passive Learning," *Journal of Financial Intermediation*, 1992, 2, 27-235.

Lee, T. "Spread and Volatility in Spot and Forward Exchange Rates," *Journal of International Money and Finance,* 1994, 13, 3, 375-383.

Lee, C. and M. J. Ready, "Inferring Trade Direction from Intraday Data," *Journal of Finance*, June 1991, XLVI, 2, 733-746.

Lehalle, C. A. and Laruelle, S, eds., *Market Microstructure in Practice,* Hackensack, New Jersey: *World Scientific, 2013.*

Loopesko, B., "Relationships Among Exchange Rates, Intervention and Interest Rates: and Empirical Investigation," *Journal of International Money and Finance,* 1984, 3, 3, 257-277.

Lyons, R., "Tests of Microstructural Hypotheses in the Foreign Exchange Market," September 1993, *NBER Working Paper No. 4471.*

Lyons, R., "Foreign Exchange Volume: Sound and Fury Signifying Nothing?," January 1995, *NBER Working Paper No.4984.*

Lyons, R., "Optimal Transparency in a Dealership Market with an Application to Foreign Exchange," September 1993, *NBER Working Paper No.4467.*

Lyons, R., "A Simultaneous Trade Model of the Foreign Exchange Hot Potato," *Journal of International Economics,"* 1997, 42, 275-298.

MacDonald, R. and M. P. Taylor, "Exchange Rate Economics: A survey," *Staff Papers,* International Monetary Fund, 39, 1-57, cited in Almekinders, G. J., *Foreign Exchange Intervention: Theory and Evidence,* Vermont: Edward Elgar Publishing Limited, 1995.

MacDonald, R. and I. W. Marsh, "Currency Forecasters are Heterogeneous: Confirmation and Consequences," *Journal of International Money and Finance*, 1996, 15, 5, 665-685.

Madhavan, A. and S. Smidt, "An Analysis of Changes in Specialist Inventories and Quotations," *The Journal of Finance,* 1993, 48, 5, 1595-1628.

Marston, R., *International Financial Integration,* Cambridge: University Press, 1995.

Marston, R., "Exchange Rate Policy Reconsidered," in M. Feldstein, (ed), *International Economic Cooperation*, University of Chicago Press, 79-136, cited in Schwartz, Anna J, "US Foreign Exchange Market Intervention Since 1962," *Scottish Journal of Political Economy*, September, 1996, 43, 4, 379-397.

Melvin, M. and X. Yin, *Public Information Arrival, Exchange Rate Volatility, and Quote Frequency*, Research Paper, June 1996, Department of Economics, Arizona State University, 1-19.

Mussa, M., "The Role of Official Intervention," *Group of Thirty Occasional Papers,* 1981, 30, New York, cited in Almekinders, G.J., *Foreign Exchange Intervention: Theory and Evidence,* Vermont: Edward Elgar Publishing Limited, 1995.

Neal, C. and G. Tanner, "Central Bank Intervention and the Volatility of foreign Exchange Rates: Evidence from the Options Market," *Journal of International Money and Finance,* 1996, 15, 6, p.853-878.

Norusis, M. J., *SPSS for Windows: Base System User's Guide, Release 6.0*, SPSS Inc.

Obstfeld, M., "The Effectiveness of Foreign Exchange Intervention: Recent Experience," December 1988, *NBER Working Paper No.2796.*

O'Hara, M., *Market Microstructure Theory*, Oxford: Blackwell Publishers Inc, 1997.

Osterberg, W. P., "Intervention and the Bid-Ask Spread in G-3 Foreign Exchange Rates," *Economic Review,* Federal Reserve Bank of Cleveland, 1992, 28, 2, 2-13.

Ostle, B., *Statistics in Research,* Iowa: The Iowa State University Press, second edition, 1963.

Peiers, B., "Informed Traders, Intervention, and Price Leadership," *Journal of Finance*, September 1997, LII, 4, 1589-1614.

Ramanathan, Ramu, *Introductory Econometrics with Applications,* Orlando: The Dryden Press, third edition, 1995.

Rasmusen, E., *Games and Information: an Introduction to Game Theory,* Massachusetts: Blackwell, fourth edition, 2007.

Rasmusen, E., *Games and Information: an Introduction to Game Theory,* Massachusetts: Blackwell, second edition, 1994.

Rivera-Batiz, F. L. and Luis A., *International Finance and Open Economy Macroeconomics,* Macmillan. Inc, second edition, 1994.

Robert, A. Z., "Monetary Independence Under Floating Exchange Rates," *Journal of Finance,* May 1975,30, 365-376 cited in Glassman, D., "Exchange Rate Risk and Transactions Costs: Evidence from Bid-Ask Spreads," *Journal of International Money and Finance,* 1987, 6, 479-490.

Schwartz, A. J., "US Foreign Exchange Market Intervention Since 1962," *Scottish Journal of Political Economy*, September, 1996, 43, 4, 379-397.

Shapiro, A. C., *Multinational Financial Management,* Massachusetts: Allyn and Bacon, fourth edition, 1992.

Sincich, T., Business Statistics by Example, New York: Macmillan, Inc, fourth edition, 1992.

Smidt, S., "Which Road to an Efficient Stock Market: Free Competition or Regulated Monopoly?," *Financial Analysis Journal,* 1971, September-October, 18-20, 64-69.

Spulber, D., *Market Microstructure: Intermediaries and the Theory of the Firm,* Cambridge; New York: Cambridge University Press, 1999.

Stoll, H., "Inferring the Components of the Bid-Ask Spread: Theory and Empirical Tests," *Journal of Finance*, March 1989, 44, 1, 115-134.

Stoll, H., "The Supply of Dealer Services in Securities Markets," *The Journal of Finance,* 1978, 33, 4, 1133-1151.

Suvanto, A., comment in Hsieh, David. A. and Kleidon, Allan W., "Bid-Ask Spreads in Foreign Exchange Markets: Implications for Model of Asymmetric Information," in Frankel, J., Galli, G. and Giovannini Eds. "*The Microstructure of Foreign Exchange Market,*" NBER, 1996.

Taylor, M. P., "The Economics of Exchange Rates," *Journal of Economic Literature,* March, 1995, XXXIII, 13-47.

Wang, Jianxin, *"Asymmetric Information and the Bid-Ask Spread: An Empirical Comparison between Automated Order Execution and Open Outcry Auction,"* Working Paper, School of Banking and Finance, University of New South Wales, 1998, 1-18.

Wei, S. J., *"Anticipations of Foreign Exchange Volatility and Bid-Ask Spreads,"* May 1994, NBER Working Paper No. 4737.

White, H., A Heteroskedasticity-consistent covariance Matrix Estimator and S A Direct Test for heteroscedasticity, *Econometrica,* May 1980, 48:4, 817-837.

Zivot, Eric and Donald W. K. Andrews, "Further Evidence on the Great Crash, the Oil-Price Shock, and the Unit-Root Hypothesis," *Journal of Business and Economic Statistics,* 1992, 10, 1, 251-270.

About the Authors

Dr. Nevi Danila
Department of Finance
STIE Malangkucecwara
Malang, Jawa Timur, Indonesia
Email: nevida@staff.stie-mce.ac.id

Professor Sardar M. N. Islam
Professor of Business, Economics and Finance (2007-2017), and
Director, Decision Sciences and Modelling Program
Victoria University, Australia
Email: Sardar.Islam@vu.edu.au

INDEX

A

Asia, 97, 100, 101, 102, 107, 141, 143, 148, 153, 154, 156
assets, 11, 13, 24, 25, 26, 140
asymmetric information, 16, 38, 78, 79, 208, 212, 213
authorities, 3, 4, 6, 12, 13, 14, 16, 20, 26, 27, 30, 33, 34, 65, 72, 133

B

Bank of Japan, 11, 19, 31, 32, 65, 68, 69, 132
bid-ask exchange rates, vii
bonds, 14, 22, 23, 24
Bretton Woods Agreement, 29
Bretton Woods era, 29, 30
Bundesbank, 18, 19, 20, 28, 30, 31, 32, 33, 34, 203

C

central bank, 2, 3, 10, 11, 12, 13, 14, 16, 17, 18, 19, 20, 26, 27, 28, 29, 30, 31, 33, 34, 48, 61, 65, 68, 69, 79, 132, 141, 204, 205, 207, 211
central bank intervention, 17, 18, 19, 20, 28, 34, 35, 69, 204, 205, 211
continuous market, 75
coordinated intervention, 28, 29, 30, 31, 33, 34, 60
critical value, 57, 59, 118, 119, 120, 121, 122, 123
currency, 6, 9, 10, 11, 12, 13, 16, 17, 19, 21, 22, 23, 24, 25, 26, 28, 30, 32, 36, 48, 53, 61, 66, 69, 72, 73, 74, 76, 80, 81, 82, 87, 94, 105, 141

D

decentralized market, 75
depreciate, viii, 5, 23, 33, 36, 53, 65, 66, 69, 82, 134
depreciation, 16, 21, 22, 23, 24, 25, 27, 28, 29, 30, 36, 60, 61, 65, 71
Deutsche mark (DM), viii, ix, 2, 5, 7, 18, 19, 20, 28, 30, 32, 33, 51, 54, 55, 56, 57, 58, 59, 60, 62, 63, 64, 66, 67, 68, 70, 71, 82, 84, 94, 112, 117, 118, 119, 120, 121,

122, 124, 125, 126, 127, 128, 129, 130, 131, 132, 134, 136, 185, 200
domestic output, 22
double-auction, 75, 76

E

economics, vii, 1, 133, 135, 203, 204, 206, 207, 208, 209, 210, 211, 213, 215
equilibrium, 13, 22, 23, 25, 35, 46, 48, 55, 61, 64, 66, 71, 83, 84, 85, 87, 88
equilibrium price, 87, 88
equity, ix, 2, 18, 41, 80, 102, 103, 104, 105, 135, 137
equity market, ix, 2, 80, 102, 103, 104, 105, 135, 137
Eurodollar rate, 52
Europe, 97, 100, 101, 102, 107, 141, 145, 150, 153, 154, 158
excess demand, 10, 14, 23, 24
excess supply, 10, 14, 23, 24, 25
exchange market, viii, ix, 1, 2, 3, 5, 6, 9, 10, 11, 12, 13, 14, 15, 18, 23, 25, 26, 28, 29, 31, 35, 36, 47, 75, 78, 79, 80, 81, 86, 88, 89, 98, 99, 100, 102, 103, 104, 105, 133, 135, 136, 137, 141, 203, 204, 205, 206, 207, 208, 210, 211, 212
exchange rate(s), v, vii, 1, 3, 5, 7, 10, 12, 14, 15, 16, 17, 18, 19, 20, 21, 22, 23, 24, 25, 26, 27, 30, 32, 33, 36, 37, 48, 51, 55, 57, 59, 60, 61, 64, 65, 66, 69, 71, 77, 80, 81, 83, 84, 85, 86, 88, 89, 93, 117, 120, 131, 132, 133, 136, 203, 204, 205, 206, 207, 209, 210, 211, 212, 213

F

Federal Reserve, ix, xi, 3, 7, 11, 12, 13, 14, 18, 19, 27, 28, 30, 31, 33, 34, 51, 61, 68, 69, 79, 104, 105, 131, 136, 203, 204, 205, 206, 209, 211
Federal Reserve monetary policy, 27
finance, vii, 1, 2, 11, 16, 30, 31, 33, 41, 69, 83, 203, 204, 205, 206, 207, 208, 209, 210, 211, 212, 213, 215
finance ministers, 33, 69
flexible-price monetary model, 23
floating exchange rates, 30, 81
fluctuations, 26, 38, 39, 78, 84, 85
foreign bonds, 14, 22, 23, 24
foreign currencies, 11, 13, 22, 28, 30, 33, 82
foreign exchange, viii, 1, 2, 3, 4, 5, 6, 9, 10, 11, 12, 13, 14, 15, 17, 18, 20, 23, 25, 26, 28, 29, 31, 35, 36, 47, 51, 75, 77, 78, 79, 80, 81, 84, 85, 86, 88, 89, 98, 99, 100, 101, 102, 103, 104, 105, 133, 135, 136, 137, 141, 205
foreign exchange bid-ask, viii, 135, 137
foreign exchange intervention, v, 1, 4, 9, 10, 12, 13, 21, 23, 47, 133, 203, 204, 205, 206, 208, 209, 210, 211
foreign exchange market, viii, 1, 2, 3, 5, 6, 9, 11, 12, 13, 14, 15, 18, 25, 26, 28, 29, 31, 35, 36, 47, 75, 78, 79, 80, 81, 86, 88, 89, 98, 99, 100, 101, 102, 103, 104, 105, 133, 135, 136, 137, 141, 204, 205, 206, 207, 208, 210, 211, 212
foreign exchange quotes, 51
France, 31, 32

G

G-5 countries, viii, 6, 31, 32, 34, 60, 63, 65, 69, 72, 135
G-6 countries, 33
G-7 countries, 32, 33, 36, 60, 69
Germany, viii, 6, 20, 31, 32, 61, 69, 134
government intervention, v, vii, viii, 2, 3, 5, 6, 13, 17, 18, 22, 25, 26, 34, 49, 50, 51, 53, 54, 59, 60, 61, 66, 79, 80, 104, 117, 124, 126, 133, 134, 135, 136, 204
Great Britain, 208

grosso modo, 27

H

Hong Kong, 112, 114, 115

I

information-motivated traders, 77
interest rate differential, 16, 48, 50, 54, 57, 59, 60
interest rates, 14, 24, 32, 48, 52, 80, 84
International Monetary Fund (IMF), 11, 29, 30, 81, 140, 210
intervention, vii, viii, ix, 1, 2, 3, 4, 5, 6, 7, 9, 11, 12, 13, 14, 15, 16, 17, 18, 19, 20, 21, 22, 23, 24, 25, 27, 28, 29, 30, 31, 32, 33, 34, 47, 49, 50, 51, 52, 53, 54, 57, 58, 59, 60, 61, 62, 63, 64, 65, 66, 67, 68, 69, 70, 71, 72, 79, 80, 104, 105, 115, 117, 123, 124, 126, 127, 129, 130, 131, 132, 133, 134, 135, 136, 137, 141
inventory cost, vii, viii, 2, 3, 5, 6, 72, 73, 78, 87, 93, 100, 101, 110, 115, 117, 134, 135
inventory-control mechanism, v, 47, 51, 117
investors, 14, 15, 16, 22, 23, 48, 68, 84
Italy, 32, 33

J

Japan, viii, 6, 11, 14, 19, 20, 31, 32, 61, 65, 68, 69, 132, 134
Japanese yen, viii, ix, 2, 5, 7, 11, 14, 15, 19, 20, 28, 32, 33, 34, 36, 37, 51, 52, 54, 55, 56, 57, 58, 59, 60, 62, 63, 64, 65, 66, 67, 68, 70, 71, 82, 117, 118, 119, 120, 121, 122, 123, 124, 125, 126, 127, 128, 129, 130, 131, 132, 134, 136, 192, 200

L

Latin America, 205
least squares, 51, 55, 56, 58, 59, 62, 63, 64, 65, 67, 68, 98, 119, 120, 127, 128, 129, 141, 175, 181, 186, 187, 188, 189, 190, 191, 192, 193, 194, 195, 196, 197, 198, 199
limit-book, 76
Louvre Accord, vii, 2, 3, 33, 60, 66, 67, 68, 70, 71, 121, 134

M

models of intervention, 4, 21
monetary policy, 4, 14, 16, 26, 27, 28, 30, 132
money supply, 13, 21, 22, 23, 89, 141
money-market effect, 23
monopoly power, 78
multiple regression, 50, 53
Mundell-Fleming Model, 21

N

New York Federal Reserve Bank, 68
New York Stock Exchange, 39, 95, 102
noise trading channel, 19

O

oil, 30, 65
open economy, 9, 27
open-bid, 76

P

Plaza agreement, vii, viii, 2, 3, 31, 32, 60, 61, 62, 63, 64, 65, 70, 121, 134, 135, 185, 190, 192, 197

portfolio balance model, 15, 24
pre-Plaza Agreement, 60, 62, 63, 70
price level, 21, 22, 23, 24, 25, 26, 83, 84
purchasing power parity theory, 21

R

regression result, 55, 58, 96, 97, 98, 107, 108

S

Singapore, 36, 204, 207
single-auction, 75, 76
speculative motive, 39
spot exchange rate, 48, 66, 77
spot market, 10, 13, 80
sterilized government intervention, 22
sterilized intervention, 13, 14, 15, 16, 19, 21, 22, 25, 28, 29
sticky-price monetary model, 23
stock, viii, 6, 13, 14, 29, 30, 38, 39, 40, 41, 42, 43, 44, 45, 46, 69, 78, 108, 109, 110, 121, 134
stock price, 78, 108
stock value, 110
stock-flow interaction, 24
Swiss National Bank, 30

T

trade, 9, 10, 11, 16, 24, 25, 26, 31, 32, 40, 42, 45, 46, 68, 69, 74, 77, 78, 79, 80, 83, 88, 92, 94, 99, 103, 104, 105, 106, 109, 110, 111, 112, 113, 140
trade deficit, 26, 31
trading partners, 31
transaction costs, 43, 76, 77, 81, 109
transactions, 10, 17, 23, 42, 43, 45, 46, 52, 76, 77, 79, 81, 82, 84, 87, 89, 90, 94, 95, 108, 113

U

unilateral and coordinated intervention, 29, 34
United Kingdom, 31, 32, 94
United States (USA), viii, 6, 14, 20, 27, 29, 31, 32, 60, 65, 68, 69, 132, 134, 204
unsterilized intervention, 22
US dollar, vii, viii, ix, 5, 6, 7, 13, 18, 19, 28, 36, 37, 50, 51, 52, 53, 54, 55, 56, 57, 59, 61, 62, 65, 66, 70, 71, 72, 73, 94, 123, 126, 127, 129, 131, 132, 134, 136, 204
US Treasury, 11, 12, 29, 61, 68

V

volatility, ix, 5, 7, 10, 18, 19, 20, 26, 30, 81, 83, 84, 85, 86, 100, 105, 117, 120, 131, 132, 136

W

wages, 22, 26
Washington, 31, 69, 206

Y

yen exchange rates, 19

International Financial Institutions, Climate Change and the Urgency to Facilitate Clean Energy Investment in Developing and Emerging Market Economies

Author: Hilmar Þór Hilmarsson, Ph.D. (University of Akureyri, Akureyri, Iceland)

Series: Economic Issues, Problems and Perspectives; Financial Institutions and Services

Book Description: This book focuses on those challenges, mainly using geothermal energy projects as examples, but also by providing an example of a large hydropower project to illustrate how the funding and risk mitigation instruments of IFIs, as well as national agencies such as export credit agencies (ECA)s, have been used to mobilize funds in a difficult investment environment.

Hardcover ISBN: 978-1-53610-045-7
Retail Price: $95

Financial Management: Methods, Outcomes and Challenges

Editor: Emily Ramirez

Series: Financial Institutions and Services

Book Description: This book examines the extent to which exchange rate changes have potentially impacted perceptions of the rate of change in the global financial influence of the United States and Europe.

Hardcover ISBN: 978-1-53611-827-8
Retail Price: $95